There is . . . a voice inside me that urges caution. It tells me to be careful, to keep my head, not to go too far, not to burn my boats. . . . I don't want to be carried away into any resolution which I shall afterwards regret, for I know I shall be feeling quite different after breakfast. . . . This is my endlessly recurrent temptation: to go down to that Sea [which is God], and there neither to dive nor swim nor float, but only to dabble and splash, careful not to get out of my depth, and holding on to the lifeline which connects me with my things temporal. . . . Of course that lifeline is really a death line.

C. S. Lewis, "A Slip of the Tongue"

The CALVIN INSTITUTE OF CHRISTIAN WORSHIP LITURGICAL STUDIES Series, edited by John D. Witvliet, is designed to promote reflection on the history, theology, and practice of Christian worship and to stimulate worship renewal in Christian congregations. Contributions include writings by pastoral worship leaders from a wide range of communities and scholars from a wide range of disciplines. The ultimate goal of these contributions is to nurture worship practices that are spiritually vital and theologically rooted.

Published

The Pastor as Minor Poet
M. Craig Barnes

Touching the Altar: The Old Testament and Christian Worship
Carol M. Bechtel, Editor

Resonant Witness: Conversations between Music and Theology
Jeremy S. Begbie and Steven R. Guthrie, Editors

God Against Religion: Rethinking Christian Theology through Worship
Matthew Myer Boulton

From Memory to Imagination: Reforming the Church's Music
C. Randall Bradley

Essays on the History of Worship in America
James D. Bratt

Inclusive yet Discerning: Navigating Worship Artfully
Frank Burch Brown

What Language Shall I Borrow? The Bible and Christian Worship
Ronald P. Byars

A Primer on Worship
William Dyrness

Christian Worship Worldwide: Expanding Horizons, Deepening Practices
Charles E. Farhadian

Gather into One: Praying and Singing Globally
C. Michael Hawn

The Substance of Things Seen: Art, Faith, and the Christian Community
Robin M. Jensen

Our Worship
Abraham Kuyper, Edited by Harry Boonstra

Wonderful Words of Life:
Hymns in American Protestant History and Theology
Richard J. Mouw and Mark A. Noll, Editors

Discerning the Spirits:
A Guide to Thinking about Christian Worship Today
Cornelius Plantinga Jr. and Sue A. Rozeboom

Voicing God's Psalms
Calvin Seerveld

My Only Comfort: Death, Deliverance, and Discipleship
in the Music of Bach
Calvin R. Stapert

A New Song for an Old World: Musical Thought in the Early Church
Calvin R. Stapert

An Architecture of Immanence:
Architecture for Worship and Ministry Today
Mark A. Torgerson

A More Profound Alleluia: Theology and Worship in Harmony
Leanne Van Dyk, Editor

Christian Worship in Reformed Churches Past and Present
Lukas Vischer, Editor

We Have Seen His Glory: A Vision of Kingdom Worship
Ben Witherington III

The Biblical Psalms in Christian Worship:
A Brief Introduction and Guide to Resources
John D. Witvliet

FROM MEMORY
TO IMAGINATION

Reforming the Church's Music

C. Randall Bradley

WILLIAM B. EERDMANS PUBLISHING COMPANY

GRAND RAPIDS, MICHIGAN / CAMBRIDGE, U.K.

Published 2012 by

Wm. B. Eerdmans Publishing Co.

2140 Oak Industrial Drive N.E., Grand Rapids, Michigan 49505 /

P.O. Box 163, Cambridge CB3 9PU U.K.

www.eerdmans.com

Printed in the United States of America

17 16 15 14 13 12   7 6 5 4 3 2 1

Library of Congress Cataloging-in-Publication Data

From memory to imagination: reforming the church's music /
C. Randall Bradley.

p.   cm.

Includes bibliographical references and index.

ISBN 978-0-8028-6593-9 (pbk.: alk. paper)

1. Music in churches.   I. Title.

ML3001.B75   2012

264′.2 — dc23

2012020288

The author and publisher gratefully acknowledge permission to quote material
from the following sources:

The text of "All Are Welcome" by Mary Haugen. Text © 1994 by GIA Publications,
Inc., 7404 S. Mason Ave., Chicago, IL 60638. Website: www.giamusic.com. Phone:
800-442-1358. All rights reserved. Reprinted with permission.

The text of "When There Is No Star to Guide You" by Thomas Troeger. Text © 1986
by Oxford University Press. Reproduced by permission of Copy Cat Music Li-
censing, LLC, on behalf of Oxford University Press. All rights reserved.

Unless otherwise noted, the Scripture quotations in this publication are from the
New Revised Standard Version of the Bible, copyright © 1989 by the Division of
Christian Education of the National Council of Churches of Christ in the U.S.A.,
and used by permission.

Contents

Acknowledgments

No project of this scope happens without the support of a community. Throughout the writing of this book, many have given me encouragement — some intentionally, and others without knowing they were helping. While I cannot acknowledge everyone, and any attempt to do so is bound to fail, all of those below are in some way represented in the pages of this book, and I want to offer them my thanks.

To Brenda, Hannah, and Isaac, my beloved family, who patiently allowed me to be away from home for many writing retreats and to often be at home but not fully present, and to Brenda for reading and revising this work and all my writing. Hannah and Isaac, you are such grace gifts in our lives.

To Don Haile for allowing me to stay many days at his family's old home on the farm in Hamilton, Texas, where the coyotes and cows were constant companions; to Hulitt and Sheila Gloer for loaning me their second home in Kerrville, Texas, when I was preparing the book's proposal; and to Abby Jimenez and the Cedarbrake Retreat Center staff in Belton, Texas, for their hospitality on my frequent writing retreats.

To my Baylor Church Music colleagues — Swee Hong Lim, David Music, and Terry York — for their support and regular feedback, and to Will May, my dean, and Jean Boyd, my division chair, for granting me a reduced teaching load for the spring semester of 2011 that allowed me to complete the manuscript. To Melinda Coats, our administrative assistant, whose prayers often sustained me.

To my former staff colleagues at Calvary Baptist Church — Sharyn Dowd, Deb Fernandez, Jonathan Grant, Eric Mathis, Julie Pennington Russell, and Kelly Shushok. Without their constant search for what it means to be a community of faith, many of the ideas in this book would never have developed. It was a privilege to walk that road.

To Brenda Bradley, Sharyn Dowd, Eric Mathis, John Woods, and Kelly Shushok, who painstakingly read the manuscript and offered scores of helpful suggestions.

To graduate students Aaron Vanvalkenburg, whose research assistance and insightful suggestions are evident throughout this text, and Karl Utz, who assisted with revisions. To graduate assistants and office workers Tyler Brinson, Chason Disheroon, Mike Eller, Austen Heatherly, Jared Longoria, Stephen Mulkey, Chris Pillsbury, Jacob Sensenig, Lauren Shively, Martha Simmons, Jill Sims, Harry Smith, Jason Terry, John Woods, and Adam Visconti, whose efforts to share my load allowed me time and energy to write. Your energy and commitment always inspire me.

To John Bell, Emily Brink, Carl Daw, Marva Dawn, David Crowder, Harry Eskew, Gloria Gaither, Keith Getty, Helen Kemp, Don Hustad, Roberta King, I-to Loh, Ken Medema, Alice Parker, Don Saliers, Pablo Sosa, Thomas Troeger, Karen Ward, Paul Westermeyer, and Carlton Young, who have been campus guests in the last few years. Through conversations with them, my views have been expanded.

To the churches I've served throughout my ministry: Mt. Pleasant Baptist Church, Georgiana, Alabama; First Baptist Church Benbrook, Benbrook, Texas; Maywood Baptist Church, Independence, Missouri; University Baptist Church, Shawnee, Oklahoma; and Calvary Baptist Church, Waco, Texas. And to Columbus Avenue Baptist Church, Waco, Texas, and First Baptist, Valley Mills, Texas, where I've served recent shorter-term interims. Remnants and stories from each of you are within these pages.

To Zipporah (Zippy) and Daniel Sindiyo, Paul and Donna Tocco, and Mike Wachira, our Kenyan friends who have opened doors for experiencing God more openly and fully.

To the students I've encountered in classes and rehearsals — for the privilege of living life together, and for the many discoveries we've made. You have touched my life deeply.

To John Witvliet for perceiving this project as worthy of being included in the Calvin Institute of Christian Worship Liturgical Studies Series, and to Mary Hietbrink at Eerdmans for her many helpful suggestions and for making the entire manuscript more succinct and logical.

June 18, 2012   RANDALL BRADLEY
(the 29th wedding anniversary for my wife, Brenda, and me)

Introduction

For as long as I can remember, I have loved the music of the church. When I was growing up in a small rural farming community in southern Alabama, going to church was the highlight of my week. As a small boy, I fondly remember sitting on my daddy's lap and singing the gospel hymns that were staples of worship at our little Baptist church. The thrill of singing "Love Lifted Me," "Leaning on the Everlasting Arms," and my favorite, "When We All Get to Heaven," brought great joy to my young life. In those early days, we had only an old upright piano to accompany our singing, and I thrilled at its sound. From my earliest days, I intended to play the piano for church, and every time I was near a piano, I tried to play it. As soon as I started school, I begged to take lessons, and finally, when I was almost through the third grade, a woman who worked with my Aunt Peggy had a piano for sale for thirty-five dollars, and my parents decided that this piano was one that they could afford on their modest salaries. Before I started lessons the next fall, I was already playing hymns using shaped notes that I had learned from my granny. In 1971, in the summer after I finished the fourth grade, I started playing the piano regularly for church.

Those early experiences shaped my life, and I've been deeply involved in the music of the church ever since. Some years later, I felt God stirring within me, and one night during our summer revival, my mother and my granny hosted the visiting preacher and song leader for dinner. Shortly after supper, Brother C. B. Raley asked me to step out into the fox-trot hall of my granny's house, and he said to me, "Randall, I've been wondering if God might just be calling you to give your life to the music of the church." Brother Raley's words connected with the unrest already within me, and that night at the end of the service, I stepped from the piano bench and went over to the pastor and shared what I thought God might be doing inside my heart and my head.

A couple of weeks after graduating from high school in the summer of 1978, I became the minister of music in a small church about fifty miles from Troy State University, where I was to begin college that fall. As I played in the Sound of the South Band, sang with the Collegiate Singers, participated in the ensemble group called Rejoice, acted in operas and musicals, and studied voice, piano, and all that comes with majoring in music, my world grew larger, and my experiences richer. During the five years that I served Mt. Pleasant Baptist Church in Georgiana, Alabama, God worked miraculously in that congregation. We worshiped God in profound ways, and youth from all around came to our church to sing in a youth choir that eventually sang the Christmas portion of Handel's *Messiah*. Those years confirmed the deep passion for the music of the church that God had planted within me as a small boy.

After teaching high school band for two years, I married Brenda Livingston, and we moved to Fort Worth, Texas, where I became a student at Southwestern Baptist Theological Seminary in the fall of 1983. During the next five years, I earned two degrees in church music and continued to serve a local church. As I studied the church's history and its worship, traveled the United States with seminary choirs, and tried to make sense of the changes that were beginning to impact the mainstream of the church's music, my understanding of the church and its music grew immensely, and my desire to affect the church's future blossomed. In the fall of 1989, with a newly earned doctorate in hand, I became an assistant professor of church music at a seminary in Kansas City, Missouri. Not long before the fall term, the person who taught worship was unable to continue, and I was asked about the possibility of teaching the required worship course. I gladly agreed. In addition to preparing for my seminary courses, I developed denominationally related materials, designed worship services for the seminary community, and continued to serve in a local congregation. Along the way I began to write down some of what I was discovering. This newfound passion for writing resulted in the publication of my first book in 1996 — a revision of the standard Baptist worship text by the late Franklin Segler. However, the impetus for the present project actually began in the late 1990s. Then teaching at a small, private liberal arts college in Oklahoma, I was asked to write a journal article to chronicle the music of the church in the last few decades of the twentieth century. I dutifully wrote the article and submitted it, adding a few of my own reflections and projections to the conclusion.

In the early days of 2000, I went to Baylor University to interview for a position in church music. As part of the interview, I was asked to bring along some of the projects that I had recently completed or was working on at the time, and I put the article in my bag to re-read in preparation for the interview. The night before the interview, I re-read the article, and I was struck by my own words, as I had ended the article with projections for the future of the music of the church. The following lines in particular captured my imagination: "The changes that have occurred in church music in the latter part of the twentieth century are continually calling for the church's music leaders to re-define their philosophy related to music's function in worship. Questioning by all involved in Christian music must happen in order for progress to take place. Philosophies long held to be true are breaking down in unlikely places. There is need for prophetic voices to lead these discussions."[1] These words that I had written just months earlier caused me to view the position at Baylor with fresh interest and spurred me to imagine more fully what might occur through the music of the church if given renewed energy. Ultimately, I took the position at Baylor, and the last eleven years I have spent thinking, imagining, refining, sifting, and listening as I have tried to discern just what it might be that God wants to do within and through the church's music.

However, monumental in this process was the ministry that developed at Calvary Baptist Church in Waco, Texas, in which I was privileged to participate. Agreeing in the summer of 2001 to serve a brief interim position at the church, I soon found a deep worship connection with the church's pastor, Julie Pennington-Russell, and we spent many pleasurable hours discussing the church, its worship and music, and our desire to see the church move in directions that neither of us had yet experienced. Over eight years, my belief in the church was strengthened, my vision of the church's worship expanded, and the weekly drama of worship that we planned and led grew to include nearly every imaginable style of music, various art forms, intentional involvement of the senses, and a profound stirring of God's Spirit that at times was

---

1. C. Randall Bradley, "Changes in Church Music," *Southwestern Journal of Theology* 42 (2000): 53.

nearly tangible. At a time when I was most deeply searching for how the role of music could be refined, God allowed me to serve in a congregation where innovation was nurtured, risks were encouraged, and change was welcomed. Out of this rich experiential worship exploration I cultivated many of the ideas in this book.

What you will read within these pages is written out of my deep love for the church, for when we love deeply enough, we are willing to take risks for the sake of those we love. Such is the case with this book. Because I love the church and have spent my life serving it, I have chosen to step into places, offer suggestions, present well-meaning critiques, and propose directions for the church to consider as we, with the Holy Spirit's bidding, chart the church's future. I am hopeful that you'll read the entire text carefully and that you'll interact with the words as they find a place within your own experience. My deepest desire is that God will use this book to bring renewal to the church through its music and its worship. While I have endeavored to write with utmost respect for all Christians, I have not shied away from expressing critiques of the church or of its music. Although you will likely not agree with all that I have written, and you may find some of it challenging to read and difficult to accept, I hope that you will give these ideas, concepts, and stories time and thought in order to discern if there is a message here for you.

The church and its music is the mission and vocation to which I have committed my life, and it is the ministry that I am confident will continue to bring me immense personal, spiritual, and professional joy. I believe the church's best days are ahead, and I believe that the church's music will be a catalyst for moving the church into the future. For the last forty or so years, no aspect of the church's life has received more attention or critique than its music. However, much of the church's internal critique of its music has gone unchecked, and few have stepped back far enough to consider the broader implications for the changes that have occurred and continue to occur. This book attempts to explore these implications. The last forty years have been among the brightest and darkest for the history of the church's music. Could it be that these years have been God's way of preparing the music of the church for its finest moment? Could it be that the element that has been most divisive in the last portion of the previous century will offer the church its greatest unity within the next? Could it be that the dormancy of the long winter of musical discontent offers the church its greatest possibility for an extended and flower-filled spring?

CHAPTER 1

From Memory to Imagination:
Beginning the Journey

Let us build a house where love can dwell
And all can safely live,
A place where saints and children tell
How hearts learn to forgive.

Built of hopes and dreams and visions,
Rock of faith and vault of grace;
Here the love of Christ shall end divisions . . .

All are welcome, all are welcome,
All are welcome in this place.

Marty Haugen, "All Are Welcome"

Memory is something that you never want to be without. Memory is foundational — it gives life meaning. Memory keeps us grounded, contextualizes our experiences, helps to facilitate emotional responses, provides a conduit for connecting to new experiences, helps us to feel safe, deepens our current experiences by situating them within other times and places, helps leaders provide continuity, lets us share our stories, and allows us to connect to the stories of others. Memory permits us to be part of a metanarrative that connects us to all people and all places. Without memory, we would not be connected to God's redemptive story throughout history.

However, memory can be a liability when we depend too heavily on it, and aren't willing to move past our memory to imagine what God may want to do in the present. When we're not willing to move beyond memories of the past, we risk not experiencing new forms of worship, new ways to view God; and our bank of memories ceases to accrue new experiences to add to our personal and collective story of God's redemptive love in our lives and in our communities. Too often we get stuck in memory, which eventually degenerates into sentimentality. Memories that were pulsing with relevancy, life, and wonder become stagnant and murky, and their lack of clarity can cause them to take on unhealthy meaning and power. To remain vibrant, our memories need regular rejuvenation. Without new stories to experience and share, we are unable to experience God's continual work in our lives and our communities. Instead of moving along a grand continuum of God's design, we are stuck in a particular place and time; and so we fail to experience God as dynamic, forever being revealed, and continually moving. At its best, memory should give us confidence and strength to experience God in new ways; however, when we linger too long on specific memories without replenishing and refurbishing them, our faith experience can become petrified. Once living trees, we eventually turn to stone.

In order to experience the freshness and newness of God, we must be continually moving past memory toward imagination. However, moving beyond memory doesn't mean that we forget our past. Memory informs and provides context for the present, but it is tempered by our recent and current experiences and by those of our community. We know that we are stuck in memory when our most significant God stories are in the distant past, when we find ourselves clutching the memories of God from another time too tightly, when our view of God has not changed in many years, when we become skeptical about new God stories, and when we are unable to imagine God as dynamic in our present and future.

Being stuck in memory reveals our brokenness, and we are unable to move ourselves into imagination. We must trust God to move us forward. We must recognize our "memory stuck" condition and ask God to give us new vision and the ability to imagine again. We must depend on our community of faith to help us by encouraging and challenging us. Sometimes we can find ourselves in a "memory box" in which all the faith we seem to have depends on memory. During these times, memory can keep us standing until we find our way to God's next memory-filled place. Being stuck in memory is not a matter of age: whether you're stuck in the 1990s, at last summer's youth camp, or in the seventeenth century, you're still stuck and, because of that, lacking imagination.

God's best is always in our future, for while we have one foot here, we also have one foot in eternity. For the Christian, life is lived in the state of "already" but "not yet." God has already done God's salvific work in our lives by redeeming us through God's son, Jesus, and we are on the journey toward being with God in eternity. But we are not with God in eternity yet, and we must fully live in the confidence of what God has already done with the hope and assurance that God will fully complete what God has begun. Being stuck in memory allows us to live only in the "already" without experiencing either the present or the "not yet" — the stuff of imagination.

Memory is always a part of our faith, for it is in remembering that we are drawn back to God's work in history — both cosmic history and individual history. To understand God in our contemporary context, we must consider God's actions in the past, for it is in doing so that we are often able to see God working contemporarily. As worshipers, we acknowledge God's eternal being and offer praise for God's saving work and faithfulness. We give thanks to God because of what God has done and because of God's being; and we understand God's being primarily by God's revelation of God's self in history.

True faith in God is always connected to the story of God's redemptive work in history — both the history of the church and our own individual history — for we are continually finding our story in the greater narrative of God's story. As followers of Christ we are always connected to Christ-followers throughout history through whose faithfulness we are called to be faithful. Through God's self-revealed act of sending God's son, we know of God's love for us; through the life of Jesus, we are challenged to live sacrificially and serve others; and through Christ's death and resurrection, we are assured of our own resurrection.

Despite memory's importance in defining us as Christ-followers, informing what we know about God, and contextualizing the present and the future, memory is not enough, for it is grounded in the past. Memory interprets the present and informs the future, but it is neither the present nor the future. The present must be fully lived, and the future must be heartily anticipated. God is always moving us toward the future — life in eternity — and our lives are focused on the hope found in Christ's resurrection. We are first and foremost people of the Resurrection, and our focus is on the risen Christ, who is alive and forever calling us toward God.

God alone is God. What we bring to worship is always based on our feelings, our impressions, our hunches, our leanings, our experiences, our memories, our community, and more. While we interpret and relate to God based on our own experiences, relationship to those around us, and our memories and recall, our subjective memory does not alter God's being. While we do our best to keep God's "Godness" in perspective, we are incapable of worshiping God objectively, and to think we can is idolatrous, since we are incapable of understanding God in ways that transcend our own biases and contexts. Since worship is for and about God, worship has an objective dimension — God. The dialogue of worship always involves communion between God, who is beyond our understanding, and we humans, who are always flawed and broken.

All memory is subjective. While it is based on actual moments in time, it is laced with interpretation and forgetfulness. New experiences are always interpreted within the context of our biases, prejudices, needs, and previous experiences. As time passes between events and our telling of them, we tend to alter stories to make them more as we wish they were or to make them fit the particular context in which we are telling them. Over time, we begin to believe the stories as we have told them rather than returning to the original events which spawned them. As time passes, our pain becomes less hurtful, our transformation more dramatic, our words more profound, and our response more measured. One has only to hear his/her own experience told by someone else to know how memories become distorted once they are shared. Memories are constantly in flux; they ebb and flow, and they do not remain consistent throughout our lives or the lives of others who share them. Furthermore, we can never go back to authenticate a memory fully because the place and circumstance of the memory can never be fully re-created. The passing of time changes everything around us — the people, the places, the circumstances, and the context.

Although memory can never be fully trusted as accurate, it is vital to our faith because it is what we know. As flawed as it may be, it is our personal and communal story, our faith journey. The importance of memory is not primarily in the accuracy of facts but in the connection of story from individual to individual and community to community. As our memories connect in recognizable patterns, our individual and group narratives are authenticated, and the similarity of my story to yours substantiates both of our stories and can allow both of us to trust God more fully.

Memory is more than being sentimental. Memory is an important spiritual exercise because so much of our faith is informed by memory. Memory is reliving our experiences. Memory can be active storytelling, individual reflection, or shared silence surrounding mutual encounters. Memory allows our current state to be contextualized, and it provides a launching place for new experiences. Individual memories combine with the memories of others to form larger narratives which form our human story. Because individual memories are usually flawed and incomplete, they are most important when interwoven with the stories of others within communal settings. Just as family stories are made more complete when several family members work together to remember important events, our personal faith stories need others within our faith community in order to find their fuller meaning.

God's plan for humankind was to create a memory for us on which we can hang everything. From the beginning, God designed a covenant with his creation through which we were able to remember God's love and actions on our behalf. This covenant of assurance was designed to launch us on our journey to fulfill God's plan. Throughout the Old Testament, God continually called his followers to remember, to allow their memory of God to inform all that they did. Though humankind continued to forget, they did so despite constant reminders to remember — through prophets, stories of failure and redemption, songs of faith, signs and wonders, and every other imaginable strategy. Likewise, the New Testament encourages us to remember in the taking of bread and wine that God is good for his promise, and that God will return for us in God's time. God created and redeemed, and everything else stems from that memory.

Sacrament is an act that connects the power of a past event to a present experience, and this connection is at the heart of our faith and worship. Without memory, we easily fall into re-creating what has already been created (our memory of a moment), believing that it is new. Memory should inform and change our present and future, and it should give us the freedom to create and take risks in order to continue God's creative work within us and within our faith community. In other words, we already live in the past (the already), but we must take the already (our memory) into the not yet. Far too often, however, our worship is based on our re-creating an experience from another time and place rather than allowing our memory of a past experience to launch us toward what God may want to do in the present. Stated differently, the moment or event that created our memory is not the important component of our memory; the ability for the memory to become a vehicle to create a similar outcome is far more significant. We are often guilty of regularly retracing our steps instead of imagining new paths toward similar outcomes. Musically speaking, a significant spiritual moment may be tied to a particular song; however, instead of continuing to sing the same song for the rest of our lives and expecting to re-create the same experience, we can use the memory of the original experience to serve as a catalyst to create other paths that can lead to new spiritual experiences. When I was a college student, I vividly remember my piano teacher, Violet Ervin, discussing her eccentric husband and his bent toward traveling. She told me, "While some people like to travel the world and see many places, Dr. Ervin loves to see the same place many times." We are often like Dr. Ervin: instead of allowing our memory to launch us toward imagining and basking in the vastness of God, we let our memory become myopic, and we spend our lives experiencing the same God-place many times.

Imagination is built on experience, on our story, and the connection between memory and imagination is similar to carrying two five-gallon buckets filled with water. When you carry both buckets, the load is balanced, and the buckets are interdependent; but if you drop one bucket, that makes the weight of the other bucket nearly impossible to sustain. The resulting imbalance sends you swerving around, and in the process, you spill water, waste time, and often lose your way — unable to deliver the water to its intended destination. In a parallel way, imagination is dependent on memory, and memory is dependent on imagination. Without both in balance, neither functions as intended.

Because memory is so important to imagination, we cannot take it for granted; it has to be nurtured, developed, and rightly understood. While for some, memory has become distorted and idolized beyond its intention, for others it is absent or lacking; therefore, they continue on, unaware of their loss and its handicapping effect. Memory is vital to our faith and worship, and without a solid repository of experiences, our faith is likely to be anemic. However, faith memory is more than a series of sound bites from the past: it is the accumulation of deeply lived experiences in which we are able to see God through intentional reflection. Often our worship is unimaginative because our leaders are lacking in memory, and our faith is shallow because our faith memory-banks are either depleted or were never filled in the first place. Most often, the corollary of a strong imagination is a deep well of memory.

Likewise, creativity also finds its source in memory, because creativity builds on a rich foundation of memories. Since all new ideas find their inspiration in past experiences, a repository of stories is vital to a strong imagination. When creating music, a thorough knowledge of the story of music enhances creativity. An understanding of music history, theory, performance style, instruments, forms, and more can provide a secure launching pad for creating new music. One will likely never write a popular ballad without hearing many songs that intricately weave story and song, compose a great symphony without experiencing the grandeur of orchestral instruments, write a beloved praise song without participating in the unity of group singing, or compose a masterful oboe concerto without understanding the oboe's range, timbre, and idiosyncrasies. Imagination builds on significant memory, so filling our individual and collective memories with the important stories from our past initiates the potential for creativity. If we don't do this, we may write music, sing songs, and preach sermons; but instead of choosing notes, sounds, and words from a broad repository, we will be drawing from our thin experiences, and our creative output will reveal the transparent shallowness of our memory pool. Rather than drawing from the unlimited palette of God's imagination, our creative efforts will draw only from the limited colors of our bleak experience. An illustration comes from a friend's story about taking voice lessons from a seasoned professor. When my friend complained about the songs that he was required to sing as a part of his lessons, the teacher simply remarked, "I grew up eating peas and cornbread myself, but along the way I've learned to enjoy lots of other foods." While we all begin life with few experiences, life fully lived and realized provides a rich repository of memories from which imagination can flourish.

Both our worship planning and our worship leadership depend on our ability to absorb the experiences around us that give voice to our thoughts about God, form our understanding of God's kingdom, and generate our deepest prayers. When I was a young teacher, I regularly planned and led worship for the seminary community. In those early years, I listened carefully to the profound prayers that my seasoned colleagues offered to God as a part of chapel worship experiences, and I longed to express my thoughts to God with similar insight and reflection; I felt inept when I was asked to pray in that public context. But eventually I realized that in order to pray with greater insight, I had to live longer and experience God more fully. As a result, I began a process of writing prayers and regularly reading the prayers of others. Over time, these practices, coupled with worship and other spiritually rich experiences, gave me a greater theological understanding and framework and a richer prayer vocabulary.

Similarly, when I started playing the piano for our church's Sunday-night service the summer I was ten years old, I knew only four hymns the first Sunday night I played. To avoid repeating hymns, each week thereafter I learned four new hymns. I continued this regimen for many months until I felt that it would be acceptable to repeat some of the hymns. By the following summer, I felt confident allowing the congregation to choose their favorites, which was our church's Sunday-night tradition. Now, decades later, most of those hymns are safely locked in the memory of my fingers, and I could play many of them solely through the power of touch. The tireless work I invested as a young boy has fed my spirit for a lifetime. That deposit in my memory bank still inspires my creativity and imagination both in personal ways and within the communities I serve.

Memory often breaks down when we fail to look beneath the surface to discern memory's meaning. What made the memory significant? What set this memory apart from others? What was the role of other memories in creating this memory? What was the memory's context? What happened within the memory that was organized, controlled, and planned? What was spontaneous, unplanned, and unexpected? Beyond the surface meaning, what is the memory's essence? What was the goal and purpose of the experience that launched the memory? What was it about this memory that set it apart from other experiences? How might this memory inform current practices? What about this memory should be re-created? Why? These and other questions can open us up to see God within our memories and to create an inroad through which God can work.

A friend of mine recently shared her experience in working in her church's Vacation Bible School. The team of leaders decided on a theme, purchased a curriculum, and recruited teachers. Interestingly, they poured their greatest energy into decorating the building to interpret the theme. As the beginning of Bible school approached, they spent countless hours turning large parts of the church into various kinds of outer-space-related scenery and its paraphernalia. Building likenesses of spaceships, robots, planets, solar systems, and control panels, they were thoroughly exhausted by the time Bible school began; some workers were burned out and questioned whether they would have the time and energy to work in Bible school in the future. Based on their memory of how Bible school should look, the team re-created their memory rather than probing the purpose of the decorations that consumed so much of their time, energy, and creativity. At the bottom of this elaborate memory-inspired operation was a desire for the children to feel welcome and for their parents to know that the teachers were well-prepared. But the Bible school team had failed to grapple with questions below the surface. What can we do to assure each child that he/she is welcome? How will parents know whether their child's teacher is well-prepared and their child is learning? How should we most appropriately invest the time and energy with which we have been entrusted? What are the purposes of Vacation Bible School, and how should we accomplish those goals? It's possible that the team thoughtfully decided on their plan of action. But it's likely that a different and better outcome might have resulted from asking probing questions instead of acting unilaterally from memory.

Now let's look to the church's music and its need for re-imagination. The church's music is in need of prophetic re-imagination and reformation. Because it has been subjected to years of wear and tear and hundreds of cosmetic updates, layers of wallpaper, coats of paint, and numerous facades, a cover job will not suffice anymore. The music of the church must to be stripped back to the rafters and re-formed. Walls that have been erected within the once-spacious rooms must be taken down and the rooms re-shaped. Windows long covered with heavy drapes must be opened to encourage fresh winds of imagination to blow freely and to allow the sun's warmth to diffuse the damp and haze. Re-imagining the church's music seems like renovating an old house: one update calls for another, and there seems to be no stopping once the process has begun.

Speaking about the church, Dwight Friesen says, "We have systemic problems, which is to say the problems facing the church and all of humanity are a series of interconnected, interanimating, and interdependent problems."[1] Physicist Fritjof Capra adds, "There are solutions to the major problems of our time, some of them even simple. But they require a radical shift in our perceptions, our thinking, our values. And, indeed, we are now at the beginning of such a fundamental change of

---

1. Dwight J. Friesen, *Thy Kingdom Connected: What the Church Can Learn from Facebook, the Internet, and Other Networks* (Grand Rapids: Baker Books, 2009), p. 22.

worldview in science and society, a change of paradigms as radical as the Copernican revolution."[2] In order for paradigms to shift, we must first recognize that there are unanswered questions that deserve exploration. As we probe these unanswered questions and begin to discover resolution, a paradigm shift eventually results. Once one paradigm begins to shift, other aspects of what we believe to be true invariably begin to re-align as a result. Thomas Kuhn defines a paradigm as "the entire constellation of beliefs, values, techniques, and so on shared by the members of a given community and used by that community to define legitimate problems and solutions."[3] A paradigm represents a belief within a given community that is coherent and consensual. A paradigm shift occurs when the accepted and generally unquestioned norms are left behind, making it impossible to return to "the old way."[4]

When I was going into the eleventh grade, my dad's job changed, and my family moved to a different region of Alabama. Near the end of my first day in the new school, I joyfully went to band class, took out my euphonium, and warmed up for rehearsal. When the band director gave the downbeat for the first march, I started to play, but I quickly discovered that the other students had stopped playing and were listening to me. Apparently my volume and tone were different from what my bandmates had heard before. Shortly afterward, we went to the marching field, and similarly, my marching technique was novel and foreign. After two weeks my parents and I decided that the music program of this school would probably not adequately prepare me for my intended college major, and I returned to my previous school and completed high school while living with my granny. During my senior year, I became good friends with a young woman who played clarinet in the band I had briefly joined. In one conversation she said to me, "Before you came to our school, we thought we were good, and I enjoyed playing in the band. But after you came, we all knew that we weren't good anymore. Band was never the same after that." While I've always regretted my part in lessening the pleasure of some of the students in their high school band, I've often reflected on that conversation, the paradigm shift that it described, and its implications for the music of the church.

2. Fritjof Capra, *The Web of Life: A New Scientific Understanding of Living Systems* (New York: Anchor Books, 1996), p. 4, quoted in Friesen, *Thy Kingdom Connected*, p. 23.

3. Thomas S. Kuhn, *The Structure of Scientific Revolutions*, 2nd ed. (Chicago: University of Chicago Press, 1970), p. 175, quoted in Friesen, *Thy Kingdom Connected*, p. 24.

4. Friesen, *Thy Kingdom Connected*, p. 24.

In essence, once new experiences and new knowledge are added to our pre-existing situation, we have to respond to what we have encountered. Once we "know," we cannot return to our previous naïveté.

New paradigms always force us to reconfigure how we perceive our surroundings. History is replete with people who were early adopters — that is, people who were able to see what was coming and respond earlier than others. These prophetic voices play an important role in our world, and they have guided the church toward previous re-formations. Regarding the music of the church, many of us have experienced the feeling that everything is shifting and the uneasiness of not trusting what we previously believed to be reliable. When our training seems outdated, the rate of change accelerates, our memory is flawed, and our imagination appears inadequate, we are tempted to retreat. However, while embracing every new fad is foolish, failing to listen to the hearts, motives, and leanings of early adopters is also ill-informed. Early adopters play an important role, and they are often catalysts for change. Still, the church must also value those who genuinely critique change and do not embrace it readily or easily. As the church faces re-formation of its music, all voices are needed in the conversation.

We are all intricately connected, and our dependence on each other has never been greater. Often referred to as the Small World Theory,[5] and used in a number of movies and games, the theory demonstrates that all people are connected to all other people around the globe by about six degrees of separation. Connecting with a friend who then connects with another friend, and so on through six "hops," as they are sometimes called, you can connect with anyone, anywhere. Similarly, jobs are found, Internet connections are made, products are sold, music is disseminated, and more. Therefore, our movement within our own sphere of existence and influence can quite quickly affect a large group of people.

Reforming the church's music will require the best that all of us can offer. No one will have all the answers, but within all of us will be some hunches and some fresh ideas about where the wind of the Spirit is blowing. As a part of this process, we must acknowledge that God is faithful as we venture on this journey. God will be with us as we discern what new paradigms to embrace. Furthermore, all re-formation of the

---

5. Duncan Watts, *Small World: The Dynamics of Networks between Order and Randomness* (Princeton: Princeton University Press, 2003), quoted in Friesen, *Thy Kingdom Connected,* p. 35.

church's music will be made on behalf of the entire church. We are not isolated within our own individual or smaller communal locale; what we discuss in this book and the changes that we embrace will impact all people who make up Christ's church. As elaborated later, we will need the entire community, for decisions regarding the church are never unilateral but communal. Genuine dialogue will assure that the process remains communal. Just as an athletic team huddles before and during a game, we must continually check in with each other to be sure that our efforts are pulling in the same direction.

Addressing the challenges of the music of the church must always be viewed as a family discussion. As we do at a family conference, we must discuss challenges within the context of those who share our values and commitments and love the church as we do. Healthy families frequently discuss ways in which their quality of life, their interactions, and their communication can be improved. In much the same way, the church's music needs to be discussed regularly. A problem should be viewed as a family challenge, and the ownership of the problem and its solution belongs to all of us. Whatever affects the church's music is my challenge, your challenge, our challenge, the church's challenge — and it is most certainly God's challenge.

George Bernard Shaw's maxim was quoted by Edward Kennedy at the funeral of his brother Robert: "There are those who look at things the way they are, and ask why. . . . I dream of things that never were, and ask why not?" The sort of questioning that this quotation implies keeps us continually re-forming and re-shaping the church's music, and it eliminates the possibility of complacency. This book seeks to view the challenge of the church's music as an adventure. It is an adventure into the unknown where no one knows the way, and we are not sure whose steps to follow. Becoming discouraged is likely, becoming momentarily lost is certain, and mistaking shadows for harmful beings can cause us to become afraid and disoriented. Still, we must, like explorers, find the way.[6] As new directions for the music of the church are charted, no one has a sure map, and we are all a part of an ongoing journey of exploration.

Each of us can develop the ability to view challenges from different perspectives. How would it be to see things from a different perspective? What if you were born at a very different time? What if you had different

6. John D. Caputo, *What Would Jesus Deconstruct? The Good News of Postmodernism for the Church* (Grand Rapids: Baker Academic Books, 2007), p. 39.

education and training, different experiences? What if on a Sunday morning you were touching the hands of people in a different culture? What if the soundtrack of your life was the same as the soundtrack of someone from a different time and place? Assuming different perspectives, John Caputo says, "requires the ability to imagine ourselves otherwise and hence to concede that while we firmly stand on the idea of the rock of ages, different ages rest on different rocks."[7] We are on a journey, and those who insist that they know the way have already programmed their lives — they can put their lives on automatic pilot. They will be spared the potential for getting lost. Unfortunately, they will also miss the likelihood of misreading the map and the possibility of discovering new relationships while taking a detour, and they will be the lesser for it.

Each of us can choose to begin the journey from memory to imagination or to sit it out. Diogenes Allen expresses the journey from memory to imagination well in commenting on the play *A Sleep of Prisoners* by Christopher Fry: "We remain captives within a mental framework that has actually been broken. We are like prisoners who could walk out of a prison because all that would enclose us has been burst open, but we remain inside because we are asleep. Christopher Fry, however, tells us that this is the time to wake up."

> The human heart can go the lengths of God.
> Dark and cold we may be, but this
> Is no winter now. The frozen misery
> Of centuries breaks, cracks, begins to move;
> The thunder is the thunder of the floes,
> The thaw, the flood, the upstart Spring.
> Thank God our time is now when wrong
> Comes up to face us everywhere,
> Never to leave us till we take
> The longest stride of soul men ever took.
> Affairs are now soul size.
> The enterprise
> Is exploration into God.[8]

7. Caputo, *What Would Jesus Deconstruct?* p. 41.

8. Diogenes Allen, "The Fields Are White for the Harvest," in *Evangelism in the Reformed Tradition,* ed. Arnold Lovell (Decatur, Ga.: CTS Press, 1990), pp. 17-18, quoted in *Missional Church: A Vision for the Sending of the Church in North America,* ed. Darrell L. Guder (Grand Rapids: Wm. B. Eerdmans, 1998), p. 17.

CHAPTER 2

Why We're in Crisis Now

Instead of telling our vulnerable stories, we seek safety in abstractions, speaking to each other about our opinions, ideas, and beliefs rather than about our lives. Academic culture blesses this practice by insisting that the more abstract our speech, the more likely we are to touch the universal truths that unite us. But what happens is exactly the reverse: as our discourse becomes more abstract, the less connected we feel. There is less sense of community among intellectuals than in the most "primitive" society of storytellers.

Parker J. Palmer, *A Hidden Wholeness*

The worship of the church is in crisis now because we have denied that cultural shifts have been occurring and that these shifts have been affecting the church. Many of us have been unprepared for the changes that have occurred, so we have retreated to the safety of the past and the security of the memory of a time that no longer is nor shall ever be again. With the shift toward postmodernity,[1] the vast shift in worship has been inevi-

---

1. Postmodernity is determined more by what it isn't than what it is. Defining postmodernity is challenging because codifying postmodernism would set ideological boundaries, build philosophical fences, and hem in a worldview whose survival depends on lack of boundaries, fine-edged arguments, and sharp lines that have the potential to exclude. Valuing absolute truth, researched knowledge, careful order, emotional restraint, organized programs, outlined sermons, logical worship, fully orbed song texts, structured music, and methodical operational procedures, modernity served the church well for a long time, and it will remain a defining force in Western churches for many

table, and signs of its coming have been evident for a long time. Although the shift will take many more years to be fully realized, rapid change is likely a permanent characteristic of what will be "the new normal."

Is resuscitation possible? Will it be possible to save the tradition that formed and shaped us? While we will discuss this question more thoroughly, some changes may be irreversible and inevitable. However, before answering this question, we must further explore whether we would want to return to the now-faded glory of what was, for what we would miss in exchange might make for a poor trade. While returning to a relative point of safety in the past might seem appealing, a full return to any previous moment or point in history is always a flawed romantic notion replete with problems and inconsistencies.

For the last half of the previous century, changes were occurring slowly and deliberately, and at first they were hardly recognizable. As more time passed, the changes became more pronounced, and in time they were fully visible, as we will see. In the 1980s and 1990s, issues regarding worship were referred to as battles over style, worship wars, and style wars. Today, a "breach" metaphor no longer seems valid because the changes are now being viewed as more the result of a cultural shift than as a breach between the traditional and the contemporary church. The changes that have occurred and are occurring are greater than those brought about by other historical breaches or battles over particular issues within the church; they are part of a broader cultural shift whose magnitude is affecting all elements of society, not just the church.

How We Got Here from There

In the last half of the twentieth century, the center of power shifted from the academy, through the church, to the community. In the 1950s, a period of relative stability, the church's power center was in the academy and the educated clergy; today, the power center is more commu-

---

years to come. Amid the changes brought about through postmodernism, signs of hope abound, for postmodernism includes all, explores all perspectives and viewpoints for answers, values the perspective of the whole person and his/her ideas, and places no strictures on how we interpret and interact with God. Postmodernity's value for meaningful relationships, deep authenticity, significant experiences, unexplainable mystery, and broad diversity make it a ready fit for the radical Christ about whose life the New Testament bears witness.

nally based. The effect that this power shift has had on all elements of worship is significant, and all churches — regardless of size and scope — have been influenced.

The 1950s: The Halls of Academia

Some consider the 1950s to be a period of relative stability within the church. The church, like society in general, had survived two world wars, and it enjoyed a decade of safety and increased prosperity. In retrospect, the changes that were to occur over time were brewing under the surface, but they were not visible to most until much later. The power within the church was primarily held by the educated clergy. Partly due to the GI Bill, which allowed military personnel returning from World War II to attend institutions of higher education at the government's expense, seminaries equipped more clergy than ever before, and churches were the recipients of these newly minted, highly educated ministers. Armed with knowledge and training, these ministers went into the churches where more sophisticated liturgy, well-crafted sermons, and classically based music were received positively by congregants, who themselves were becoming more affluent and more highly educated than their parents. Writers and thinkers such as Erik Routley were influential in the musical philosophy that churches espoused, and many denominations published materials that encouraged congregations to deepen their faith through learning about worship and music. Churches started choirs for all ages, music participation increased, and many churches installed new pipe organs and hired classically trained musicians to supplement their volunteer core. Choral music flourished, and hymns began to nudge out gospel songs even in some evangelical churches. Church musicians flocked to summer training institutions to learn the latest repertoire and techniques. The foundation that was established during the 1950s and before would support the music of the church for decades, and the power that it wielded would prove to be influential.

The 1960s: The Church Basement

In contrast to the 1950s, the 1960s was a decade of instability and rapid change. What was dormant in the 1950s surfaced in the 1960s. With the civil rights movement gaining momentum, the Vietnam War entering the world stage, and the emerging rebellion of younger people catching the establishment off-guard, the age of questioning and instability gained momentum. Meanwhile, life in the sanctuary progressed as usual with few changes evident. However, in the basement of the church, young people were beginning to play guitars in ways that mimicked the early stars of rock and roll and the newly rediscovered power of folk music. They wrote songs which they played and sang for youth gatherings, for fellowships, and in their private worship; and they also sang the protest songs of their non-churchgoing counterparts. By the end of the decade, some church youth choirs that had cut their teeth on the classics were now singing youth musicals that were written in a pseudo-popular music style. Younger people were attracted to the music, and youth choirs grew at an unprecedented rate well into the next decade. For the first time, churchgoing young people had their own music.

The 1970s: Up the Stairs

The youth music that sprouted in the 1960s gained momentum in the early 1970s with more youth musicals, the Jesus movement, and the publication of songbooks such as *Sing and Celebrate!*[2] and dozens of others. As the young people of the 1960s matured, they wanted music for worship based on the music they had experienced in the basement and around campfires as youth. Particularly in churches such as the Vineyard Fellowship in Anaheim, California, and Calvary Chapel in Costa Mesa, California, new songs were written, and the sounds started to rise from the basement up the stairs; this is how praise and worship music took root. And then came Watergate, the bitter ending of the Vietnam War, and the youth rebellion against the status quo with wild hair, "groovy" clothes, and liberal ideas. Clearly, the 1970s was a decade in which shock was commonplace.

Meanwhile, producers began to publish and market this new music and the groups and individual artists who sang it. For the first time, young people had access to mass-produced music that mimicked the

---

2. This book was a staple of youth music ministry in the 1970s and beyond. Its publication was followed by *Sing 'n' Celebrate II* and others. See Kurt Kaiser and Sonny Salsbury, *Sing 'n' Celebrate* (Waco, Tex.: Word Music, 1971).

popular sounds of the day with Christian lyrics; this was the birth of what became known as contemporary Christian music.

While little seemed to change in the sanctuary itself, perceptive congregants couldn't ignore the sounds from the basement that seemed to be coming up the stairs. However, with no imminent threat audible, worship in most congregations experienced little change.

The 1980s: Now Where To?

The 1980s were a time of transition in which the music of the church was ripe for change; still, the changes were easy to ignore and usually perceived as an intermission in the broader drama of the church. Pervading the 1980s church was the notion that denying change would cause it to disappear. Most in academia viewed musical changes as a temporary deviation or the farthest trajectory of a normal pendulum swing. Staying the course — continuing to propagate "standard" music and worship practices — would assure that momentary changes would remain short-lived. No one spoke of cultural shifts, and postmodernity was rarely if ever discussed. While church members sometimes advocated change, and students sporadically campaigned for the ever-broadening "popular culture" of the music of the church, their presence was scattered, and their voices were not prominent. In retrospect, inevitable signs of noteworthy change were visible and audible, but many retreated to older, more secure paradigms.

The 1990s: In the Sanctuary

By the mid-1990s, there was no denying that the church was changing, and many began to believe that change was anything but temporary. Newer worship forms and models had now fully reached the sanctuary, and there was no longer any possibility of denying that change was imminent. The place of newer musical forms gained solid traction in the 1990s, and what were by then decades-old shifts began to be viewed as shifts with deep roots and possible permanence.

Also, prominent in the early 1990s was the church growth movement. It had a "worship as the front door of the church" mentality; it viewed worship as a commodity for drawing people to church. Even the outreach techniques deeply entrenched in evangelical churches began to give way to this use of worship as a means to church growth.

Additionally, as the 1990s progressed, the term "worship wars" began to appear. By the close of the decade, many churches were divided over worship and music styles. As churches attempted to pick up the pieces from battles over worship, they also began to explore different streams of worship — liturgical, traditional, blended, contemporary — in an attempt to find their way along the ever-broadening worship path. On the positive side, worship was a regular topic of discussion, and the body of scholarly literature related to worship that had been growing since the 1980s reached its peak.

The Year 2000 and Beyond: Opening the Doors

As we entered a new millennium, the church gradually opened its doors, and over time, fresh winds of the Spirit have begun to blow through the church and its worship. As worship wars have begun to calm[3] and churches either have decided what style(s) of worship they will authenticate or have opted for a blended model, the emphasis has shifted from obsession with the local body gathered in a building to a focus on a missional model in which God's center of gravity is imagined in the world instead of the sanctuary. In the new millennium, churches have begun to recognize the vast size and scope of the cultural shift of postmodernism and other shifts. Churches are exploring community as a biblical model for church, and small groups, cell groups, and home worship have resulted. Churches are recognizing the importance of making communal decisions and are exploring those implications for worship.

However, old paradigms die slowly and painfully. Several years ago at a family reunion, I was discussing church music with my cousin, who is a worship leader in his faith community. As we discussed his church's resistance to change related to the role of women in worship leadership, he quoted his mother as having once said, "Some people will have to die before change can occur." My cousin added, "At the time I never imagined it was my death that she was referring to."

---

3. The March 2011 cover of *Christianity Today* proclaimed that the worship wars are over.

Holding up the Myth (The Stories We Tell Ourselves)

A myth is a legend or story that we believe to be true. A myth is usually based on an event or a person — possibly a hero or heroine. While the myth may contain truth, it can also be based on indeterminable evidence. Because myths develop over time, they accumulate additional stories, beliefs, and ideas until their multiple layers are nearly impossible to sift through in order to reveal the often-forgotten core. As a culture, many of our actions and our worldviews are based on myths that we believe and trust and often don't question. Myths embody the ideals and institutions of a society, they move us to act, and they form our reason for being.

Consider this possibility: the church's music, the institutions it embodies, the ideals it upholds, and the legends and stories that surround it are a multilayered myth that the church and its musicians have served without pausing to question its origins, its contextual truth, or its relevance to the future. As the music of the church has become more diverse and complex, the ability of the church music myth to sustain myriads of new stories and legends has caused great strain, and stress fractures and fissures have developed as a result. As we've continued to add to the existing church music structure, the additional weight has outstripped the myth's original load limit, and it can no longer sustain the strain. Perhaps the complexity and scope of the church's music can no longer be served by the existing myth, and new repositories must be imagined and created.

Holding up a myth is a difficult task. Once the myth has either outlived its intent or assumed more baggage than its load limit can sustain, the myth becomes a burden, no longer a freeing story whose purpose is to encourage, inspire, and provide context. Once the myth's story is too complex, unbelievable, or incoherent and can no longer sustain itself, it has to be buttressed externally. Buttressing a myth is a complex task, and it can't be accomplished by an individual. It takes communities of people to sustain an ailing myth, and once the myth is dead, the strategies for making it appear to live become even more dysfunctional. Is it possible that the church has spent years resuscitating a dying myth? Could it be that the church, the academic community, and organizations that support the church's music have collaborated in an epic comedy in which we have tried to breathe life into a failing myth without recognizing the obvious farce?

If we have participated in the buttressing of this myth, we must step back and consider the price we have paid. Nothing is more taxing and life-sucking than breathing new life into the dead! To breathe new life into a dead entity, one has to breathe both to sustain one's self and to try to raise the dead. No individual can sustain this stifling act, and eventually others have to be enlisted to help. In addition, the focus on propping up the dead firmly roots us in the past and allows no space for imagining the future. Because this great effort exhausts us, we have no energy for sustaining new ideas. Consequently, we harbor anger against the obligation to which we believe we are called, and we are defensive when our actions are questioned. Our responsibility to bolster the dead becomes so routine and normal for us that our dysfunction cannot be called out or recognized.

Yet, we can be freed from the burden of buttressing this myth. Being true to heritage and history is valuable, but it isn't worth our lives. The message of the resurrected Christ is to give us life and freedom, not to deplete them. Ultimately, God is good for what ails the music of the church. God can sustain what God wants to sustain. God doesn't need our efforts. God remembers so that we don't have to. To trust our own memory and our own breath to sustain the life of the church's music myth is idolatry; we have trusted ourselves as if everything depended on us.

When we're able to acknowledge the inevitable death of a myth that we've loved and sustained, we can recognize that death is a gift and future life is possible. Then space can be created for new life to develop. The repositories that are cleared and the space that opens up allow for new stories to be created, new ideas to sprout. While myths are important in making sense of our world, they can also hinder imagination and dwarf the future. Owning our myths but discarding what is worn out, allowing light to shine into curtained rooms, and burying what is lifeless create space for God to indwell and create a better future. The memory of what was then becomes the catalyst that launches us into the imagination of what can be.

What Inhibits Recovery

Like a twelve-step program, the path to recovery from the dysfunctional myth of the church's music is paved with honesty. Acknowledging that the myth is on life support and exploring the aspects of the myth that have allowed us to function dysfunctionally provide a logical starting place for recovery. But certain stumbling blocks can inhibit recovery.

Denial

The church's music has been shrouded in denial. Those within traditional circles have denied that "their" music often failed to connect with the people the church is called to serve, that historical music is not always best, that well-crafted tunes may not be singable, that theologically rich texts may be too dense, that newer music was filling many of the gaps that resulted, and so on. Those within more contemporary circles have denied that music existed before "their" music, that the new texts were sometimes weak and trite, that tunes were often unsingable, that extreme volume discourages participation, that popular-sounding tunes may not be able to carry theologically rich texts, and so on. Furthermore, we have denied that the church's music is in crisis because denial protects us from that larger reality. We have ignored our participation in the larger body of Christ, where when one part is in pain, so is every other part. We have denied that our misinformed words about the musical preferences of other brothers and sisters within Christ's body were hurtful and counter to the church's mission. We have denied that we have not listened to others and communicated across imaginary lines. We have also failed to recognize what is good in the position of the other or to admit what troubles us about our own position. Our obsession with denial has allowed us to prop up the part of the myth about which we were unwilling to be honest and forthright. The first step toward recovery is to discontinue denial.

Provincialism

Provincialism leads us to think about only the part of the world that most readily affects us. Provincialism allows us to be safe within our own relatively small sphere while ignoring the problems of the larger body to which we are connected. Within the music of the church, our local attitudes have allowed us to ignore the larger world (the songs that Christians sing around the world or even down the street), to inflate the "success" of the music we prefer while minimizing the importance of the music we like less. For years we have expended untold money and energy in publishing mostly denominational hymnals rather than working together for the good of the whole. In order to make recovery possible, we must surrender provincialism to the God of all people and all places.

Recent Memory

The music of the church has existed in relatively recent memory. Even younger people are enslaved to recent memory. For example, college students are able to imagine only that for which their memories provide context. They're often stuck in the memory of high-school youth-camp worship or the worship experience of last week's college gathering. Similarly, older adults may be trapped in the relatively recent memory of their young adult years and the music popular during those decades. In essence, most of the church is trapped in recent memory, and our ability to look deeply into the church's historical forms is often limited. We must begin to look beyond recent memory to the historical church, and we must look beyond the pragmatism of today toward the eschatological imagination of God.

Retreating

When challenged, the musicians of the church have often chosen to retreat toward security. Rather than using challenging situations and tense moments as vehicles for growth, we have tended to retreat toward the safety of those whose thoughts we perceived to be most like ours. As a result, we have forfeited the possibility of open exchange, the opportunity to think creatively together, and the prospect of cross-pollination. While retreating is a natural response and sometimes necessary in the face of inappropriate behavior, the losses that are incurred are difficult to recoup.

Posturing

Posturing occurs when we expend more energy defending our views than listening to the perspectives of others. Insecurity is usually intrinsic in posturing. Posturing shows that fear controls us — the fear that authenticating the experience of another might weaken our position. When we posture, we subtly admit that our thoughts are already entrenched, and that embracing the perspectives of others would threaten the structures we have erected to support the myths we prefer. Posturing limits recovery because it feeds the very source that needs to starve in order to create space for openness and dialogues.

Control

Our ability to move toward recovery is severely limited by our need to control ourselves, our environment, and those around us. When pressed, we are sometimes capable of extreme behavior in order to maintain control. Retreating and posturing are often methods of maintaining control, of recognizing that we are vulnerable to the control of others. To surrender control of an aspect of the church's music might mean that we make ourselves vulnerable to other types of music and worship forms that don't fit within our myth.

Power

Power is at the heart of all of the church's music. Our desire for power upstages most other motivations. For instance, to have power over others means that they don't have power over us; to have power over our finances lulls us into believing that we have power over our destiny. Obsession with power is fueled by lack of trust in others and God, and it reveals a lack of regard for the community of faith that nurtures us. Addiction to power limits our ability to learn from others, inhibits our willingness to collaborate, and stunts our future growth and usefulness. Maintaining power suffocates our ability to recover because recovery is dependent on vulnerability, and dependence on power doesn't allow for vulnerability.

Self-Sufficiency

Like being obsessed with power, believing too strongly in self-sufficiency inhibits change. When I believe that I'm invincible, I'm closing myself off to the power of God to do more through me than I could have imagined. Self-sufficiency is the enemy of community, because when we're self-sufficient, we don't need others to guide us. Self-sufficiency is the antithesis of collaboration: we don't need to work with others when we can do it ourselves.

Measurable Outcomes

To need to control the outcome of the music of the church is to assume a control that is not ours. Nevertheless, we are addicted to measuring outcomes in terms of numbers, participation, perceived emotional response, and level of understanding. The church has been obsessed with growth, measurable outcomes, and quantitative data. Spurred on by capitalistic notions of "bigger is better" business practices and the need to sustain our large and cumbersome institutions, we have often exchanged the way of Christ for the way of commerce. But God cannot be measured on our terms, and the impact of music can never be quantified fully. When we surrender the leadership of the church's music to the Spirit, we are no longer responsible for all outcomes.

The Key Players

Considering the key players in the church's music is an important step in understanding the challenges facing the church. The music of the church is multilayered and involves many different entities. Each plays a different role, and each must be examined to make the full picture visible.

Church Music and the Academy

Church music and the academy have traditionally been closely linked, as we saw above; in fact, in some periods, the academy controlled the music of the church. During the last half of the twentieth century, the academy lost some of its influence as it failed to adjust to the changing culture that influenced the church's music. On many fronts, the academy offers only minimal input regarding the church's music today, and at times the input is not pastorally offered by the academy or readily welcomed by the church. While in the past most professional church musicians were trained within the confines of academia, many musicians today learn through hands-on training from practitioners that more closely resembles apprenticeship models. If the academy is to re-establish a significant role in the church's music, the academy must create new paradigms that serve the church rather than exalt itself.

Church Music and the Church

Oddly enough, the church itself, while utilizing music in all of its services, has often abdicated its voice regarding music. Rather than deciding how music can best serve the church and its mission, the church has often failed to discuss music, teach congregants about music, realize music's power, or explore its musical options. Churches tend to be influenced by tradition or pragmatism, and both can be helpful, but they are harmful if employed to the extreme. For instance, some churches have experienced only minimal changes in their worship despite the music changes occurring outside the church and within the church universal. By contrast, other churches have embraced nearly every form of new music with little discernment concerning their local context, music's place in worship, and music's power to shape lives.

In moving toward the future, the church itself must reclaim its rightful position of discernment regarding the music that it embraces.

Church Music and Artists

Prior to the 1970s, fewer professional artists depended primarily on the church and its members for support. Since the 1970s, artists within the church have played an increasingly significant role in determining the church's musical diet. From the meager beginnings of a few bands, vocal groups, and soloists have come numerous Christian music makers; today, hundreds of Christian artists represent every imaginable genre of music. This music and the systems that support it — radio stations, publishing companies, agents, producers, and the Internet — exert a formidable influence on the worship music of many churches. Many view this music as "Christian music" rather than "church music"

— that is, music performed and produced by Christians for Christians. They maintain that it isn't primarily designed for the church; nevertheless, this music plays a significant role in the repertoire of Sunday's worship.

Church Music and Performers

The role of people who perform music for others has increased continually. From the organist who spends more time each week preparing a stunning prelude and postlude yet gives minimal attention to the hymns, to the band who refines its sound to the degree that congregants are subtly encouraged to listen rather than participate, the church is full of musical performers. Coupled with a culture that enjoys cheering for others (think sports) rather than participating, this single aspect of the church's music may very well be the most potentially dangerous.

Instead of performers, the church needs leaders who are able to "enliven," who are able to infuse songs with life and to encourage others, through their winsome spirit, to participate. Worship is based on participation, not observation. We must discover ways for the church to move past its lethargy toward full-bodied engagement.

Church Music and Commerce

The commercial interests involved in the music of the church are many and varied — musical instruments; music publishing; technology; sound, lighting, and audio; recording; promotions and public relations; transportation; and so on. Companies continually develop new products and market both these and their existing products to the church and its music ministries. The decisions that churches make regarding music are strongly influenced by the products that are available and by the ways in which they're marketed. Many churches have large budgets which they spend on the products they perceive to enhance ministry, and each of these products has influenced the worship in which it is involved.

Church Music and the World

Everything that happens in the world influences the music of the church. When we worship, we don't check our "worldly" selves at the door. Natural disasters, political decisions, elections, recessions, cultural shifts, fashion — all have a direct or indirect effect on the church's worship. Songs are written in response to world events and natural disasters, church budgets are cut during recessions, and worship attire shifts with fashion. The world of the church cannot be separated from its surrounding culture; in fact, worship typically mimics its cultural surroundings.

Who Holds the Power of Change?

Ultimately, all power within the church should reside with the people, in the voice of the community both locally and globally. However, as we have seen, the entities that influence the church and its music are many and varied. Like family systems, the church seldom assumes a proactive stance. When times are good, the church relishes stability. Only when it is in acute crisis does it embrace change — although some local congregations may even choose death over change. Change in the church always trails change in society in general, and the church's overall makeup and governance make it unwieldy when change is required. Since the church is mostly responsive to models that "work," it will be more likely to change as current models fail and are replaced by new and more efficient ones. However, we must never discount the work of the Holy Spirit in empowering and propelling the church and its worship toward meaningful change.

Coming to the Table

For worship and its music to move forward, people who love the church and its music must come together for dialogue in order to imagine a better future. A hopeful development for this future conversation is a growing body of thinkers, artists, creators, and church lovers who are both invested in the church and committed to creatively imagining the "not yet." In order to lead in meaningful change, leaders within varied

constituencies must set an example of inclusion, respect, open dialogue, and mutual exchange. Even the Protestant Reformation wasn't
led by just one person; several leaders blazed new paths within their
own developing sphere of influence. Donald Miller makes an interesting point about the difference between that reformation and the next
one — which he sees as already underway:

> I believe that we are witnessing a new reformation that is transform-
> ing the way Christianity will be experienced in the new millennium.
> This reformation, unlike the one led by Martin Luther, is challenging
> not doctrine, but the medium through which the message of Chris-
> tianity is articulated. . . . These "new paradigm" churches have dis-
> carded many of the attributes of established religion. Appropriating
> contemporary cultural forms, these churches are creating a new genre
> of worship music, restructuring the organizational character of insti-
> tutional religion, and democratizing access to the sacred by radicaliz-
> ing the Protestant principle of the priesthood of all believers.[4]

The primary way in which the conversation will move forward is
through the creation of opportunities that continually bring together
leaders who would not ordinarily be together. When leaders interact
and meaningful dialogue occurs, change will eventually result.

The future will probably be very different from what we are able to
imagine, but this book seeks to imagine a better future than the one
that will result from our present trajectory. The future of the church is
certain, for as broken as it is, the church is still God's best hope for the
world.

Unexpected obstacles will appear along our way. But true signs of
hope for the church are in its future, not in a return to any "glory days"
of the past. While God has always encouraged God's people to be firmly
grounded in memory, memory must also help us to imagine and shape
a better future. And as Paul Tillich reminds us, our "future depends on
the way [we] will deal with [our] past, and whether [we] can discard into
the past elements which are a curse!"[5] How we deal with these elements

---

4. Donald E. Miller, from the Web site *Thunderstuck — A Truck Stop for the Soul,*
quoted in Phyllis Tickle, *The Great Emergence: How Christianity Is Changing and Why*
(Grand Rapids: Baker Books, 2008), p. 155.

5. Paul Tillich, *The Eternal Now* (New York: Charles Scribner, 1963), p. 128.

of the past will form the basis for the upcoming re-formation of the church's music. This music must be stripped down layer by layer. Each layer must be celebrated for what it contributed to a particular time in the church's past, and it must be respectfully filed away in our collective memories to remind us of our rich heritage and to provide evidence of our stories when future generations are curious about the stories on which the present rests. However, our relics must not be given more power than they deserve, for at the core of the music of the church we must find Christ himself revering the sacred symbols of the past, all the while ruthlessly revising them. Once we have rediscovered Christ himself, we must stand back as the Incarnational power of Christ moves among us and re-conceives the church and her song from the moment of conception. After a time, we will be stunned at the miracle of the re-birth that will transpire!

CHAPTER 3

The Mess We're In

A chalkboard is a lot like memory; often jumbled, unorganized, and sloppy. Even after it's erased, there are traces of everything that's been written on it.

Andy Selsberg, "Teaching to the Text Message"

No one likes a mess, and no one likes to clean one up — especially a mess they didn't create. Yet, at this historical juncture we find ourselves in the middle of a mess. With theological baggage yet to be resolved, radioactive fallout from the bombs thrown about musical style, discarded costumes of long-gone fads, cans of worms that have never been opened, sediment from musical disputes that have never been resolved, dust from styles abandoned too soon, paper from statements about others that should never have been penned, and sand from words misspoken, we have a mess to clean up that isn't ours. We have repeatedly ignored it and pushed it into yet another corner. But we are no longer able to work around the mess, and the debris must be acknowledged for what it is. Logically, we want to find out who created the mess and have them clean it up. However, because the mess represents a multilayered heap from years of neglect and denial, tracking down the trashers is impossible and wouldn't be helpful. Because this mess is hindering us and the church we serve, it is our collective garbage. Past the statute of limitations for casting blame, it is ours to fix. Yet, in every pile of rubble, treasures await.

During spring break of 1997, I traveled with Oklahoma Baptist University's Bison Glee Club to inner-city Chicago to sing and participate in mission projects. Working with the Lawndale Community Church, we were asked to clean up a vacant lot to create space for their ever-expanding social ministries. As we surveyed the lot, tightly lodged between two tall, dilapidated buildings, all we could see was recent garbage covered with a light coat of late snow. As we began to pick up trash and place it by bucketfuls into a Dumpster, the trash seemed to multiply. Before we took a break for lunch, we had discovered vintage bottles, cans, shoes, and household items dating back several decades. Shortly after lunch, still in search of soil, we began to see what appeared to be a large piece of rusted metal. Like a group of eager archeologists, we began removing the trash around the metal object now taking shape. By the end of the day, we had fully uncovered a 1968 Pontiac that had been completely submerged in the layers of rubble.

In the end, the car was sold for "junk iron," and the proceeds helped the mission. Hundreds of bags of cans and glass bottles were recycled, and eventually soil was discovered under about fifteen feet of layered refuse. Recently, when the choir who traveled to Chicago met for a reunion, this story and the lessons it taught surfaced. As the group reflected, they realized that the lessons of working together, persisting through virtual impossibility, sticking together though snow and rain, and feeling unexpected joy in work well-accomplished were treasures they discovered in that trash heap.

The trash heap that the church faces is in part caused by post-modernism. Postmodernism is a shift of seismic proportions. It is not a fad or a cultural period. It is changing all that we are. The very foundations of our society and the church are shifting, and the music of the church is not immune to these shifts. Currently, most music/worship practices are primarily based either on historical practice or on relatively new ideas that are moored in pragmatism, in what works. Both models are inherently flawed because they depend on faulty suppositions, one on the power of cultural capital and the other on expediency. With the cultural shift of postmodernism,[1] the worship of the church will transform, and the changes we see now are only the tip of the ice-

---

1. The last similar shift occurred about five hundred years ago with the Protestant Reformation. Although signs of this shift began long before Luther nailed his 95 theses (on October 31, 1517) to the door of the Castle Church in Wittenberg, Luther's public announcement incited change that spread quickly. For a discussion of the "Great Reformation," see Phyllis Tickle, *The Great Emergence: How Christianity Is Changing and Why* (Grand Rapids: Baker Books, 2008), pp. 43-61.

berg. While little within the church will likely survive in its current form, the change will be slow at first. It will happen over several decades and with the passing of generations. However, there is no denying the mess we're in at the moment. We can no longer pretend that nothing is changing. And as those invested in the worship and music of the church, we find ourselves in a difficult position: we can no longer hold tightly to the myths of the past, nor can we move wholly into the future.

In this chapter we will deconstruct two elements (preaching and music) and one tool (hymnals) of worship that are held in common among most faith traditions. We will begin to recognize that some of our presuppositions, elements, and tools are flawed. While we cannot (nor would we want to) change any of these things too quickly, we can no longer prop up our presuppositions with outdated and flawed logic and reason. Fortunately, the changes that will ensue are not altogether dependent on any one of us. The future direction of the church's music and worship will be decided by the community of the faithful as they live out God's call on their lives in their specific context, one locale at a time. And treasures will be uncovered in the process.

Why Preaching Can't Survive (As It Is)

Because It's Based on Power

Like the music of the church, preaching is also based on power, although the power structures that support preaching are different and even more deeply rooted — at least in some traditions. Beyond the preacher's role as Bible teacher, expositor, proclaimer, moral authority, prophet, priest, and more, the preacher employs many power-invested trappings — the Bible, the authority of the church, ordination, education, and the power of the position itself. Furthermore, in many faith practices, the preacher is invested with the power of being "the spokesperson for God," while in other practices the preacher represents centuries of tradition and thus represents the church's hierarchy. To disagree with the preacher may be to risk feeling as if one has disagreed with God, the church hierarchy, or the tradition of the faith itself. The layers of preaching power are many, and each is formidable. In fact, there are few roles in our society that potentially have more power than that of chief proclaimer in a faith community.

Because It Lacks Opportunity for Input and Shared Ownership

Inherent in the structure of most preaching and sermon preparation is a lack of opportunity for input and shared ownership. Most sermons do not allow for accessible feedback, discussion, questioning, or dialogue. In addition, asking questions about sermons can be daunting for parishioners because the nature of sermon preparation and delivery has little built-in opportunity for community input. When input is not sought from the outset, input may not be easy to offer or to accept. Sermons are usually conceived by the preacher, prepared in isolation, and delivered with minimal assistance or input from other ministers. While the Lectionary does allow for contributions from the broader Christian community with regard to Scripture, Free Church ministers often depend exclusively on personal preference or on whatever "God has laid on their heart" as they decide what to preach. Further complicating matters is the proliferation of sermons available on the Internet; they may diminish the well-crafted, congregationally specific sermon.

Because a Sermon Is a Monologue

With the exception of the classes of a few university teachers who haven't updated their teaching strategies and the President's State of the Union address, sermons are the last vestige of monologue and lecture approaches to disseminating information. Nowhere else but in church do regular people listen to between fifteen and forty minutes of oratory. While the field of homiletics has an active scholarly research community, holds regular conferences in many parts of the world, and has made significant progress in many areas of preaching (including story-telling, preaching as performance, and others), sermons have remained relatively static in terms of delivery, despite the constant changes in information delivery of the larger society. While some preachers/lecturers are able to maintain the attention of a congregation for twenty-plus minutes, this is an increasingly difficult task, and most preachers aren't able to achieve this feat, nor should they be expected to do so. In a society where conversation is valued, different viewpoints are respected, and technology is usually available, preaching's failure to incorporate these priorities and to adapt to culturally preferred communication styles must be questioned. While music has been discussed openly, even to the point of contention, preaching has survived largely intact. Why? Is preaching considered too sacred to question? Is the power of preaching held so tightly within a closed community (preachers and the seminaries that train them) that it is impenetrable? With the current shortage of ministers in some denominations, wouldn't younger women and men who are pursuing ministry vocations be more likely to imagine proclamation as a part of their vocation if more collaborative and innovative models were encouraged, developed, and implemented?

One must wonder why preaching hasn't been more frequently practiced as a collaborative act in which two or more proclaimers share the role of proclamation during a given worship experience. Other worship elements, such as silence, song, and reflection, could easily punctuate each smaller sermon. If proclamation within worship were a shared experience, no one person would bear the full responsibility for it, collaboration would be modeled, and a truer voice of God (most often expressed communally) might have a better chance of being heard.

Because It's Leader-Centered

Preaching is the only part of most worship services that is exclusively leader-centered. While all worship models call for maximum congregational participation and extol the congregational community as the primary reason for gathering, preaching remains largely a solo activity. Imagine for a moment that you come to worship on a Sunday morning and there is no congregational singing — a single soloist (although the most highly trained and gifted person) does all singing. In addition, imagine that there are no congregational prayers, no congregational readings — that all readings are done by our most gifted and well-trained dramatic artists. While the scenario proposed above sounds outlandish, the point regarding preaching is well made. None of our congregations or their pastors would agree with this model theologically, psychologically, or in terms of group dynamics, yet they practice this model through preaching.

Because It's Not Multi-sensory

While there are exceptions, most preaching is limited in multi-sensory possibilities. Largely based on auditory models, preaching minimally involves other senses — seeing, smelling, tasting, and touching. Furthermore, since preaching is primarily auditory, it seldom engages other learning channels — visual, tactile, or kinesthetic. And even though preaching is primarily auditory, it is limited here as well. It is normally limited to speaking and fails to explore fully other forms of auditory stimuli, such as music, other voices (testimony, readings, dramatic arts, etc.), soundtracks, video, and environmental sounds.

Because It Doesn't Belong to the People

Ministers often wonder why the congregation seems minimally involved in the sermon, why response seems low, and why they themselves are pressured and feel as if much of their work is done in isolation. The reason is that sermons in most churches fail to belong to the people; they are not shared communal experiences. While congregational members are invited to listen and respond, they sometimes fail to engage fully with the sermon because some don't know how to absorb and process this potential auditory overload. As we will discover in a later chapter on the role of hospitality in the church, gifts given in worship should be reciprocal. They should be evenly exchanged. Since most models of sermon preparation and delivery don't allow for open exchange, they are not perceived as shared communal experiences. Unfortunately, the gift of the sermon, which involves untold hours of preparation, is sometimes not accepted in the spirit in which it is intended. Consequently, the art of preaching needs to be re-envisioned and re-imagined.

Because It's Male-Dominated

Most preachers — even in denominations that are open to women as ministers — are male. In contrast to most other arenas of society where women are recognized for their abilities and skills, many churches deny women access to ministries involving proclamation. Although this practice claims to be based on biblical interpretation and tradition, it will not stand the ongoing shift from modernity to postmodernity because churches that don't allow full access for women will be perceived as using power to repress the voice of women. Perhaps one of the reasons that preaching has remained relatively static while surrounded by unprecedented change is partially due to the failure to involve women in the process of re-imagining the art. The qualities sometimes associated with being female have often been omitted from preaching; hence, preaching has not benefited from women's perspectives, few models for younger women have emerged, and preaching as an art has been dominated primarily by masculine oratorical content and delivery. This cannot continue. Women have much to say, and the church needs to hear the voices of all who are called — even to places and positions that might make some uncomfortable.

Because "Preaching" as a Word Is Flawed

In most areas of society, the word "preaching" is perceived negatively. For instance, when someone says, "Please don't preach to me," they're stereotyping preaching as a one-dimensional, top-down, moralistic platitude. For many people, preaching is perceived to be done "at you" rather than "with you," which explains the phrase "preaching at me." Unfortunately, the term "preaching" has suffered from sermons which are non-conversational in their approach, fail to exhibit gentleness, and seem to have all the answers for every problem. While this sort of preaching is uncommon in many churches, "preaching" as a term to describe the act of proclamation in worship may carry too much negative baggage to be redeemable. The more formal term "homiletics" also fails to communicate the intent of proclamation because it is perceived as formal and academic and is not a term which most parishioners understand or identify with.

In summary, proclamation will survive, but "preaching," as it has been traditionally done, will not. While groups such as the Academy of Homiletics and the Academy of Evangelical Preachers are discussing the latest innovations in preaching, fresh books are continually being published, and renewed attention is being given to preaching as a performance medium, there seems to be little attention given to the possibility that "preaching" is inherently flawed and must be reconceived from the inside out. In order to communicate with the next generation of worshipers, the act of proclamation must be re-imagined and must emerge with fresh forms and updated presentation models.

Why the Music of the Church Can't Survive (As It Is)

Because It's Based on Power

The music of the church is based on modernity's systems of power, and postmodernism is suspicious of real or perceived power structures. Yet the current structures undergirding the music of the church are power-dependent. For instance, traditional church music is based on the power of education — more highly educated people, and the musical forms that they espouse, wield greater power than people with less education and the more vernacular musical forms that they may prefer. Furthermore, with education comes status, and some musical forms receive preferential treatment because of their perceived higher status. Similarly, churches that choose music in popular styles use the power of commerce, suggesting that "this is the music that everyone likes" (meaning "purchases") to justify their preferences. Likewise, both systems are based on top-down leadership models. In both models, worship is centrally controlled by a leader (a music minister or an organist choirmaster) or an elite team (a praise band); but neither model typically enlists broad-based community input or collaborative planning. Both models are based on hierarchical structures in which the power is held and controlled by a few leaders who are highly talented, well-educated, and/or charismatic.

Because It's Leader-Dominated

Postmoderns fully endorse collaborative leadership models that are relational, and they bristle at hierarchical, top-down models. Yet the music of our churches usually depends on the latter. In traditional services led by an organist choirmaster, the music is managed from a central control system — the organ console. In a traditional evangelical church model, the upfront leader and the large choir that stays fully in the background become the face of the church's worship, and the success of the service is largely on the leader's shoulders. And in the praise-and-worship model, the music is managed by a small band of experts with few, if any, places for other gifted people to use their talents in worship leadership.

Because It's Elitist

When only the most educated, most talented, or most charismatic are empowered, elitism is at work. When the leadership base (in a larger congregation) involves only a few people, elitism is at work. In the three models described above (organist choirmaster, leader and choir, and band), elitism is clearly visible. When the focus of worship revolves around leadership instead of the people, the model is internally defective.

Because It's Non-communal

All that the church does should be communally conceived. As we will discover more fully in Chapter 7, the music of the church usually functions best when the community has a voice in it, and decisions about music are made within a communal context. But most music programs in churches don't use this broad-based communal model. The voice of the community should be apparent in the conceptual stage as well as in the execution of worship. Planning teams should reflect the congregation for whom they plan, and worship should be led by people who embody the make-up and context of the worshiping community. Too often, worship is conceived without meaningful exchange between planners and congregation, and worship is led by people who do not represent the gathered community generationally, ethnically, or socio-economically.

Because It's Personality-Driven

Many worship services in our culture are personality-driven. When churches seek worship leaders, they often use words like "dynamic" and "charismatic" to describe the leaders that they desire. In fact, many churches are looking for youthful people, and some churches fail to consider people who exhibit obvious signs of aging.[2] Positivity and en-

2. Recently, a middle-aged friend of mine told me about the interview he had with a church in Houston, Texas, about a possible worship leader position. During the process, he was asked if he would be willing to color his hair if he were hired. When he said no, the church never contacted him again.

gagement are important to enliven congregational song, and all leaders should maximize the positive qualities of their personality through leadership. But in mimicking the entertainment industry, the church has fallen into the trap of chasing after the novel and the unusual. We have become addicted to the personality-driven models of our culture and have embraced the idea that those who lead us should be more energetic, more youthful, and more unusual than we are. Closely linked to this issue is our tendency to sit back and evaluate worship instead of participating in it fully. Our romantic obsession with creating heroes and imagining that our association with them will in some way also cause us to be larger-than-life creates unrealistic (and sometimes strange) expectations for those we call to lead us.

Because It's Male-Dominated

The most unexplored territory for worship leadership of the future is in the area of gender inclusivity. While women have entered the ranks of most professions and the ratio of women to men is becoming more evenly matched, the church continues to lag behind the world in embracing women as leaders in worship. In all worship styles, men strongly dominate the worship leadership landscape. Our male-dominated models of church music leadership are counter to the emerging postmodern culture and to God's valuing of all people, and they cannot survive. Churches and their leaders must find ways to empower women in music leadership.

Because It's Performance-Driven

Performance rather than participation captures the essence of many worship services in our culture. Those of us in Western culture seem addicted to passivity. In many homes, participation in the family means controlling the remote, and we sometimes expect little more in worship. We are also infatuated with applause. We are eager to offer it, and the performers we exploit in our churches are eager to receive it! While applause may not be inherently wrong, the performance mentality that it suggests is dangerous. One only has to walk into a typical worship space to encounter subtle performance implications. Non-congregation-friendly acoustics, dimmed congregational lights, spotlights on the platform, and extreme volume send not-so-subtle messages to the congregation that the primary action is not expected to be from them, and the musical offering isn't really about them. These auditorium-like performance accoutrements discourage even the most tenacious worshipers. Furthermore, the language we use influences our behavior. Using "auditorium" (a place to listen) rather than "worship space," and "stage" (a place from which people perform) rather than "platform" (a place from which a leader can be seen) — these choices shape us and our worship. Similarly, applauding for God or "giving God a hand" can put God on the same level of needing approval as the rest of us.

Because It Lacks Imagination

At its root, the church's music lacks imagination. We have lost the wonder of God's creative imagination embodied in us, God's creative creatures. Our busyness consumes us, and there is little time for activities and processes that encourage imagination. We are often too focused on the present to spend time imagining a better future. We are content with things the way they are, for what we know is good enough. We have rarely been challenged toward more imaginative worship. Our obsession with what "works" has lulled us into imitating perceived success while sacrificing creativity in the process. We are actually starved for the imagination of God, but we are unaware of our hunger. Church leaders serve congregations of imaginatively malnourished people who are unaware of the lack of imaginative balance in their worship diet. But there are ways to correct this imbalance. What if we were to utilize the entire worship place instead of just the platform? What if readings were altered among different ages, written in narrative form, or read theatrically? What if worship began or ended differently? What if songs were interspersed with Scripture? The possibilities are as endless as our imaginations can be.

Because It Lacks Memory

While we lack imagination, we also lack longer-term memory. Many of us are "stuck" in short-term memory. Like some older folks, younger people are also trapped in memories of earlier days — but their "earlier days" are more recent. Simply put, we are ensnared in what we know and what has worked. We are enslaved to sentimentality and emotionalism. We have learned to rely on feelings, and when feelings fail us, we are helpless. We continually sing the same songs expecting the same emotions, and we are unable to trust the imagination of God and rely on the Spirit for renewed energy and breath. Furthermore, our short-term memory has caused us to ignore the rich repository of the historic church in favor of newly conceived material, and it has caused us to be so satisfied with what is that we fail to imagine what could be. We fail to continue to explore and learn in order to create ongoing memory, which will feed our imagination in the future.

In summary, the song of the church will survive because the people of God will always sing, but "church music" with all its trappings will not.

Why the Hymnal Can't Survive

The use of hymnals has been declining since the 1970s and 1980s, when new songs began to be written and marketed faster than hymnals could be revised and published. At first, churches that wanted to utilize newer materials not available in the hymnal printed the texts in their worship bulletins or published in-house hymnal supplements. As technology became available and churches worked to avoid extra printing of this material, they began to use overhead projectors, transparencies, and makeshift screens to allow newer songs to be accessible to their congregations. With the widespread availability of computer technology and the continuing evolution of video projection, churches began to install permanent screens in their worship spaces, and PowerPoint, MediaShout, ProPresenter, and other worship presentation software continued to fill in the void left by the hymnal's inflexibility. Along the way, many worship leaders and their congregations began to prefer screens for reasons often unrelated to the hymnal's lack of flexibility. The ability to change the projection quickly, to allow the congregation to look up instead of down, to show photos and video, and to make everyone less paper-dependent were just some of the reasons. What began as a way for worship's music to respond more quickly to recent developments has evolved into a preference for newer technology over hymnbooks.

Just as the invention of the printing press in 1440 eventually revitalized the church and its congregational song by allowing each congregant to view his/her own hymnal, recent technology has made possible an equally significant shift in the way in which congregations receive information. Once the information shift is made, a return to the old way is not possible. While hymnals will survive for a long time, and some congregations will use them for many years to come, many younger people (who are minimally dependent on printed media) will fail to see the validity in hymnbooks when there is no similar model anywhere else in society. With the burgeoning popularity of electronic books, audio books, and other delivery systems for traditionally printed media, hardcopy books will eventually be considered quaint.

Many within academic circles have long defended the use of the hymnal, and some of their claims are valid and substantive; yet, despite this defense, the hymnal continues to be used less and less. Whether or not we prefer a hymnbook doesn't change the reality of its decline.[3]

Because It's Not Communal

A traditional hymnal is not a communally conceived book. From its conception and design it lacks the input of the local community. While it may represent a larger denominational entity, it is not a local book, and it rarely contains all of the songs which represent the local story of a congregation. While congregations of the past fully depended on their pastors to choose the hymns they sang in worship, today's congregations want to offer input. Taking advantage of current technology and marketing, congregants often listen to potential congregational songs in their leisure time, and they frequently have preferences about the songs that are meaningful to them. Given the sheer volume of congregational songs that are accessible, the rate at which they become available, and the numerous songs that a single local congregation may appreciate, hymnals may not be able to meet the very specific needs of a local worshiping community.

---

3. According to Claire Cain Miller and Julie Bosman, who co-wrote the article "E-Books Outsell Print Books at Amazon" (*New York Times*, 19 May 2011), e-books are outselling traditional printed books at the rate of 105 to 100. While print books have been around for hundreds of years, the Kindle e-reader is less than four years old.

Because It's a Closed Book

The hymnal is by design permanent, complete, and fixed. Traditionally, once the hymnal is published, it is finished — that is, the canon is closed and the collection is permanent and complete until a new hymnal is published.Traditionally, hymnals were designed to include what was good for us — a balanced musical, historical, and theological diet. When hymnals were our only source for congregational song, a denomination and its thinkers could design a hymnbook with the songs that were believed to be most helpful to the congregation theologically, historically, biblically, and thematically. Meanwhile, the denomination's marketers pressed to include the songs that would sell the book. For hymnals of the past, these entities and the compromises that they negotiated were primarily responsible for the content of hymnals. However, it has always been left to the local congregation to choose to buy a particular hymnal or to sing the songs!

Once the hymnal is published, change isn't possible until a new hymnal is published — usually in about twenty years. It's true that recent hymnals and their supplements have been published more regularly in an attempt to respond to changes in congregational song. Recent hymnals also offer newer materials through their Web sites and through their online presence, and these efforts may extend the use of hymnals. But in time the hymnals' "virtual presence" may be seen as unrelated to the "real" hymnals, and that presence will likely outlive the hard-copy books.

In short, hymnals are flawed for current congregations because by design, they lack flexibility and fluidity — qualities that society and churches today prize highly.

Because It's a "Power" Book

A hymnbook is a power book because it's conceived within power structures. The process of creating a hymnal is primarily a political process rather than a communal process. Hymnals are usually designed by a committee, and one has to be invited to committee participation by whoever is in charge or through an application process. The make-up of the committee is limited by the number of people needed to represent certain constituencies — women, minorities, younger people, older people, academics, practitioners, and so on. Becoming a committee member is not unlike becoming a political delegate or participating in a political caucus, because committee members are selected according to influence, groups they represent, and who they know. Once the process of gathering materials for the hymnal has begun, content is determined through consensus votes by a majority of the voting members. People are allowed to speak about the merits of a song, and the vote then usually becomes binding.

Because It's Designed for Denominational or Niche Markets

Because they are limited in scope through their number of pages, hymnals are not designed for mass appeal. They're designed to appeal to a niche market, usually one with a particular denominational, liturgical, or theological perspective. By design, hymnals cannot be inclusive, since they appeal to subgroups within Christendom. Consequently, as the larger church has moved away from denominational identity and toward greater inclusivity, hymnal publication and distribution have been negatively affected.[4]

Because It's a Commercial Book

In addition to serving worship, hymnbooks are designed to make money and contribute to the financial coffers of those who publish them. While some hymnals have been funded primarily through the generosity of a benefactor, hymnals must be conceived as a commercial enterprise, and they must meet a financial bottom line. Since hymnals must be designed to sell, they must rely on what they perceive their customer base will purchase; and most recent commercially successful hymnals have depended on market research to guide their content, presentation, and supplementary products. Historically, churches tended to buy the new hymnal of their denomination when it was published, but churches are no longer so denominationally loyal.

---

4. In response to this change, a number of hymnals are now published in two or more versions, with one cover reflecting the denomination and a different cover designed to appeal to a nondenominational market.

Since hymnals are profit-dependent, the material that they include must appeal to their market niche, and the songs they include must be limited by how many copyrights they can afford. For this reason, hymnals usually contain larger numbers of their publishers' copyrights and an inordinate number of hymns written by people who serve on their editorial boards.

Because It's Elitist

Hymnals are generally perceived as representing the more highly educated element of their intended constituency. Many hymnal committees are often comprised primarily of the educated insiders within the denomination, and it is certainly valid to have knowledgeable people involved in the process. However, hymnal committees have sometimes failed to adequately consider the average person in the pew and have catered to the more highly educated. This process has sometimes resulted in hymnals that have failed to connect at the grassroots level; as a consequence, they haven't sold enough copies to effectively replace their predecessors.[5]

Conclusion

Practices and symbols that embody our beliefs become sacred, and can become as important to us as the faith realities they represent. Since our stories are deeply embedded not only in their narrative but also in the forms in which we have told them and they have been told to us, altering either the method of presentation or the method of delivery can be frightening. However, running deeply beneath our individual and collective faith is the narrative of God's continual redemption through Christ's birth, life, death, resurrection, and ultimate reign. A walk

---

5. While the reasons why one hymnal is more widely received than another are complex and deserve thorough investigation, many hymnals have not out-sold their predecessors. For instance, the widely used *Broadman Hymnal* sold over ten million copies and in 2001 was still selling seven to nine thousand copies per year; meanwhile, its successor, *The Baptist Hymnal 1956*, sold fewer than seven million copies. See "Glorious Is Thy Name" (a pamphlet published in celebration of the sixtieth anniversary of the Music Ministries Department of the Southern Baptist Convention), Lifeway Christian Resources, 2001.

through history always reveals ongoing change, and this progression cannot be stymied. God's work throughout history and in the present time is assured, and the message of God's redemption can fully transcend any form or symbol in which it is embodied.

CHAPTER 4

A Clearer Picture

Precious memories, how they linger,
How they ever flood my soul.
In the stillness of the midnight
Precious, sacred scenes unfold.

John Braselton Fillmore Wright,
"Precious Memories"

In the previous chapter we have clearly seen that the music of the church is in a mess, and as a result, change is inevitable. At first the idea that everything must change seems grossly overstated, yet closer examination reveals that when one component changes, the larger picture changes as a result. When one element within the field of the music of the church shifts, the shift eventually impacts all of the church's music, whether the shift is acknowledged or not. For some ideas, philosophies, and groundings to change and others to continue fully intact will only increase the mess we're in. In fact, attempts to empower the opposing forces of reformation and entrenchment are partially responsible for the current quagmire. The picture of the church's music is multidimensional and is often hard to see up close. Moving farther away from the issues at hand can help us to see more clearly.

What We Need to Remember

God doesn't necessarily value one type of music more than another. While we may place different values on different types of music, we can never be fully confident of God's value. Of course, we must consider aesthetic qualities, compositional techniques, text appropriateness, biblical integrity, poetic quality, and others aspects of music. However, these standards are ones that we have come to value over time, and they may or may not be as valuable to God as we perceive them to be. Since our best thoughts related to God's ideas are filtered through the church and are authenticated within community (with the continual consideration of the Bible, tradition, reason, and experience), a new approach should be based on open dialogue, healthy respect for God's working in each of us, personal and corporate humility, and a willingness to learn.

Historically, church-music philosophy has most often been approached from the top down. The direction of the church's music has been studied, discerned, and articulated primarily by scholars and theologians — often without primary consideration for how God seemed to be working in local faith communities. A new approach must be advanced communally and must involve conversations, shared stories, and consideration of how and where God is working through music. Priority must be given to music's ability to move freely among different contextual settings. Regarding the music of the church, there will not be a right way and a wrong way, a winner and a loser. Trusting more fully in God for discernment in the church's music could mean that God will simultaneously urge two leaders in separate congregations to move in directions that seem in opposition. In a new model, we will walk shoulder to shoulder with our eyes on God — our shared goal — rather than looking at those around us who are like us, and looking away from those who are different from us. Instead of looking within the family to share old times and receive confirmation, we will be moving toward the imagination that is present with God. Shared beliefs for the future direction of church music should include the following:

Music must first please God. While music is pleasing to us, and it can meet many of our social, spiritual, and psychological needs, music in the church is primarily meant to please God and honor God. Granted, music can meet our needs and please God at the same time; but sometimes we forget that God is our priority, and we seek to serve ourselves first and foremost. While pleasing God is our highest priority, knowing whether God is pleased or not is not up to us. Our privilege is to offer our best gifts with our purest motives.

God is the source for all music. God created all music and declared it good, and it seems likely that all music in some way represents God's creative work among God's people. While most music will never reach the category of "work of art," it nevertheless represents an offering from someone God loves.

Worshiping God is our most important goal. We were created for worship, and worship is our chief aim. Consequently, the music of the church is servant to the worship of God, and music offers us one of the best ways to express ourselves to God, and for God to speak to us.

God can be worshiped in many different ways through many different forms. To limit the ways in which God can be worshiped would indeed limit God; therefore, we continually seek to embrace different ways in which others worship God. To do so is to more fully understand and communicate with God.

The Bible can be read and perceived differently by different individuals and faith communities. While most Christians agree that the Bible is central to the Christian faith, they do not agree on how the Bible is to be read and interpreted, or on what constitutes truth.

We must not use the Bible to camouflage our own preferences and opinions. Too often we have used the Bible to defend what we believe to be true or wish were true, and we have often used the Bible as a trump card of sorts in our conversations and our writing. To say that we are speaking biblically or that we are always true to the Bible can be a way for us to shut down much-needed conversation.

We must openly share what God is doing in our own context in order to help others. Sharing our faith stories with others is a way that God has used throughout history to tell God's story. Open dialogue with others about what God is doing in our local contexts is a much-needed addition to the field of worship studies.

All Christians are a part of God's family; we must not speak ill of our brothers and sisters and their worship practices. To speak disparagingly about our Christian sisters and brothers dilutes the voice of God in our world. And it's hypocritical, because we use such conversation to put ourselves in a position of greater access to God's mind than we perceive others to have.

Worship must center on participation by the congregation. Participation is at the heart of Christian worship, and all worship reform must have full-bodied participation at its core. Participation also involves creating and imagining worship, and in order to do that, the congregation must be taught about music. Giving the community music is not enough. If the community is going to move beyond spectatorship, they must be taught about music too.

Music must be viewed as a source of theological formation, and leaders must be good stewards of this trust. Both music and the texts we sing form our theology both in ways we can authenticate and in ways we have yet to discover. Worship leaders must become aware of music's ability to shape our theology, and like all leaders and proclaimers, they must fully acknowledge this sacred trust.

We must recognize the power that we hold through music. Music has the power to move us emotionally, deepen us spiritually, enrich us intellectually, and stir us toward missional living. The church's music leaders must be good stewards of the power that has been invested in them.

We must repent of our continual misuse of music's power. Music has been wrongly used both within the church and elsewhere, and we must continually repent of the ways that we intentionally or unintentionally misuse music. To minister within the world of music leadership is to always be at risk of misuse.

We must focus on the church catholic, and begin to assume an ecumenical spirit. A spirit of valuing all other Christians must permeate every discussion about the church's music. While we come from many perspectives, speak many different languages, and represent many different aspects of God's being, we are all God's children, and God values each of us. We must value each other as well.

What Are the Biggest Issues?

Perhaps the church's most significant challenge regarding music for worship is its frequent failure to represent the broader body of Christ through its selection of music. If music is as important to shaping our theology and missional outlook as we believe it to be, then the music chosen — the style, theological content, and source — must represent a larger view of God. The widening gap between different styles within church music and the resulting intolerance of Christians who worship differently are surely hindering the church in its worship, outreach, and influence. To worship in a single musical genre and vocabulary can result in a one-dimensional view of God, which can lead to arrogance. Failure to experience God through different musical styles and genres can limit our ability to vicariously join the worship of others both around the world and down the street.

Here are two hopeful signs: many who are involved in the more traditional stream of church music, such as hymns and choral music, are searching for ways to shore up this component of the church's music, and some involved in the more contemporary side of the church's music are realizing their failure to involve larger groups of people in specialized singing within corporate worship and are looking to the choir as a possible solution. In addition, recent hymnal projects have all included a sizable body of material from more recent congregational songs written in more popular musical styles. With potential bridges moving in multiple directions, a significant exchange of ideas could occur in the near future, and the church could quickly begin to develop new life and energy in its worship. If history is an indication of the present and the future, our energy is best spent on finding new ways of worshiping and involving others in worship that moves beyond our current or historical understanding. Stated differently, what we need is not to return to the past but to forge new paths for the future — paths that move in yet-to-be-discovered directions. If organists, guitar players, choral conductors, drummers, and singers of all stripes can pool their wisdom and passion, new approaches can be forged. Given the openness that seems to be emerging from both the traditional side of church music and a younger set of worship leaders, the time may be ripe to bring together these music and worship gatekeepers for healthy and productive dialogue. Among the most promising signs of the timeliness of these conversations are the following:

- The frequent use of hymns and older materials on many albums points to a return to discovery of the old. Particularly noteworthy is the work of Chris Tomlin and David Crowder. Their work to breathe new life into beloved hymns from the past has resulted in the rediscovery of many important texts and tunes by a different group of worshipers.
- Many hymnals and collections that are designed for more traditional-

leaning congregations have recently included contemporary songs that are written in a popular music vein.

- In a time when many consider hymnals passé, many denominations have published new hymnals. While time will tell how effective these new books are, their emphasis on the church's song and its need for revitalization is nevertheless a hopeful sign.
- There is a greater inclination among leaders within the popular music genre to consider texts more deeply.
- Some traditionalists are making an effort to find and write more singable tunes.

The above are hopeful signs. Continued challenges include the following:

- *A lack of consideration for the music of other cultures.* Many churches seldom sing songs from cultures other than their own, even though they are committed to sending congregants to visit other cultures and interact with Christians there. When we are unwilling to accept someone's music, we are failing to accept him or her as a follower of Christ.
- *Churches failing to consider the music of their surrounding culture while being willing to consider the music of cultures across the world.* While some churches are willing to sing songs from around the world, they aren't willing to sing songs from the people who live right around them.
- *A deep lack of honesty about what it is about different styles of church music that makes them non-compatible.* For example, traditionalists most often cite repetition of texts and poor lyrics as the major problem with much contemporary music. However, they hypocritically use repetitive songs from other cultures, historical periods, and from Taize. The *style* of contemporary music is what they don't like, but they're unwilling to acknowledge this bias. Similarly, leaders and stakeholders within contemporary churches are also highly concerned with style. Perhaps it's time to consider the reasons why texts within the contemporary church frequently lack breadth, depth, and poetic imagination.

It's time to submit the issue of style to God and allow the Holy Spirit to begin working among us as we discuss how to come together.

Such discussions are never easy, and they must be approached with prayer and with a view to the worship of all of God's people and the proclamation and dissemination of the gospel around the world. We can no longer afford to be only local-centered in our discussions of the church's worship. Recognizing some of the inherent challenges involved in these discussions can be helpful. First, the church's musicians often have different training — musically, theologically, and liturgically. While some hold advanced music and theological degrees, others have been trained through hands-on mentoring within their churches and other support systems. Second, musicians come from many contexts, and since we all worship and lead within our specific context, it's often challenging to fully consider the larger picture. Third, musicians work within different communities where they are nurtured, formed, and influenced. We're all comfortable with the group that surrounds us, and moving out of relative safety will require hospitality from us all. Fourth, musicians work within different power structures. These structures can be denominational, economic, academic, social, cultural, racial, or ethnic. Musicians are tacitly charged by their constituencies to represent their interests. Fifth, musicians fail to recognize their differences and similarities. Because we each own our differences and have worked over our lifetime to develop our training, contexts, cohorts, and power structures, our differences are deeply ingrained, and we usually can't see ourselves as others see us. Now it's time to acknowledge these differences as we focus on our similarities.

It is likely that these important issues are being ignored because they're difficult and challenging. In addition, the nature of the leadership calling often breeds an unhealthy ego which isn't given to self-examination — and the result is that leaders are unlikely to observe these truths in their own contexts. Dialogue is important, but leaders within various worship styles and traditions have rarely discussed these issues. We don't know each other. We rarely attend the same conferences and workshops. And we often lead separate, protected ministries insulated by those who are like-minded.

What about Our Power Structures?

If the predictions and signs that the church will lose its prominent position in the mainstream of society and be banished to the margins are true, the church and its music/worship leaders must begin to take notice. Some music and worship leaders wield immense power, and churches in many communities also hold significant power — political, commercial, educational, and cultural. How would the church and its worship function outside this power structure? Attempting to acknowledge our power structures and imagining ourselves without them can be a helpful exercise, one that could be a wake-up call for many churches. If our current power structures were non-existent, how much of our current ministry would remain intact?

What are the trappings of power in music and worship ministry? A list readily comes to mind: opulent worship spaces, access to advanced technology, cutting-edge instruments and equipment, recording studios, money to purchase music and printed materials, What effect do these trappings have on the ministries we lead? Are we equipped to lead worship when we don't have access to the power of the latest technology, the newest downloadable music, the trappings of nice buildings, and the money to hire support teams? How connected are we to other Christian artists in our communities who aren't a part of our particular worshiping community? Are we primarily dependent on ourselves and the people that currently form our small circle? Are we nurturing those who are able to artistically imagine worship with minimal resources? Are we connected to Christians outside our own theological/liturgical praxis with whom we should already be interacting? Are we able to serve the church if/when the church may not be able to pay us salaries that are commensurate with those of other professionals? Are we developing the next generation of the church's musicians who can function in varied cultural contexts? If the trappings of our worship were stripped away, would we be able to lead worship from our deepest core?

What Are Our Core Theological Values?

If the church were banished to the margins of society, what theological tenets would hold importance for us? What core values would sustain the church in a different cultural context? We must be prepared for a time when out of necessity we become far less concerned about possibly minor theological differences and focus instead on the theological underpinnings that unite us. We may move toward a time in which Christians will not have the luxury of working independently or in competition with each other but will need to work together as a minority faith on a mission field — our new context. In the face of this possibility, *all* Christians must develop an ecumenical spirit. We must show less concern for theological, denominational, and liturgical differences, and show more concern for the core truths of our faith: Christ has died, Christ has risen, and Christ will come again! Overemphasizing denominationalism and being hyper-concerned about theological orthodoxy and differences in liturgical practice must be replaced by valuing shared beliefs and goals. It's important to recognize that the differences which often consume much of our energy are often associated with affluence; if we were stripped of our economic, social, and political capital, they would be negligible. If our Christian identity were less dependent on being authenticated by non-Christian social, economic, and political entities in our communities, we would out of necessity develop greater connections with our brothers and sisters in Christ who may interpret the Bible differently and whose liturgical practices may differ from ours. The luxury of holding on to our minor differences will not exist in the future, and the church will be the better for it.

How will greater interdependence among Christians and less reliance on secular culture for validation affect the church and its ministry? If collaboration were to replace competition within and among faith communities, how could the gospel be celebrated and proclaimed more effectively? When we move past the familiarity of size, superiority, success, and power, we will discover that our self-sufficiency has left us lonely without knowing it, bankrupt of new perspectives, and lacking vital community. There is a better way.

What Difference Has Technology Made?

Our ability to quickly access the texts and tunes of most hymns and songs, liturgical readings, multiple translations of the Bible, video clips, musical arrangements with various instrumentations and keys, and much more has changed the way worship is planned and will be planned in the future. The ability to readily view what churches across the world are doing in their worship and to instantly download an audio and/or visual file of a new song impacts worship leaders and congregations. The vast increase in information cannot be ignored, and it will continue to affect the church's worship. While some might prefer to return to an earlier time when worship could be planned with the Bible, the denominational hymnal, and other denominationally specific liturgical resources, these times are past and will never return. Once we gain ready access to worship materials, we must use these resources or be responsible for not using them.

In an earlier time, ministers and worship leaders had access to worship-planning books and resources that congregants usually couldn't access. It took more money, time, and energy to pursue new songs and other resources than it takes now. They had to be discovered in journals or magazines, ordered, and then received. Accordingly, professional clergy and worship leaders accessed and maintained materials in their field of worship, and laypersons trusted the content of liturgy primarily to their leaders. But today's parishioners are often keenly aware of new songs and resources at the same time as or even before their worship leaders are.

Today, people can learn about their symptoms, possible diagnoses, and potential medications prior to seeing their physician. Congregants have similar access to worship materials. They often know much of what is available prior to discussions with their worship leaders. Just as wise physicians realize the benefits of knowledge and information for their patients, wise clergy work together with their well-informed parishioners to determine directions for the worshiping community. The faith community must be involved in the process of worship planning, and they must also be involved in discovering what God might be doing in other parts of the world that might need to be incorporated locally. Worship leaders must empower others within the congregation to continually bring forth new ideas. At the same time, we must all recognize the realities of information overload, and we must empower others to help us wade through and sort out the best of what is useable in our particular context.

Where Is Technology Going?

Technology isn't inherently bad. In fact, technology can be good, and God wants us to use all that is good to reflect God's goodness. We must continually imagine how technology will further the cause of Christ in our world and how it will help us to worship more effectively.

Technology isn't going away, either; in fact, its use will continue to accelerate. It has made a major impact on the way we worship, and its full impact is yet to be experienced. Discussions of newer technology will continue because technologies that we are not yet able to comprehend will be discovered, and they too will impact our worship.

Before the invention of the printing press in 1440, congregational members had no ready access to printed materials, and the educated clergy held the power of literacy. As primary disseminators of knowledge, they were able to share this power as they chose. All that changed with the advent of the printing press. The church was thrust into a new era, and it had to decide how to steward the congregation's access to books and other printed materials. Over time, as books became less expensive and more accessible, congregants became more educated and informed. Consequently, parishioners were less dependent on the educated clergy for spiritual formation. Similarly, with the advent of the computer and the Internet, twentieth-century congregants gained significantly greater access to information, and they became even more informed about the church across town and around the world. This new learning required new ways of viewing Christian community. The continual development of technology will challenge the church of the future as well.

Prior to the printing press, there were no hymnbooks available in pew racks — such books were handwritten and available only to clergy. There were no pew Bibles — Bibles were scarce and usually accessible only to clergy. Prayer books and other worship sources were also scarce, and most people were unable to read them. But now, after nearly five hundred years of having hymnbooks, Bibles, and other resources easily accessible to them in their pew racks, many Christians are understandably hesitant to move toward newer ways of disseminating information. As a consequence, some churches have spent untold time discussing screens, sound systems, and electronic instruments. Churches have made significant monetary investments in printed resources, and they are understandably hesitant to replace these resources with newer methods of information dissemination. And it's interesting to recognize that once we're used to receiving information in a particular form, changing the form does in fact change the message for some. To remove the tactile elements of worship from a tactile learner by eliminating books and paper can significantly alter his or her ability to worship effectively. Eventually, however, the use of technology in worship will be as accepted as printed materials were in previous centuries. In the meantime, churches should consider intermediate steps to integrate technology in ways that allow all worshipers to adapt at varying rates.

However, because technology will continue to evolve at an increasingly fast pace, there will not be a period of relative stasis like the one that followed for several hundred years after the development of the Gutenberg press. The discussion of what sort of technology to use and how to use it effectively will continue, but the discussion about using technology as a useful and necessary worship tool is almost finished.

What Are the Major Dichotomies within the Church's Music?

While most congregations worship in a hybrid style or in a mixture of many varied musical elements, it is helpful to look carefully at the major dichotomies in the worship music of the church.

Organ leadership for congregational song	Praise-band leadership for congregational song
Low use of technology	High use of technology
Low sound amplification	Highly amplified sound
Music in a traditional style	Music in a popular music style
Choral music	Solo or small-group music
Classically trained vocal production	Popularly trained vocal production
Cognitively based texts	Emotionally based texts
Distant approach to God	Up-close approach to God
Traditional language	Folk language
Natural light	Controlled theatrical lighting
Low congregational participation	High congregational participation (singing)
Prepared remarks or no remarks (leadership)	Informal remarks (leadership)
Leader-focused direction	Shared leadership
Minimal physical participation	Frequent physical participation
Closed song structures	Open song structures
Minimal use of rhythm instruments	Frequent use of rhythmically driving music

The new approach will proclaim that all or most of these dichotomies are acceptable within the church, and they can all be used effectively within a specific context. Congregations should be encouraged to explore models outside their familiar paradigm, since cross-fertilization is often a catalyst for new worship models and forms.

Why Are We Afraid of Worship Outside of Our Paradigm?

Many leaders seem to have experienced so much change that they are weary and afraid to embrace more change. With immense change, people can feel as if they have lost their liturgical home. Even doubts about God's nature can develop as worship practices shift and morph. Some Christians have experienced little worship change, but they've seen worship in neighboring parishes lose its sense of history and tradition, and they may be fearful of losing what they have come to trust. While our fears can be justifiable, change will occur and continue to occur at an ever-increasing speed. If we embrace our fears, we will find ourselves paralyzed, unable to consider the future that God intends for us. While fear is not rational, it is real. Below are some of the common fears that inhibit our ability to embrace change.

- I will be tainted. Involving myself in worship that's different from what I'm accustomed to might taint the ideal worship that I've embraced in the past.
- I might be robbed. If I consider and participate in new types of worship and worship music, my past preferences could be taken from me and no longer valued.
- I might have to change. To explore new kinds of worship and music might force me to make changes that will be painful for both me and others. This is pain that I want to avoid.
- I might lose my current status. My status within my current group of peers will change, and eventually I might lose the place I have earned or inherited.
- My friends might think poorly of me for talking with these "new ideas" people. If I explore new worship ideas with people who are different from me, my friends won't understand, and they'll think that I've compromised my belief system.
- I might be misunderstood. Exposing my thoughts and ideas to oth-

ers who think differently from me may cause me to be misunderstood by both my new friends and my current ones.

- I might have to learn something new. Learning new songs, following new worship practices, and embracing new paradigms is difficult and can be painful.
- I might have to forgive. If I discover that I've been wrong about the motivations and goals of others, I might have to ask their forgiveness for disrespecting them.
- If I lose my fears, I may have nothing left to hold on to. When I'm fearful, I have a purpose and something to protect.

Since we are on the cusp of a cultural shift of epic proportions, change will come whether we embrace it or not. Our choosing to be a part of impending change and to follow God into new paths gives us hope for a better future.

What Happens if We Don't Reform?

Whether or not we choose to embrace worship and music reform, the reality is that reform will happen. However, if we choose to play a role in our local community's response to change, we can help to shape our worship in ways that represent our story as we have known it. The best reform model will involve as many people as possible on the local level who are sharing their stories as they participate in shaping worship in their specific context.

CHAPTER 5

Worn-Out Paradigms, Unquestioned Myths, and Threadbare Clichés

Memories are important. They give us a way to understand the present, what's happening now. They define us, not just the memories, but what we choose to remember, how we remember it, what we leave out.

Peggy Leon, *A Theory of All Things*

What do we really believe about the music of the church's worship? How much of what we believe is actually based on biblical principles, theological insights, and best practices? Like other institutions, the church has a tendency to pass along practices without carefully analyzing them. Ideas that were valid for a particular time or context have gathered baggage so that they're no longer applicable today. Particularly in light of the immense changes in the church's music in the last quarter of the twentieth century, it's time to reconsider what we've accepted as accurate in light of changing cultural contexts, evolving theological insights, and developing forms of worship.

Imagine the church's music as a wonderful old house with many beautiful rooms, intricately carved moldings, beveled glass, ornate fixtures, solid oak doors, carefully crafted mantels, and virgin pine floors. Once standing as a testament to fine craftsmanship and artistry, the house no longer reveals the original workmanship. Over time, layers of paint have filled in the intricate wood carvings; carpets now cover the native wood luster of the floors; the beveled glass has been broken and replaced by reproduction glass; and the ornate brass fixtures, once polished, have been painted. More recently, the rooms, too large for smaller families, have been divided into easier-to-maintain units. Alas, the house has been cordoned off into apartments where multiple families live out their days, never recognizing the original grandeur of the home's earlier life.

This chapter attempts to strip away the paint, carpeting, and even the walls that divide us, allowing us to see the original beauty inherent in the music that God has created. Once we have removed all that hides the original structure, we will attempt to reconstruct the music of the church so that it is free, creative, and functional, as it was originally created to be.

The call for continual assessment of the state of the church's music and worship is not new, for many of the best thinkers and writers in the field — Harold Best, Marva Dawn, Nathan Corbitt, Michael Hawn, Donald Hustad, Calvin Johansson, Austin Lovelace, William Rice, Robert Mitchell, Erik Routley, and others — have expressed concern over the condition of the church's music and its need for re-formation. In many ways this chapter stands squarely on the shoulders of these thinkers and writers, who have begun our journey of imagining a philosophy of church music that breathes new life into the body of Christ.

In his book *Unceasing Worship,* Harold Best sets forth the need for evaluation when he states, "The Church desperately needs an artistic reformation that accomplishes two things at once: (1) it takes music out of the limelight and puts Christ and his Word back into prominence; (2) it strives creatively for a synthesis of new, old, and cross-cultural styles."[1] Similarly, Marva Dawn offers hope for the church to move beyond its current condition and to embrace creativity and boldness when she says, "It is right to reject moribund tradition — its keepers have not had the boldness to be creative with it. On the other hand, those who spurn tradition itself, instead of the atrophy of tradition, forget that real creativity is impossible without the grounding in truth that tradition conveys."[2] She goes on to encourage a variety of musical styles and intergenerational worship in order to develop spiritual maturity: "Because the people who come for worship represent an immense diversity of ages, emotions, concerns, and spiritual maturity, authentic

---

1. Harold Best, *Unceasing Worship* (Downers Grove, Ill.: InterVarsity Press, 2003), p. 75.

2. Marva Dawn, *Reaching Out without Dumbing Down* (Grand Rapids: Wm. B. Eerdmans, 1995), p. 147.

worship requires a variety of musical styles to convey an assortment of moods and convictions."[3]

Donald Hustad emphasizes the need for the church to accept many styles and genres of music as well as both newer and older music: "From both a theological and a musicological viewpoint, we should be slow to condemn any style of music created by God's creatures as intrinsically evil. A study of the world's folk musics reveals many sounds which sound strange, even weird, to those outside of the culture. Yet missionaries have often used indigenous music to express Christian worship."[4]

In his seminal work *Music and Ministry: A Biblical Counterpoint,* Calvin Johansson imagines the music of the church as a melding of the new and the old, housed under the umbrella of God's creative work through humankind: "We are on a pilgrimage — always moving, wrestling, creating. The painful travail of the new must be a part of the church music program. . . . We are being ever called, even in our day, to 'sing the praise of God freshly.'"[5] Further expanding Johansson's ideas, Nathan Corbitt explains, "Congregations that protect their music boundaries run the risk of raising walls against the very people they seek to reach. On the other hand, some Christians appear to identify with the culture of the street rather than offering a faith for the street."[6]

Indeed, the journey has begun, and a vision has been cast; yet the evolution of the music of the church continues to unfold, and further changes must be considered. In the intervening years since some of the aforementioned works were published, the church has moved from liturgical and traditional streams to those such as contemporary, blended, and emergent — and these streams and their tributaries continue to develop. During these intervening years of immense creativity and exploration, instead of coming together to discuss differences and consider new paradigms, the church has often splintered and in the process only strengthened its constituencies' positions. The church must renew its vision of worship and must re-imagine worship so that it may once again breathe new life into the body of Christ. To this end, the

---

3. Dawn, *Reaching Out without Dumbing Down,* pp. 179-80.

4. Donald Hustad, *True Worship* (Carol Stream, Ill.: Shaw Books, 1998), p. 175.

5. Calvin M. Johansson, *Music and Ministry: A Biblical Counterpoint* (Peabody, Mass.: Hendrickson Publishers, 1984), p. 18.

6. J. Nathan Corbitt, *The Sound of the Harvest: Music's Mission in Church and Culture* (Grand Rapids: Baker Books, 1998), p. 26.

music of the church would greatly benefit from healthy dialogue and cross-fertilization.

To see where we might be able to go, we need to see where we've been. Let's look at some of the suppositions upon which the music of the church has been constructed.

What We Can Learn from Bach, the Model Church Musician

Bach has long been viewed as the model church musician. First, Bach was an amazing musician. A consummate organist and composer, he wrote the finest and most intricately conceived music that we know from his time. Second, Bach was a student of theology. He is known to have studied his Bible frequently, marking it with additional theological considerations. Third, Bach was an educator. He functioned as a schoolteacher and a church musician in a local parish. Lastly, Bach was a family man who was committed to his large family.

On a recent trip to St. Louis, Missouri, I visited a former student who's now studying at Concordia Seminary, where Bach's Bible (The Calov Bible) is housed in the library. There I was privileged to actually see that Bible and some of his handwritten notations. For instance, in the margins beside 1 Chronicles 25, Bach penned, "This chapter is the true foundation of all God-pleasing church music." A few chapters further, beside 2 Chronicles 5:12-13, Bach scribbled, "In devotional music, God is always present with His grace." Bach was a student of the Bible, and later in the New Testament, he even filled in words that were missing in the written text.

What if Bach were living today? How might he function in a modern context? Would he live up to all the expectations for church musicians today? Would he be open to different styles of music from his past? Do we have any evidence that Bach used the music of his predecessors while at Leipzig — the works of Palestrina, Byrd, and Monteverdi, or even the works of other German Lutherans who predate him, such as Schultz, Schein, and Scheidt? These are key questions to ask about this important church music model.

What we know of Bach is that he was a man of his time. He used the texts of his day, primarily those being written by his contemporaries, who, like himself, were influenced by Pietism — a prominent theological perspective in Germany at the time. While he surely understood the music of the period that preceded him (what we call sixteenth-century counterpoint), he aggressively moved forward, forging new concepts of tonality, counterpoint, terraced dynamics, and form. Bach used his intellect and exceptional work ethic to explore and create new ideas for his time. And, although we often use Bach as an icon for traditional music styles in the church, he also exploited the newest instruments of his day: the organ, the harpsichord, stringed instruments, brass and percussion. Bach moved beyond *a cappella* vocal music, which was the music used prior to his time, to create music for the church using varied forms and instruments. Ever an innovator, he most often employed instruments that had been used only minimally in the church prior to his context.

While Bach's musical genius is never lost on any well-informed listener, it is doubtful that he could survive the scrutiny of many today who are critical of repetitive texts on the one hand and music that is too technical and not accessible to the untrained on the other. Bach likely would be unpopular, criticized and underappreciated by those who hold either of these perspectives exclusively. Clearly, Bach was a man of his own day who responded to the ideas of his time using contemporary texts, the latest musical ideas, and the latest instruments and conventions. And he wrote music that reflected his time.

More to Learn: Exploring Our
Wrongheaded Ideas about Church Music

The above gives us a clear picture of Bach's ideas about worship and music, and how he thought Scripture shaped them. But now we must explore some of the ideas — worn-out paradigms, unquestioned myths, and threadbare clichés — about the church's music. Once we deconstruct them, we'll have a clearer idea of what we can retain in church music's "old house."

The Bible Is Clear Regarding the Music We Should Use for Worship

Although we often make such statements as "We must turn to the Bible as our guide for worship" and "Our church bases its worship on the Bible," the Bible is rarely prescriptive on the subject of music and worship. While the Old Testament indicates instrumentation and occasional forms used in Israelite worship, the New Testament provides little substance in this regard. While we must study the Bible carefully, using it as a centerpiece for worship, we must not pretend that it justifies individual ideas and preferences related to the music of worship. Many biblical principles influence the music of worship in a general sense, but the Bible offers great latitude regarding details. Churches often choose either Luther's method or Calvin's method of interpreting the Bible regarding worship. Luther believed that all practices in the church should be patterned after Scripture. He proposed that whatever is not forbidden by Scripture is allowed if, in the judgment of the church, the practice is thought helpful. However, Calvin took a more restrictive approach and declared that whatever is not taught in Scripture is not allowed in worship. It is between these two poles that the church finds itself. While worship leaders and their churches might stake territory on one side or the other, most churches are much closer to Luther's model than to Calvin's. The Bible should always be a source for decisions made about worship. But not all musical decisions can be squarely based on Scripture because many times it offers minimal guidance.

Some Instruments Are Not Suitable for Worship

There is no doubt that certain instruments can carry connotations of good or evil. In the Western tradition, instruments such as guitars, drums, and saxophones have occasionally been associated with secular music and have been considered by some as unsuitable for worship. Yet in other churches pipe organs carry the stigma of wealth, extravagance, and opulence, and could be barriers to worship. In still other churches, a piano might be seen as unfit to lead in congregational song because of its association with evangelical worship and revivalism. Nevertheless, instruments do not carry power that we do not give them. They are neutral — neither inherently good nor inherently evil. God can redeem any instrument from its cultural trappings and use it to glorify God and lead in worship. The church should be active in breaking down stereotypes and should strive to redeem any negative ideas associated with particular instruments.

Classically Trained Musicians Can
Easily Adapt to Any Style of Music

Many have maintained that classical music training prepares church musicians to fully engage in the different styles of music that the church encounters. But, given how the music of the church has evolved, this notion can be shown to have two inherent flaws. First of all, classical music typically has simple rhythms in comparison with jazz and rock music styles. Classical training typically doesn't teach the "feel" or "groove" (the subtleties of these rhythms) present in these styles. And second, extensive classical training for many musicians actually limits their ability to participate in popular music styles. For instance, when classical singing technique is followed too strictly, it can inhibit good or "proper" singing in jazz, folk, and other styles. Focusing primarily on operatic and art song technique, classical music training sometimes fails to teach the flexibility needed for singing a wide variety of styles authentically. A more healthy approach might be to view this singing technique as just one of many techniques. While some of the basic elements of an operatic style apply to rock, jazz, and folk styles, other elements can be disruptive.

The Best Church Music Is That Created
within the Church's Classical Tradition

While there is much great music within the Western art music tradition, this music is only one component of the church's repertoire. For much of the studied history of church music, Western art music was virtually the only music explored. But the fact that other styles and forms of music received minimal attention doesn't mean that there were no other musical styles and forms being used in worship in other parts of the world. In our not-so-distant past, Western culture was believed to be superior. Early missionaries not only shared Christ with their converts — they also taught them about Western culture and its styles of worship. Consequently, this prevailing perspective sometimes stunted the growth of indigenous church music in other parts of the world. Church leaders in some parts of the world are presently working to help Christians learn to express the gospel in their own language, cultural idioms, and particular musical styles and forms. Fortunately, many Western

Christians have realized that while God has been at work in Western churches, God has also been active around the world, and a sharing of music from many cultures flourished in the last half of the twentieth century. Many churches have begun to use music from other cultures as a reminder of our need to be missional. This multicultural music connects us to Christians worldwide and allows us to stand in solidarity with them.

Also notable is the failure of some church musicians to recognize church music from folk and popular music idioms within the United States. The near-absence of African-American spirituals in denominational hymnals until the late twentieth century, the neglect of the gospel song tradition among many denominations until the present, the failure by many in the academic community to acknowledge the contemporary Christian style and the praise and worship style — these things seem unconscionable to Christians who consider reaching out to all of God's people a core value of their faith.

Only the Best Music Is Good Enough for God

While on the surface this sounds like a noble statement extolling the greatness of God and our desire to please God by offering God our best, in reality this statement is sometimes used as a weapon against certain styles of music. For what is often meant is not necessarily the "best music" but the music that we know and trust. Since most of us (even trained musicians) like what we know best, we defend our favorite style and genre as "the best." In reality, there is "good" music in many categories; however, we must *understand* the music in order to assess its value. Since many of us are not adept in several musical styles, we often don't understand other musical styles well enough to accurately critique them.

Additionally, the statement above begs the question of God's taste. If only the best music is good enough for God, then whose "best" does God like most, and what is God's preferred style? Does God value imaginative and well-crafted music in all styles? If this is the case, then who gets to decide what is best? It appears that our initial statement leads us nowhere. And what does this statement say about presentation? Isn't it true that God values the well-intentioned gifts offered by the novice as well as the heartfelt gifts of the professional musician? It would be hard to imagine serving a God who didn't value the musical gifts of children, the gifts of the congregation, the gifts of the differently abled, or the gifts of people who aren't trained as some of us are.

Music Ministry Should Be Built around the Choir

While choirs are ideal for including many people who might not be "good enough" or confident enough on their own to help lead music, not all worship music is designed to be sung by a choir. Worship doesn't inherently need the aid of a choir. Furthermore, there are situations where a choir would seem out of place: they wouldn't "fit," for example, as the centerpiece of a rhythm-based ensemble. Choirs have long been a part of the church's worship both in liturgical and non-liturgical settings. Choirs have been at the heart of historical church music literature, and they have also served the cause of evangelism well. But there is nothing inherently sacred about choirs. God doesn't like choirs or choral music better than other types of music. With that said, it must be noted that no better alternative has been found for involving larger groups of people in music-making beyond congregational singing, and that singing in an ensemble is also significant as a builder of community.

Praise Music and Contemporary Music Touch the Heart More than Hymns and Traditional Music

I've often heard people say, "I just don't like hymns." However short-sighted this view may be, many people in our churches have been exposed only to praise music and don't believe that hymns have the ability to carry the same emotional power. The issue in this argument is not the music but the attitude, because hymns can touch the heart and move the worshiper emotionally as readily as praise music. Whether one is moved emotionally by the music of worship has much to do with its communal context and its presentation. When sung in a trusting community and presented in a way that allows them to be accessible to the particular gathered body, songs of any style can surely carry emotional power.

A related issue is the body language — or lack of it — involved in music. Many who prefer praise and worship styles are accustomed to

70

hand-raising, facial expressions, and other postures and expressions that are often synonymous with this style. When these postures and expressions are lacking (as is sometimes the case with hymn singing), worshipers may experience the singing as less emotionally and physically stimulating and thereby less worshipful. On the other hand, some churches rarely go beyond standing and sitting in worship, so the postures and expressions that are readily identified with praise and worship music seem shallow and superficial to them.

While practices regarding posture, expression, and emotional content need additional exploration, worship must move toward becoming more accepting of all who worship and the varied preferences they bring with them. It's impossible to judge how involved others are in worship; we only know how involved we ourselves are. Just as we have different levels of comfort with personal space and outward expressions of affection in our private encounters, so we have different levels of comfort with public expression in worship. They often determine the degree to which we engage with God through our physical expressions and our external display of emotion. When we worship, we offer all that is authentically ours.

Worship with a Vocal Team and a Band Requires Less Time and Skill than Leading Worship with a Choir

As anyone who has led worship in both settings can testify, much time, energy, and skill are required. Rehearsing with a band of several instrumentalists and a vocal team of several singers is as time-consuming as — if not more time-consuming than — working with a choir, an organist, and a pianist. Recruiting the worship band and singers, and crafting introductions, transitions, tags, and other musical materials that are often un-notated — these tasks take immense creativity, rehearsal time, and coordination. While the result looks as if the players and singers simply got up and put the worship together on the fly, this is usually far from true. Often the casual appearance of the worship takes more preparation than a well-ordered traditional service involving a highly crafted script and predictable weekly patterns. Furthermore, writing out lead sheets, transpositions, and other materials is as time-consuming as the work that well-trained organists invest in designing transitions, interludes, and other worship music.

A side note: While a praise team is easier to rehearse than a choir because it's smaller and usually has very carefully selected members, it doesn't produce better results than a choir. The results from these two vocal ensembles aren't actually comparable, because they can and most likely should serve different purposes. While both groups serve the function of enhancing congregational song, the vocal team is usually more visible and involved in the actual up-front leadership of worship, and the choir often leads by primarily enriching the service through choral musical offerings. Both models have significant strengths and can be successfully used together.

Praise Music Appeals to the Younger Generation

This statement is an easy stereotype, and while it can be true, it isn't necessarily so. We often assume that younger people always lean more toward contemporary music, but there are many exceptions. Many older people like contemporary music, and many younger people like traditional music. Sometimes music leaders fail to challenge younger people with older music, just as they fail to challenge older people to learn newer songs. To believe that younger people are drawn only to one particular style is to fail to understand and appreciate their complexity. They're eager to learn and explore many types of music, and they may often lead older parishioners in exploring a greater diversity of traditional worship forms than their older brothers and sisters are comfortable with.

The Role of the Music Leader Is to Raise the Musical Taste of the Congregation

Many music and worship leaders were taught that it is their role to raise the level of the musical taste of the congregation. They were sent from church music programs with the mandate that they were to teach the choir and congregation "better" church music and to always appeal to "higher" tastes. They were expected to teach standard choral repertoire to the choir and standard hymns to the congregation. They were charged with transitioning churches from electronic organs (or no organs) to pipe organs, and they were to disseminate "cultured" musical tastes to the church. But many music leaders soon came to the harsh realization that leading the church's music is about working with a given group of people in a particular context. If pastors didn't agree with this view of music ministry, some music leaders became discouraged and left the ministry. While it may be true that musical taste is learned, not all people are interested in classical Western art music as the prototype for church music. While most people seem to be drawn toward excellence and seem to recognize beauty in its many forms, not all people are receptive to an outsider imposing musical taste, nor should they be. Music ministry is always about loving people into change, and it must be centered in authentic expressions.

As the Trained Musician within the Congregation, the Music Leader Should Make Decisions Regarding the Music Used in Congregational Services

While professional church musicians are trained in various aspects of worship and music, many decisions regarding worship should be collaborative or communal. The professionalization of music can cause people without musical training to think, "I don't do music. You do music because you're a professional." This attitude easily leads to spectatorship in worship, regardless of its style. Well-trained choirs and organists can think that they perform music for the congregation to observe rather than for the congregation to participate in. Likewise, a highly skilled band can give the same impression. When people begin to comment only about the quality of what happens on the platform, music leaders should be concerned. Congregants may be thinking, "I don't perform — I cheer for you."

At this point the church must be prophetic and oppose the cultural norm. The church is one of the last places where group singing is still practiced and encouraged; it is one of the last places where common beliefs are recited by all; it is one of the last places where all who are present kneel, stand, and sit together; it is one of the last places where the individual conforms to the community. Although our culture encourages individualism and unhealthy competition, Christian faith is communal, and our worship is dependent on its corporate nature. Nothing will destroy worship more quickly than individualism. The church should take cues from African culture, where singing is for everyone; singing is a communal activity, not a performance. Regarding music, most decisions should in some way be communal. Everyone should be valued.

Historical Works Are Better than Ones Created More Recently

While it's true that historical works have stood the test of time, and they've been vetted, there must always be a place for the creation of a new song within the church — and there is always the possibility that a new work can outstrip an older one. The church must balance the importance of creating a new song and its potential prophetic message with the importance of standing on the shoulders of the past, of tradition and the known. Perhaps if the church had been more open to newly created material, the body of superbly crafted church music that we have would be even larger. Rather than encouraging creative people in our congregations to write and compose on behalf of the church, we have opted for standard works that have stood the test of time or ones that we could easily import from other churches that we deem successful. We must realize that genuine creativity can occur only within a place and a space that is open to risk-taking. Exploration plays an important role in developing creativity, and risk-taking must be allowed. Nearly every congregation worships at least once a week. We're fortunate that we can always try again next week. Often the church has not nurtured a creative culture; therefore, we have only appealed to the familiar or materials that closely resemble the familiar, thus stifling the creation of new works.

The Organ Is the Best Instrument for Supporting Congregational Singing

The organ can be a superb instrument for supporting congregational singing. When only one instrument is allowed or available, many would choose the organ because of its variable registration, its flexible volume, and its ability to sustain sounds. Historically, many classically trained church musicians strongly preferred the organ over the piano to accompany congregational singing. This preference dates back to a time when, due to its portability, the piano was the primary instrument used in evangelism, whereas the organ was the staple instrument of more formal worship. For some of the church's most elite, the piano's early association with evangelistic worship left it with the stigma of an informal musical instrument better used for entertainment than for worship.

Still, the organ is a very difficult instrument to play, and to play it well, an organist must have much training and immense skill. Since well-trained and creative organists are often difficult to find, some congregations who preferred the organ have opted for other instruments to accompany congregational singing. Other congregations have chosen other instruments because they prefer them to the organ. And since organs are expensive to purchase and maintain, they're financially prohibitive for many congregations around the world.

Furthermore, the organ is often played so loudly that the congregation can't hear itself sing, and there may be little difference between an organ that's too loud and a worship band that's so loudly amplified that the congregation is inhibited from singing. Also, because of its lack of percussive qualities, the organ doesn't suit more contemporary songs and music, since they rely on percussion.

Because congregational singing is very diverse, no single instrument or combination of instruments provides the "best" accompaniment. The best instruments for supporting congregational song are as diverse as the body of congregational song itself.

The Organ Represents Formal Worship, and It's Less Emotional and God-Inspired

While organs are most commonly used in churches that employ more formal worship, in reality an organ is a very flexible instrument, and it's capable of adapting to many styles. Recognizing that the organ is likely not most effective in settings where a driving beat is desired doesn't mean that the organ and the worship it supports are less emotional and God-inspired. For people who have experienced significant spiritual moments of their lives with the sounds of an organ close at hand, organ music plays a prominent role in their spiritual and emotional soundtrack. While it's true that emotional involvement may be easier to observe in many services that use music in more popular forms, to equate the visible signs of emotion with actual emotional response is to seriously misunderstand the differences in people and how their feelings are manifested.

Hymns Are More Theological than Praise Songs

While proponents of hymn-only worship often use this argument, it isn't categorically true; only some hymns are more theologically accurate than praise songs. Furthermore, songs from the gospel song tradition (more currently referred to as hymns) are often written in the first person and are experiential, just like many songs in the praise and worship genre. If all hymns were more theological, then many of our hymns wouldn't have gone through so many editorial changes in subsequent hymnals. In fact, many standard hymns have multiple stanzas omitted, and many have been changed even in the most recent hymnals. While it is certainly true that most hymns, perhaps due to length, offer a more comprehensive theology than praise songs do, that doesn't always put the hymn at a higher theological level. Rather than being evaluated solely on their individual merits, songs must be considered by the role they play in a specific liturgical context.

Repetitive Songs Aren't as Good as Songs with More Text

Repetition is important, and repetitive songs have always been a part of the church's repertoire. However, in most liturgies, a repetitive song is coupled with another that has more text, or a series of repetitive songs are used to create a comprehensive unit. Ideally, the texts should complement each other. Context is important for any worship music, and some contexts are more appropriate for repetitive songs than text-dense songs. Unfortunately, the argument for the superiority of songs with more text has often been used to denigrate the music coming from the praise and worship movement. But it must be recognized that this argument is significantly flawed, because the same opponents of praise and worship music might readily advocate songs from Taize, repetitive songs from other cultures, and even the repetitive nature of the Kyrie or music from the Baroque period. The fact that hymns are denser doesn't necessarily mean that they're deeper.

Every Congregational Song Must Contain a Fully-Orbed Gospel Message

Several years ago, after I led worship for a large national event, a seasoned scholar took me to task for using a hymn in worship that didn't have a fully-orbed gospel message. True, the hymn contained only minimal references to Christ and strongly extolled the power of music in worship; however, seen in the larger context of the full worship event, which involved nearly a dozen other congregational songs and was thematically centered on the theme of music in worship, the hymn served a specific purpose within the liturgy. I responded that we seldom expect any other worship element to carry the gospel's full weight — not even the sermon; yet we sometimes have unrealistic expectations for the music of worship. All songs must be viewed within the larger framework of a complete worship service, not as freestanding entities.

While much is written in worship materials about Trinitarian worship, not every song needs to extol the full Trinity, nor should it be required to tell the full gospel from creation to final resurrection. However, the complete worship experience on a given Sunday should offer a rather comprehensive picture of the Christ event, and the Christian year should provide an inclusive and in-depth story. Often, poor worship planning is the culprit rather than poor song-writing. For example, a friend of mine recently told me that his church combined "I Sing the Mighty Power of God" and "What Wondrous Love Is This?" into a back-to-back song set. While both of these are superb standard hymns, they don't go together as a single musical entity, and they no doubt created a sort of musical and theological schizophrenia.

Is it true that we want every song to be fully orbed — to contain the basic tenets of the gospel? In fact, certain songs may be difficult to place within the drama of worship because they tell the whole story before we're ready to reveal the entire plot. It's more helpful to have many songs representing various theological ideas than to have every song representing every idea. Also, songs that seek to "tell all" within a few standard four-line verses often are lacking in imaginative poetic images and creative imagination.

The Problem with Church Music Is that
It Is Controlled by Commerce

While this statement may be partially true, it does need further examination. Many of the decisions that ultimately affect the music we use in worship are influenced by what will sell. Much of our music is published because it's sure to sell, not because it represents innovation and creativity or because it's useful in worship. Few companies are willing to gamble on new composers, new ideas, or new compositional techniques. The same is true for recording artists. Unfortunately, the "commerce" argument is often used to belittle a particular style of music. A traditionalist, for example, may use this argument to denigrate the popularity of praise and worship music or the contemporary Christian movement, but fail to hold choral music and hymnal publishers to the same standard. In reality, church choral composers rarely take risks with the pieces they publish, and hymnal publishers are sure to include enough tried-and-true songs to assure the hymnal's monetary success.

Fortunately, academic publishers are often more likely to take risks, and this music sometimes ends up serving the church. In addition, the Internet is providing forums for disseminating music that bypass traditional models which are dependent on volume to meet a bottom line.

Contemporary Christian Artists Are All about Performance

Although artists by nature are performers, most Christian artists deeply desire to serve the church, and their work should be interpreted accordingly. In my own experience in working with Christian artists, I have appreciated and respected their goals and motivations, and we have become friends.

To be fair, we need to look at other areas of worship which by their nature are highly artistic and performance-based. Though performance is not the goal, what are we to say about preaching? Preaching at its best is Christian oratory, and it is well-rehearsed, artistically presented, and seeks to create response. Our criticisms of Christian artists, however valid they may be, need to be considered in a broader context.

And let's consider the organ once more. If liturgy is always the driving motive for organ music, then why is so much of the organ music used in worship — particularly postludes — based on concert-organ repertoire, and why do we sometimes applaud following the postlude? Choral music can easily slip into performance as well. We often work countless hours to perfect the choral craft while ignoring the ministry potential in the music.

The House Analogy Revisited

When the old house of the music of the church is stripped of its years of cosmetic updates, what will we find? Will we find heart lumber, original masonry, and solid brass? Or will we find a destroyed inner core eaten away by termites, mice, and carpenter ants?

At the core of all songs of the church are two primary elements, text and melody, and both are critical. When one or the other is missing, song, the basic building block of the church's music, is only a shell. Recently I looked over a stack of eighteen songs that a group of trusted friends sent me for a reading session for new congregational music, and if what I saw is representative of the whole, the current state of our congregational song is disturbing. More than half of the songs didn't have a single well-stated or original idea. Musically, their melodies weren't singable by most congregants and had no semblance of continuity that would aid in memory. With texts beginning on fractions of rests, lacking regular rhyme or melodic predictability, and often using few pitches, these songs lacked the two "must haves" of congregational song — text and melody.

An effective melodic evaluation for any song is the "melody only" test. When everything else is removed — accompaniment, rhythm, backup, and so on — will the text and tune still sing? If the song won't sing or isn't singable by most congregants, then it won't effectively serve them or be memorable in their lives. Melodically and textually, this song doesn't have enough imagination for them to remember it and sing it. Songs must have something distinctive, memorable, and worth returning to. They must be simple and approachable but not trite and mundane. Good songs don't need to have everything, but they must have *something*. Good songs must go beyond individual singing styles that only a soloist can sing effectively. Melodies that are too ornamented (that have several notes on one word) rarely work for a large group.

Melody and text come together in congregational singing. Unfortunately, a performance mentality has dominated the church's music for centuries, and it's the primary inhibitor of group singing. The performance skills of trained musicians have the ability to dwarf the attempts of non-trained singers in the congregation. Both the recital-like mentality of some churches and the band model of others are built around performance. Congregants come to see and hear others. For the church to move forward in fuller worship through congregational singing, we must put the congregation at the forefront of all that we do. Music leaders must empower congregations to participate. Everything that inhibits participation must be removed — everything.[7]

As we take stock of what remains of the church music house once the deconstruction process is complete, we realize that the church will have to decide whether or not the original foundation can sustain future developments. We'll have to get our best thinkers and spiritual leaders together to discern whether we should build upon the existing foundation or start anew. Because the deconstruction is just beginning, there are still many layers to remove. We'll wait to see what lies beneath.

---

7. For more information, see *The Message in the Music: Studying Contemporary Praise and Worship,* ed. Brian D. Walrath and Robert Woods (Nashville: Abingdon Press, 2007).

CHAPTER 6

What the Bible Does/n't Say about Music

> We are half-hearted creatures, fooling about with drink and sex
> and ambition when infinite joy is offered us, like an ignorant
> child who wants to go on making mud pies in a slum because
> he cannot imagine what is meant by an offer of a holiday at the
> sea. We are far too easily pleased.
>
> C. S. Lewis, "The Weight of Glory"

To be valid, all discussions about the future of the church's music and
worship must intersect with the Bible at some point. One might imagine that the Bible offers many prescriptions for how the church's music
and worship should operate, but this is far from the case. In fact, the Bible is remarkably silent on most specifics regarding the music of the
church. Nevertheless, many detailed church music and worship philosophies have been constructed in the name of biblical fidelity. How is it
that the Bible can say so little and yet so much?

While the church has often wanted the Bible to speak authorita-
tively to the difficult questions that have faced the church and its music,
most of the New Testament references to music are descriptive rather
than prescriptive. They describe the music rather than give us specific
directions about what kind of music is acceptable. Throughout history,
the Bible has failed to answer some of the church's questions related to
music. Is polyphony acceptable? Is it acceptable for the church to sing
words of human composition (nonbiblical texts)? In what language(s)
can the church's song be sung? What if any musical instruments are acceptable for worship? Can the songs of the church be sung from texts,

or should they be memorized? According to Jeremy Begbie, "Scripture provides little direct help in answering the kinds of questions that might readily be asked: What place should music have in human life? How do we go about evaluating different pieces of music? What makes good music? It certainly does not supply anything like a 'theology' of music."[1] The church has made decisions about these and many other questions based on its best understanding of practice, history, context, and biblical interpretation. Still, the Bible has sometimes been more a source of confusion than of assistance.

What are the implications for the Bible's silence on many matters related to music? The axiom "Silence speaks louder than words" may be appropriate as we consider this question. The relative silence of the Bible on matters pertaining to music may be the loudest and most important message that the church needs to hear. We have often attempted to give the Bible power that it chose not to assume.

In a recent book on worship written by five different authors — *Perspectives on Christian Worship* — each of the writers used the Bible as the foundation for matters regarding worship.[2] However, the conclusions that the five authors reached were diametrically opposed to each other. The authors represented a spectrum of worship styles, and they used the Bible in different ways — sometimes subtly, sometimes blatantly — to support their preferences.

Leaders can be tempted to make statements about the Bible that give it responsibility that it cannot assume. These statements resonate with Christians who still expect the Bible to speak to areas that it doesn't specifically address. But to use the Bible in such a way is a disservice to the body of Christ, and it is a cowardly way to hide our own opinions and preferences behind Scripture. It is dishonest. In Dan Wilt's critique of one of his colleagues in the book just mentioned, Wilt reiterates this point:

> I have nothing against biblical culture, Jewish or otherwise. I do have a problem, however, with a Western cultural overlay being emphatically described as "biblical," over and against the diversity in the

---

1. Jeremy S. Begbie, *Resounding Truth: Christian Wisdom in the World of Music* (Grand Rapids: Baker Books, 2007), p. 59.

2. Ligon Duncan et al., *Perspectives on Christian Worship: Five Views* (Nashville: Broadman Press, 2009).

church today that I personally believe reflects the nature of God and gives Him great and lasting joy.

To think there is a singularly "acceptable" way of self-offering, in living sacrifice and utter surrender, that is instituted by God in the Scriptures and is disconnected from our "now" human contribution, imagination, and even innovation, is untenable . . .[3]

Many of the problems that result from different biblical interpretations would diminish if we would come to terms with the multiplicity of interpretations characteristic of a postmodern world. Just as fish are constantly surrounded by water and depend on it completely, so we are completely surrounded by and dependent upon interpretation for meaning. Let's briefly consider how this affects our understanding of biblical interpretation.

Looking at Biblical Interpretation

Perhaps nothing is more debated within religious studies and within the church itself than the way in which the Bible should be interpreted. While the field of biblical interpretation is constantly in flux, with new methods and forms being introduced, the shift to postmodernism is also affecting the way in which the church interprets the Bible. An exploration of biblical interpretation, also known as "hermeneutics," leads to a long and growing list which includes cultural, historical, literary, narrative, reader-response, and rhetorical criticism, along with engagements in cultural studies and theories of intertextuality, semiotics, structuralism, post-structuralism, deconstruction, postcolonialism, and cross-cultural hermeneutics. While this list is too exhaustive to consider each even briefly, we will concisely explore some of the models that specifically relate to postmodern biblical interpretation, sampling a few key ideas and figures.

The Author Model

Attempting to understand the intent of the author has traditionally been an important component of biblical criticism. Questions have been

---

3. Wilt, in Duncan et al., *Perspectives on Christian Worship*, p. 132.

asked about the author's intent, perspective, position in life, training and education, upbringing, and more. However, postmodernity has turned this perspective on its head by proclaiming that "the author is dead."[4] Simply put, this perspective postulates that the author has little or no control over the work in question and that interpretation is fully left to the reader(s). Postmoderns continue to be interested in who wrote the material that they read and interpret, but with regard to biblical interpretation, there tends to be much less allegiance to the original author or the historical author and an emphasis on "This is what I would have meant if I had written these words" or "If there were but one author of this work, what intention best accounts for the resulting composition?"[5]

Foucault's Model

Michel Foucault is a key figure in the development of postmodern thought and is a central figure in post-structuralism. This is the theory that at the foundation of all social, cultural, and knowledge systems lies not an ahistorical and unchanging structure (structuralism's view), but a historically contingent and malleable structure that is therefore no total foundation at all.

According to Mark K. George, "Foucault is primarily concerned with three major problems: (1) knowledge and how that knowledge relates individuals to truth; (2) power (the relationships individuals have with others on the basis of that knowledge); and (3) self, the way in which individuals come to understand and speak about themselves in relation to knowledge and power."[6] These three problems relate to Foucault's concept of power/knowledge. For Foucault, the dynamic flow of power relations controls what knowledge constitutes truth about both oneself and the world. Indeed, one's very identity and way of seeing the world are caught within this dynamic flux of power relations. While Foucault's contributions to biblical interpretation have been largely ignored until recently, his ideas on power shape postmodern thought and practice.

4. This was proclaimed in the article by Roland Barthes titled "The Death of the Author," *Aspen* 5-6 (1967).

5. *Handbook of Postmodern Biblical Interpretation*, ed. A. K. M. Adam (St. Louis: Chalice Press, 2000), p. 8.

6. Mark K. George, "Foucault," in *Handbook of Postmodern Biblical Interpretation*, ed. Adam, p. 92.

The Intertextuality Model

According to Timothy K. Beal, "Intertextuality is a theory that conceives of every text as a set of relations between texts, and intersections of texts that are themselves intersections of other texts and so on."[7] Every text finds itself intersecting, colliding, and overlapping with other texts. In this theory, the word "text" refers to anything that can be read. In addition to literary texts, one can also read a face or a person. Differently stated, any interpretation is a matter of exhausting, shutting down, or giving up, for there are always more intertextual connections that can be made. Intertextuality accepts "the death of the author," and it shares with post-structuralism the lack of a pure structural genesis of meaning due to the infinite number of intertextual connections.

The Identity Model

Identity in the act of biblical interpretation involves features such as race, gender, class, sexual orientation, and geography. According to Francisco Lozada Jr., this interpretive method "challenge[s] modernism's long-reigning assumption that interpretation is independent of one's identity."[8] All ways of seeing the world are situated within the flow of power relations that also have shaped our identity. Such an interpretive model challenges the "readings and interpretations that claim . . . objectivity and superiority over others."[9]

Reframing Biblical Interpretation

Biblical interpretation that claimed to use a "scientific method" objectified the text, turning it into something to be examined. Primary attention was given to the text's distinctions from other texts and the differences between the world in which the text was originally written and the world in which the interpreter lives. The text was examined,

7. Timothy K. Beal, "Intertextuality," in *Handbook of Postmodern Biblical Interpretation,* ed. Adam, p. 128.

8. Francisco Lozada Jr., "Identity," in *Handbook of Postmodern Biblical Interpretation,* ed. Adam, p. 113.

9. Lozada, "Identity," p. 113.

measured, and dissected, then reconstructed in order to perceive its meaning. Interpreters tried not to be "contaminated" by the environment around them — not to be influenced by their context. Instead, they sought to understand the text based on the evidence found within the text itself. Personal biases arising from their experiences, beliefs, faith, and context were discouraged. According to Joel B. Green, interpreters using the scientific method "seek to secure the text's 'differences,' its primary quality of 'not like us,' in order to ensure that we do not read ourselves and our assumptions into the ancient text. Its world is not our world. Its ways are not our ways. Its presuppositions are not ours. We come to the biblical text from the outside."[10] This mode of interpretation understands the biblical text in terms of the past. According to Green, ". . . the only viable history within which to construe the meaning of biblical texts is the history within which those texts were generated — or the history to which those texts give witness."[11]

As we enter postmodernity, the idea of a detached and neutral interpreter has been shattered. According to Green, "Postmodernity denies the existence of a ledge of objective truth on which the reader might stand in order to make value-free judgments."[12] Based on a theological reading of the text rather than a scientific approach, this view of Scripture acknowledges fully that when interpreting the Bible, we bring all that we are to the Scripture itself. Green summarizes, "The first question, then, is not what separates us (language, diet, worldview, politics, social graces, and so forth) from the biblical authors, but whether we are ready to embrace the God to whom and the theological vision to which these writers bear witness."[13]

Relocating Biblical Interpretation

This interpretive approach moves biblical interpretation beyond the sterility of the lab and the aloofness of the academy and relocates the center stage of biblical interpretation within the community of faith. While older critical approaches are valued, they don't have the final

10. Joel B. Green, *Seized by Truth: Reading the Bible as Scripture* (Nashville: Abingdon Press, 2007), p. 13.

11. Green, *Seized by Truth*, p. 15.

12. Green, *Seized by Truth*, p. 17.

13. Green, *Seized by Truth*, p. 18.

word, for as Green states, "No interpretive tool, no advanced training, can substitute for active participation in a community concerned with the reading and performance of the Scripture." Green proposes that interpretation must be ecclesially located, theologically fashioned, critically engaged, and Spirit-imbued.[14]

The church is involved in performing Scripture — not in the sense of play-acting but in the sense of enlivening a script through embodiment. For instance, the notes of a musical score are complete only when they're transformed into music as they're enlivened in performance. Similarly, the church doesn't plug the Bible into its existing ministries or use it to prove points in sermons; rather, it seeks to be shaped by and live out the Scripture. According to Green, the church finds its home in the whole of Scripture, which means ". . . opening ourselves within the church to the role of Scripture in shaping a people, transforming their most basic commitments, dispositions, and identities."[15] And Scripture finds its home within the church; according to Green, "The church protects the Bible, and us, from the myopia that would press us, however unwittingly, to substitute our word for God's."[16] Locating Scripture within the community allows us to hear the voices of others as Scripture is lived among us. The voices of those who are more or less learned, older or younger, richer or poorer, more or less theologically and politically conservative, and of different national origins have the potential to influence our understanding of Scripture and to shape us theologically, liturgically, and spiritually. In sum, biblical interpretation must consider the theological perspectives of both Testaments, must be read from many different perspectives (cross-cultural, canonical, historical, communal, global, and hospitable), and must always be open fully to the Spirit's working within the community.[17]

Disarming Biblical Interpretation

While the intersection of the Bible with the music of the church is tremendously important, this relationship has often been misinterpreted

---

14. Green, *Seized by Truth*, pp. 67, 66.
15. Green, *Seized by Truth*, p. 72.
16. Green, *Seized by Truth*, p. 73.
17. Green, *Seized by Truth*, pp. 79-100.

and abused in order to satisfy modernity's need to objectify and prove. As a weapon in the tool chest of the faithful, the Bible has been used as a trump card that we play when our argument is in danger of being over-powered or when we want to halt dialogue which might actually en-lighten us. However, the Bible, and faith in general, is not meant to be argued about, and as we shall see, its power is most profound in the par-adox of its weakness. Ultimately, of course, we have no power to defend God. But we have sometimes treated the Bible as if it were God rather than a component of God's revelation. We think that we're holding a di-vine power in our hands, but we're not capable of using such power with appropriate discernment. Due to our brokenness and our inability to think very far beyond ourselves, we often distort and misappropriate the power that the Bible wields.

Let's consider for a moment the title of this chapter: "What the Bi-ble Does/n't Say about Music." The title is meant to make the reader un-sure of exactly what this chapter is about. The use of the slash makes several important points that aim to situate the role of the Bible in church music and worship philosophy. The first three points of the five below have been addressed already in this chapter.

1. Of all the possible interpretations that could be offered about church music and worship, the Bible *does* "say" some of them, and *doesn't* "say" most of them. While this statement may seem overly obvious, I'm making it because it's easy for us to forget that the Bi-ble can't answer most questions about worship music.

2. Although the Bible *doesn't* "say" much about music and worship practice, this very lack *does* promote a general freedom in the ways we worship.

3. The Bible isn't a unified text with a single voice; rather, it "speaks" with a myriad of voices that occasionally conflict. It both *does* and *doesn't* "say" certain things, depending on the passage being exam-ined. Given the nature of the Bible itself, we should understand that there isn't just one biblical perspective, but rather multiple biblical perspectives.

4. Hidden beneath the text of the Bible and our interpretations of what the Bible "says" are unspoken histories (things the Bible *doesn't* "say") that make possible the very text of the Bible (the things the Bi-ble *does* "say"). We can never satisfactorily know the histories that led to, enveloped, and followed after the biblical texts, and therefore

we're left with only subjective, historically contingent interpretations of a text that is itself subjective and historically contingent.

5. To say that the Bible "speaks" or "has meaning" is misleading, since texts cannot have meaning apart from a historically situated interpretation. Although people tend to talk as if the Bible says this or that, the Bible itself cannot "speak" except through the voice of a historically contingent interpretation. So what the Bible *does* seem to say to us, it actually *doesn't* say.

I won't be exploring the final two points here. But I wanted to at least mention them here because they may be useful as we contemplate what the Bible does/n't say about music. Let's begin by first considering what the Bible *does* "say" about music.

What the Bible *Does* "Say" about Music

Music Can Be Used in Times of Celebration (Miriam)

Miriam's singing to God when the Israelites were saved from the Red Sea is an example of song being used in celebration: "The prophet Miriam, Aaron's sister, took a tambourine in her hand; and all the women went out after her with tambourines and with dancing. And Miriam sang to them: 'Sing to the LORD, for he has triumphed gloriously; horse and rider he has thrown into the sea'" (Exod. 15:20-21).

This oft-quoted canticle involves not only singing but also playing instruments and dancing. The passage serves as a memory marker for ancient Israel of an occasion when God delivered them in a powerful and dramatic manner. The celebration involved the whole community — "all the women went out after her." In addition, this passage, which has been used in many musical settings, has served to voice the church's praise and extol God's work.

Musicians Can Be Called Out and Set Apart for Service in Worship (the Levites)

First Chronicles maintains that when early worship practices were established, God called on the Levites to serve as the worship leaders for

God's people. God gave them special tasks, including accompanying singing and playing instruments: "David also commanded the chiefs of the Levites to appoint their kindred as the singers to play on musical instruments, on harps and lyres and cymbals, to raise loud sounds of joy" (1 Chron. 15:16). In a later passage, even the dress for worship was described (David wore a fine linen robe), and Kenaniah was designated as the person in charge of the choirs. The work of the Levites was further broken down into an extensive system of hierarchical leadership when Asaph, along with Heman and Juduthun, was made head of the musicians.

The Levites were involved in leading the people in times of celebration. They sang in praise to God for God's good work among them. When they offered worship to God, the glory of God filled the worship space: "The house of the LORD . . . was filled with a cloud, so that the priests could not stand to minister because of the cloud; for the glory of the LORD filled the house of God" (2 Chron. 5:13-14). The Levites also led the dedication of the first temple, using the instruments that David had made (or designed) for them, and they led in praise before the people went to battle.

The work of the Levites was organized by division and specific duties: "Hezekiah appointed the divisions of the priests and of the Levites, division by division, everyone according to his service, the priests and the Levites, for burnt offerings and offerings of well-being, to minister in the gates of the camp of the LORD and to give thanks and praise" (2 Chron. 31:2).

No job relating to worship was too large or too small for the Levites: "Some of the Levites were scribes, and officials, and gatekeepers" (2 Chron. 34:13). The Levites were willing to do whatever work was necessary to lead effectively in worship. They were skilled as singers, instrumentalists, conductors, and administrators. Their extensive leadership system assured that all tasks were carried out and completed. The text implies that commitment to the team and to the important task of liturgy motivated their ministry and enlivened their work.

A word is in order about Asaph. His descendants (who were numerous) were portrayed as leading the worship of God even after the Exile. In fact, Ezra 2:41 lists the men of Israel and numbers the descendants of Asaph as 128 people. Nehemiah 7:33-34 refers to the descendants of Asaph who were returning exiles. We read in Nehemiah 12:24 that they sang antiphonally: "And the leaders of the Levites: Hashabiah, Sherebiah, and Jeshua son of Kadmiel, with their associates over against them, [were appointed] to praise and to give thanks, according to the commandment of David the man of God, section opposite to section."

The postexilic claim was that the Levites were also brought to Jerusalem for the dedication of the wall of the city (Neh. 12:27-29). Two choirs were involved with the dedication of the wall: "So both companies of those who gave thanks stood in the house of God" (Neh. 12:40).

In summary, we read, "They [the Levites] performed the service of their God and the service of purification, as did the singers and the gatekeepers, according to the command of David and his son Solomon. For in the days of David and Asaph long ago, there was a leader of the singers, and there were songs of praise and thanksgiving to God" (Neh. 12:45-46).

Worship Music Can Be Highly Organized and Structured

The music of early worship has been portrayed as highly organized and structured: "They performed their service in due order" (1 Chron. 6:32). Also, they were organized hierarchically by families. A theocratic system regulated how tasks were assigned: "They were all under the direction of their father for the music of the house of the LORD. . . . They . . . numbered 288. And they cast lots for their duties, small and great, teacher and pupil alike" (1 Chron. 25:1-8).

The text claims that everything they made and used for worship was of the finest quality; their harps and lyres were like nothing that had been seen in Judah (2 Chron. 9:11). The importance of the singers wasn't in question, since the king himself supervised them: "For there was a command from the king concerning them" (Neh. 11:22-23).

The People of God Need a Broad Repertoire of Songs/Psalms

The Psalms are the songs of God's people, and they reflect a full range of song expression — songs of praise, songs of confession, songs of lament, songs of proclamation, songs of protest, and more. The repertoire of the church should also reflect the rich diversity that is found among God's people around the world. The Psalms give us this imperative: "Sing unto the Lord." The entire world should sing — no exceptions (Ps. 67:5). Christians are to have a song to sing, and we are to sing it wholeheartedly.

Today, however, the church fails to embrace the full range of Christian expression. It seems to be more comfortable singing songs of praise and celebration and less likely to fully acknowledge the pain and struggle that surround us. A quick survey of recent mainstream songs written for corporate expression shows a lack of themes dealing with pain, lament, justice, and poverty. In the future, the church needs songwriters to compose from the deepest places of these experiences. Others have called for new songs that cover the whole experience of the Christian faith. In "An Open Letter to Worship Songwriters" (updated), circulated on the Internet several years ago and re-posted recently, author and pastor Brian McClaren called on songwriters to write songs that include the following:

1. Eschatology: "By eschatology I mean the biblical vision of God's future which is pulling us toward itself."
2. Mission: "Many of us believe that a new, larger sense of mission . . . participating in the mission of God, the kingdom of God . . . is the key element needed as we move into the postmodern world."
3. Historic Christian spirituality: "On every page of Thomas a Kempis, in every prayer of the great medieval saints, there is inspiration waiting for us."
4. Text about God: "We need songs that are simply about God . . . songs giving God the spotlight, so to speak, for God as God, God's character, God's glory, not just for the great job God is doing at making me feel good."
5. Lament: "Since doubt is part of our lives, since pain and waiting and as-yet-unresolved disappointment are part of our lives, can't these things be reflected in the songs of our communities?"[18]

The Church's Song Is for All of Us to Sing

If the church is to fully carry out its mandate to sing, we must have songs that have tunes that are easily learned, have singable ranges, and

18. Brian McClaren, "An Open Letter to Worship Songwriters" (updated). Access this at http://brianmclaren.net/archives/blog/open-letter-to-worship-songwrite.html.

are less speech-like or recitative. People come to worship expecting that singing will occur, but they may not expect it to include them. Music leaders are responsible for removing all possible barriers to allow their full participation. Leaders must nurture and encourage the insecure person who believes that everyone else has a better voice (and that means not showcasing well-developed voices in ways that cause such a person to shrink into his/her introversion). Leaders must also cultivate inclusive leadership teams, foster an atmosphere where all gifts are valid and accepted, and create safe places where participation in song is typical and expected.

The Church Should Sing a New Song —
Be Creative and Model God's Character

The invitations to sing a new song to God are clear and numerous in the Bible. Exactly what does "a new song" mean? Why is it that new songs seem so important? It seems that God intends for us to continually model God's creative spirit as we are co-creators with God in writing, singing, and playing our new creations for God. God wants us to offer songs that express our individual and corporate experience in the here and now. Songs from the past are also valued in the Bible, and the Psalms and other books draw on the music of previous generations. But the importance of singing new songs cannot be overlooked or ignored. God wants the church to encourage its composers and poets to offer their best new creations.

What does it mean for us to create songs to offer to God in worship? For the individual writing a song, this process can be an act of personal worship as he or she contemplates aspects of God's character, God's work among us, God's silence, God's good gifts, or God's apparent absence. Offering this song to the local church can be a way of sharing one's gifts with the larger body. For the church, receiving a new song can be a way to corporately acknowledge how God is working in the local context.

Because God is continually acting among us and offering new insights of God's self, there will always be new songs to write. It is impossible to fully know God; therefore, we are continually on a quest to know God more. As we continue on the journey, we will gain new insights, and new songs will need to be written to chronicle the journey. There are many aspects of the Bible and of God's revelation that still need to be expressed in song.

But it's important to realize that not all "new songs" are newly created. Often the church discovers songs that were written long ago that become new when they are discovered in a new era. We must continually be looking for these songs as well and be ready to offer our best hospitality to them. From the book of Psalms to the book of Revelation we are encouraged to "sing to him a new song; play skillfully, on the strings, with loud shouts" (Ps. 33:3).

The People of God Should Sing God's Song in a Strange Land

> By the rivers of Babylon — there we sat down and there we wept when we remembered Zion. On the willows there we hung up our harps. For there our captors asked us for songs, our tormentors asked for mirth, saying, "Sing us one of the songs of Zion!" How could we sing the LORD's song in a foreign land? (Ps. 137:1-4)

The songs that we sing in worship should express our deepest and widest emotions. God created us capable of a broad range of emotions, and when we worship, we should explore the gamut of our emotional selves. When we're in pain, we should sing to God; when we're happy, we should sing to God. Music should be used to tell God's redemptive story from wherever we are in our lives. When we find we are in a strange land, and we are tormented, our song should reflect the pain of our present condition. When others who misunderstand our faith sarcastically ask us to sing a song of our God, we are to be ready with a song that comes from the recesses of our faith experience. When the pain is too intense to offer a song, we are to offer the best word we can muster. At other times, when we as individuals are unable to sing, we should ask the community to sing on our behalf. Once again, the Psalms speak to the pain that is sometimes too deep for expression: "With my voice I cry to the LORD; with my voice I make supplication to the LORD. I pour out my complaint before him; I tell my trouble before him" (Ps. 142:1-2).

In the New Testament, we find that even in prison, Paul and Silas were offering their praise to God: "About midnight Paul and Silas were praying and singing hymns to God, and the other prisoners were listening to them" (Acts 16:25). The passage goes on to tell the story of how

God miraculously showed up in the prison to release them and bring salvation to their captors. Our culture could lure us to believe that we affirm our faith in God because of the good that happens to us; but the biblical record speaks sharply in contrast to this notion. Throughout the Bible and the history of the church, Christ's followers have offered their songs to God in their most difficult times — through martyrdom, through slavery, through apartheid, through civil rights abuses, in prison, when underground — and God has used songs to keep them focused on God rather than on themselves or their detractors. The power of God's people singing God's song must not be underestimated.

Music Is a Significant Part of the Lord's Supper

The Lord's Supper is one of the most obvious biblical moments in which music is integrated, and in fact, Scripture's description of it was used to justify the beginning of hymn-singing in the early free church.[19] In the book of Mark, we read about the very first communion that Jesus celebrated with his disciples, and what they did after the sharing of the bread and wine: "When they had sung the hymn, they went out to the Mount of Olives" (Mark 14:26). Communion is an intimate worship time, and music should always be part of it.

As the centerpiece for the Mass, the Eucharist has inspired music from many of history's most significant composers, such as Haydn, Mozart, Schubert, and Liszt. Music is still the cornerstone of the Mass in the Catholic Church, and most Protestant churches also use music in the service of communion. From an anthem, to a departing hymn in traditional worship, to the song that the entire congregation sings while people walk forward to partake of the communion elements, music has remained an integral part of celebrating the Table of the Lord. As we take communion in the manner in which Jesus asked — "in remembrance of me" — our singing is a way we call to mind and express all that we remember about Christ. Music not only signifies the importance of this ritual; it also sends us forth and stays in our minds. Long after worship is over, songs and their texts are lodged in our memory.

---

19. See William J. Reynolds and Milburn Price, *A Survey of Christian Hymnody*, 5th ed. (Carol Stream, Ill.: Hope Publishing Company, 2010), p. 67.

How the Church Sings Is Important

> Do not get drunk with wine, for that is debauchery; but be filled with
> the Spirit, as you sing psalms and hymns and spiritual songs among
> yourselves, singing and making melody to the Lord in your hearts,
> giving thanks to God the Father at all times and for everything in the
> name of our Lord Jesus Christ. (Eph. 5:18-20)

> Let the word of Christ dwell in you richly; teach and admonish one
> another in all wisdom; and with gratitude in your hearts sing psalms,
> hymns, and spiritual songs to God. And whatever you do, in word or
> deed, do everything in the name of the Lord Jesus, giving thanks to
> God the Father through him. (Col. 3:16-17)

By far the most quoted passages regarding music in the Bible are the
above passages from Ephesians and Colossians. They are important for
every musician who serves the church, and they offer key insights into
the music of worship and education. While these passages are often
used to demonstrate the importance of embracing a wide variety of music in worship, this emphasis may not be the most important one. Much
has been written about the meanings of "psalms, hymns, and spiritual
songs" in an attempt to explain the categories and genres of worship
music currently in use — psalms, traditional hymnody, and praise music. But many believe that the passage's primary emphasis is not on
what we sing, what styles we choose, but on how we sing — on matters
of attitude and heart.[20] Ephesians 5 seems to emphasize the primary
importance of being filled with the Spirit as you sing, and it further
mentions the importance of "making melody to the Lord in your
hearts." Similarly, the Colossians passage seems to focus primarily on
the indwelling of Christ, the importance of teaching and admonishing,
and the role of giving thanks in all things.

Music Helps the Church Remember

Music plays an important role in teaching because it helps us to remember texts, and it can move us to action. It is an ideal mnemonic de-

20. For a discussion of these ideas, see Ronald Allen and Gordon Borror, *Worship: Re-
discovering the Missing Jewel* (Portland, Ore.: Multnomah Press, 1982), pp. 159-60.

vice, and it helps shape our faith. Most theologians agree that we learn a majority of our theology through the songs we sing rather than through the sermons we hear or the lessons we're taught. This point is made well by Lutheran theologian Chad L. Bird:

> Put your ear to the church's mouth — not your nose to her books — and there she will tell you what she truly believes, not just what she claims to believe. It is no coincidence, therefore, that virtually all communions within Christendom have their own distinctive hymnody. This mirrors their theology.[21]

It's much easier for us to remember text when it's combined with music. Many of us know passages of the Bible that we've learned through singing the text. When we hear the text spoken, immediately our minds start hearing music — whether it be the choruses from Handel's *Messiah* or the praise and worship songs we have sung in small groups.

First Corinthians 14:26 emphasizes the importance of building up the body of Christ through our worship. Song is at the front of the list of ways in which the word of God might be presented: "What should be done then, my friends? When you come together, each one has a hymn, a lesson, a revelation, a tongue, or an interpretation. Let all things be done for building up."

We Will Sing in Heaven

Singing is one act of worship that we will take with us to heaven. When we read the numerous passages from the Bible about heaven, music is always mentioned. Music's role in heaven will undoubtedly be very significant, and it seems obvious from the biblical account that music will occupy much of our time there. One only has to look at the book of Revelation to find many references to singing in heaven. Older hymnals that come out of times of difficulty and struggle are replete with songs of heaven — "Sing the Wondrous Love of Jesus," "I Will Sing the Wondrous Story," and more. Newer songs also speak of heaven and the role of music — "I Can Only Imagine," "Better Is One Day," and others.

---

21. Chad L. Bird, *Why Lutherans Sing What They Sing: An Apology for Lutheran Hymnody* (Kewanee, Ill.: Evangelical-Lutheran Liturgical Press, 2003), p. 9.

While much of heaven is a mystery, the fact that we will sing there seems undeniable.

What the Bible *Doesn't* "Say" about Music

We have seen that the Bible speaks frequently about music and that it offers many guidelines for how music should function within a faith community. Still, many specific musical issues about which the church has been concerned throughout history are not directly addressed in the Bible. In the section that follows we'll explore several of these issues.

The Bible Doesn't Say that God Prefers Spontaneity over Structure

Within the biblical narrative one finds examples of spontaneous worship and highly structured worship. The question of which is better is a topic that has concerned the church throughout its history. Temple worship was more formal than synagogue worship; Catholic worship has sometimes been more formal than Protestant worship; and traditionally the hierarchy of formal to informal within Protestantism goes from Anglican churches to charismatic churches. Within much of the controversy over formal and informal worship preferences and traditions is the issue of spontaneity and structure. Does God speak more profoundly through the words, songs, and liturgies of the historical church passed from generation to generation, or does God speak most profoundly in the moment? While free church worshipers have held to their rights and tradition of spontaneity and extemporaneous worship forms, liturgical churches have maintained their adherence to preparation and liturgy. But it must be pointed out that much within the free church is not really spontaneous. Many musical repetitions and verbal insertions are scripted or at least formulaic. Although these constructions aren't official "liturgy," with continued repetition many of them have become unofficially liturgical. Similarly, within liturgical congregations, leaders often go off-script. Often the free church appearance of spontaneity is just that: appearance rather than reality. And sometimes the liturgical church's adherence to form is not as rigid as it might appear.

The Bible Doesn't Say that God Has a Style Preference

There is no evidence in the Bible that God has a style preference. God does not seem to prefer choral music to congregational music, and God doesn't seem to like newly composed songs in contemporary genres more than chant and plainsong composed hundreds of years ago. God cares about our involvement in worship, about the status of our hearts, and about the attitudes we have toward other worshipers. However, God shows no stylistic preferences.

The Bible Doesn't Say that God Likes Certain Instruments Better than Others

While most of us have preferences about the instruments we like most in worship, the Bible doesn't show evidence that Gods has a preference. Die-hard traditionalists have written that the organ is the best and most effective instrument for worship, and they have justified this position rather convincingly. However, the "organ" mentioned in the Old Testament was not the pipe organ of the Baroque era. The evidence is that God has worked in the revivals of the eighteenth and nineteenth centuries, when most congregational singing was led by the more portable piano and enhanced by other occasional instruments such as the trombone or trumpet. God can be very present in worship led by guitars, drums, and a throbbing bass. While it's acceptable for us to have preferences about instruments, we need to remember that God is interested in our worship only — not in the instruments that assist our voices.

The Bible Doesn't Say that God Has a Preference for How the Music of the Church Is Organized

While the book of Chronicles, as noted above, speaks to the organization of Israel's music, there are no specific guidelines for a New Testament church on how music should be organized and implemented. From the Old Testament we might derive general guidelines such as training for leaders, an organized system of hierarchy, a specific calling, and a workable system of responsibilities, but particulars beyond these are lacking. Questions such as whether the leader should lead from the organ bench, from the piano or electronic keyboard, from a guitar or from a pulpit are lacking. Particulars such as whether we should sing from hymnbooks, screens, or by memory are not to be found. Questions regarding whether music leadership should be led by a choir, a small group, or a single individual go unanswered. The Bible certainly offers guidelines but not specific details that are applicable to twenty-first-century worship contexts.

The Bible Doesn't Say that God Cares Whether We Read Music or Play by Ear

While Chronicles does address the training of music leaders, and suggests that being skillful at the craft of music is important, how training should occur and what type of training is obtained are not specified. Important to note is that a college-educated organist can be considered well-qualified and trained while a folk musician whose style has been passed down from generation to generation can also be considered well-qualified and trained in his/her particular genre of music. The same can be said for the training that is prevalent in many churches today in which music leaders are trained through a process of mentoring — an apprenticeship model.

The Bible Doesn't Say that God Cares if We Move and How Much

There is no biblical justification for the idea that being still while we worship is preferable to moving. In fact, the Bible mentions dancing as a part of worship. God gave us bodies that move, an innate sense of movement to music which for many of us has been unlearned or suppressed, and God desires for us to use all that we are given to honor God. Also, God created us with different personalities that prefer high amounts of interaction (extrovert) and low interaction levels (introvert). We are given permission to worship God in whatever ways are most honest and authentic — we may move our bodies, lift our hands, or stand or sit in stillness as long as we refrain from judging those who worship differently. God understands our needs, and God honors our best gifts.

The Bible Doesn't Say that God Cares about the Particular Quality of Our Voices

Whether your voice has a wide vibrato or a straight tone is not of concern to God. While people with extensive vocal training typically sing with vibrato, which is the natural resting stage of the voice, it is far-fetched to think that the Bible speaks to this subject or that God has a preference. However, God does care about the health of your voice, and about your giving your particular gifts to God. It must be noted that in our youth-obsessed culture, we tend to think that older voices are inferior when in reality they are different, and the processes of aging that alter voices do not make them of lesser beauty in God's economy.

The Bible Does Say that God Prefers a Pure Heart

The Bible is clear that God prefers a pure heart. According to Psalm 51:17, "The sacrifice acceptable to God is a broken spirit; a broken and contrite heart, O God, you will not despise." Regardless of the song we sing, the accompaniment we use (or not), the sound of our voice, the style of our worship, or our worship posture, God cares about the intent of our heart. God desires our purest motives, our best intent, and our deep desire to offer God our best gifts.

From Bible Verses to Biblical Themes: The Big Picture for the Church's Music

As we have seen, the Bible is frustratingly silent on many issues regarding the music of the church. However, when we assume a different vantage point and look at the church's music through large concepts and overriding theological themes, we find that the Bible offers wisdom about what church music should be and has the power to be. As Jeremy Begbie states, "Gaining theological wisdom about music from the Scripture will come more from taking account of the whole sweep of God's creative and redemptive purposes that Scripture recounts than by scrutinizing specific biblical references to music."[22]

22. Begbie, *Resounding Truth*, p. 59.

What the Music of the Church Should Do

Our Music Should Direct Us to God Worship is first and foremost about God, so the music that we sing and the ways in which we worship should point us to God. Worship and music should encourage us to focus on God, not just each other or our own emotional gratification. In many of our gatherings, it is all too easy to think that worship is primarily about those gathered rather than about the One in whose name we are called. To curb this tendency, we must carefully evaluate what we do in worship that is not God-focused, and begin to minimize moments that focus only on ourselves.

Clearly, the texts of our songs must put their primary focus on God. In addition, our leaders must find more effective ways to minimize their idiosyncrasies and personalities and point us more directly to God. When this is done, we leave worship focused on God's greatness instead of the skill, cleverness, or charisma (or lack thereof) of our leaders.

Our Music Should Have an Eschatological Dimension As Christ-followers, we live in the reality of the already but not yet. We are already in fellowship with Christ, but we are not fully in the presence of Christ as we will be in the kingdom of God. The music of Christ should speak often and forthrightly about God's future reign and our being a part of this future reality. Our present worship and the songs that we sing should be connected to the future reality of our being fully present with Christ. We are always aware that our worship is not the last word or the ultimate experience, for we live in the hope of the fulfillment of Christ's future reign.

Our Music Should Reflect God's Creativity God created music for us to enjoy and for us to reflect back to God. God is pleased when we use the gifts God has created, and we co-create with God and offer our imaginative work back to God as a gift of gratitude. When we worship and create, we do well to imagine ourselves not as having had original thoughts, but as having tapped into a creative vein that God has already imagined. Our role, then, is to discover the dormant creation of God and to become the conduit through which God's creativity becomes apparent to us and others. Once the co-creation is re-created, we are to offer it back to God as a reflection of God's grace.

Our Music Should Represent Believers of Both the Past and the Present
Music that we use in worship should represent the timeless message of
God's love for God's people throughout history, and it should also represent the God of the present. When we sing in worship, we are not only
singing with those who are present in our particular context, but, according to Hebrews 12:1, we are joined in our worship by a great "cloud
of witnesses." We might do well to picture a gallery around our worship
space with a host of people throughout history who are joining us and
encouraging our worship even today. The assurance of the presence of
this "before our time" group helps us to see worship as both timeless
and timely. We worship the God of all time and of our time! Therefore,
the songs we sing should connect us to the story of those who are our
forebears in the faith, and to the story of those who worship beside us in
the moment. We are to sing songs written hundreds of years ago, and
songs written just yesterday.

Our Music Should Unify Christians in Worship For some, music has
become the great divider rather than a unifying force. As individuals in
churches have become overly obsessed with style preferences, music
has been used as a source of contention and division. This is one reason
why many churches have begun offering multiple services with different worship formats, and why some churches have had "splinter
groups" that left and formed new churches altogether. But music is
meant to be a force that unites a Christian community into a single
voice that speaks to God and to the surrounding community. Historically, music has been used in every great movement that inspired
change — the Great Reformation, the Great Awakening, the civil rights
movement, the dissolution of apartheid, and so on. Music's ability to
unify our goals and serve as a channel to express them with others
should be utilized in corporate worship. To sing of God's attributes
with other believers, to offer our voices corporately, attests to God's
greatness and inspires us to love God more fully.

In order for music to best serve its unifying function within the
church, we must move beyond the idea that music is to serve our individual desires and develop a philosophy of music and worship that is
based on music's communal purposes. In addition, we need to create
and write songs that bridge stylistic gaps and reinforce the musical and
theological commonality of Christians from diverse backgrounds.
These new songs will allow us to worship again with one voice.

Our Music Should Stand in Solidarity with Christians Worldwide As twenty-first-century Christians (particularly those of us in North America), we have a tendency to believe that the world started with us and will end with us. Our perception that we may be the center of the universe significantly hinders our worship and keeps us from fully experiencing God from the perspective of others — particularly Christians of other cultures. Our worship in its best and truest form should stand in solidarity with people from all nations and people groups. God is the God of all people, and our worship should be a reminder of God's work not only in our local context but also throughout the world. When we sing songs from other cultures, we are instantly reminded that God is vast and loves and cares deeply for all people. When we struggle with language that is difficult to pronounce and hard to understand, when we learn songs with tunes that are not in our musical vocabulary, when we encounter concepts of God that cause us to pause, we are standing with those in other parts of the world who are our brothers and sisters in Christ. Our struggles to sing their songs can be considered a good sacrifice of worship, and the songs themselves can be a vivid reminder that we are but a small part of God's big and creative world.

Our Music Should Express the Full Gamut of the Christian Experience While we are often effective in praise and adoration in our worship, we sometimes ignore other aspects of our faith that are also important. We often fail to recognize aspects of life that make us uncomfortable or sad. As Christ-followers, we are not immune to loss, to grief, to injustice, to abuse, to greed, and more. In order for our worship to be truly alive and representative of the full Christian experience, these and other themes must be represented in the texts that we sing. We should offer our best attempts to be honest and vulnerable in worship, and our willingness to sing texts that may sometimes make us squirm may be an important first step in this process of offering our full humanity to Christ, who became human like us.

Our Music Should Be Truly Corporate Corporate worship should be corporate — not a large group of people gathered in the same room for private worship. While we are to be personally and intimately connected to God, we are to worship with other Christians. When we do, we hear the stories of what God is doing in the lives of others, and we are inspired to better living. We are able to sing songs that we couldn't sing on our own, and others are able to sing for us when our voice cannot rise above the lump in our throat. We are able to sing with instruments and sounds that we could never create on our own, and we are able to combine our meager gifts into a God-gift that far outweighs our individual offering. The solidarity that we experience when we worship with others is an important component of our faith, one that God intended for us.

Our Church Music Shouldn't Stay in Church   The music we sing in church should be integrated into our daily lives. Every culture in the world sings, and God seems to have designed us to create songs and to have them serve as an important way of expressing our deepest thoughts, desires, and concerns. Accordingly, the music of the church should be integrally involved in our lives — the songs we sing in church should address situations that are important to us, and they should encourage us during the week as we recall their words and music. Music should also speak to us throughout life — from childhood to old age. The church should provide a soundtrack that will nurture us as we move through life's stages. We must teach preschoolers and children songs that go beyond "fun and novel." We must teach them songs with texts that fill their minds with thoughts of God and God's plan for them. Likewise, the church's music must provide nurture for people at every stage of life.

The church must offer long-term texts and music that provide sustenance for a lifelong faith. Music is a natural part of our lives, and the church must further explore ways to help Christians integrate the church's music more fully into their everyday ways of living and being.

What Music Can Do

Music Has the Power to Move Us to Show Our Love to God in Bold Ways
Music's melody and rhythm can help us to move toward becoming less self-conscious and more willing to offer ourselves to God more completely and openly. God wants us to offer all that we are to God — our full selves, body, mind, and spirit. The most poignant biblical example is found in 2 Samuel 6:14-16, 20-22:

> David danced before the LORD with all his might; David was girded with a linen ephod. So David and all the house of Israel brought up

the ark of the LORD with shouting, and with the sound of the trumpet. As the ark of the LORD came into the city of David, Michal daughter of Saul looked out of the window, and saw King David leaping and dancing before the LORD; and she despised him in her heart. . . . David returned to bless his household. But Michal the daughter of Saul came out to meet David, and said, "How the king of Israel honored himself today, uncovering himself today before the eyes of his servants' maids, as any vulgar fellow might shamelessly uncover himself!" David said to Michal, "It was before the LORD, who chose me in place of your father and all his household, to appoint me as prince over Israel, the people of the LORD, that I have danced before the LORD. I will make myself yet more contemptible than this, and I will be abased in my own eyes; but by the maids of whom you have spoken, by them I shall be held in honor."

This passage does underscore the fact that what we offer to God from pure joy and love can be misunderstood and ridiculed by others. But, more importantly, this example of unabashed offering to God (which, admittedly, goes well beyond the comfort zone of many of us) demonstrates how our worship of God can embolden us to show our love for God with our whole selves.

Music Has the Power to Create Unity within a Community Music's ability to build community is significant, because singing is an ideal way to draw a community together. Singing with others creates unity, breaks down barriers, and draws us toward common goals. Singing together is similar to working with others side by side to complete a task, because both require commitment, vulnerability, and self-giving. Indeed, the ability of music to unify has been used in major national movements to draw together large groups of people for a common cause. People who participated in the civil rights movement, for example, spoke of the power of music to draw them together even when they knew that they were facing danger. Singer/songwriter David Crosby writes,

Belafonte, Seeger, Baez, Yarrow — all of them told me that at one point each saw a scene almost identical to this: a church basement full of black faces, terrified, sweating, afraid they would die at any moment, even afraid that their babies could be murdered. Then somebody in the corner would start singing "Ain't Gonna Let Nobody Turn Me Around" or some other spiritual. It was like a lightning bolt to the soul. People went from being so terrified that they were literally huddled in a corner, tears streaming down their faces — to where they could put that child on their shoulders, walk up those stairs, walk right out the front door of that church, and confront a line of policemen with police dogs and water cannons. They could look them right in the eye and still be singing "Ain't gonna let nobody turn me 'round/God is standing at my shoulder/God is watching what we do here."[23]

Music's power helped these people face danger with little fear for themselves. Music in worship has similar power, and it can help to create common bonds with others who share our faith and mission.

Music Has the Power to Break Down Barriers   God's work through music has the power to break down barriers — literally — and change the status of a situation. Many of us are familiar with the story of the wall of Jericho, in which the Israelites marched around the wall with the priests playing their trumpets until the wall fell down (Josh. 6:1-27). Not literally but just as effectively, music can break down barriers in our own lives and the lives of others, because music can help us be more receptive to the leading of the Holy Spirit. As writer Anne Lamott recounts her conversion experience, she recalls how the power of music she experienced in a small church "wore down all the boundaries and distinctions":

> I could sing better here than I ever had before. As part of these people, even though I stayed in the doorway, I did not recognize my voice or know where it was coming from, but sometimes I felt like I could sing forever.
>
> Eventually, a few months after I started coming, I took a seat in one of the folding chairs, off by myself. Then the singing enveloped me. It was furry and resonant, coming from everyone's very heart.

---

23. Jaimee Karroll, "Twentieth-century Song as an Instrument of Activism," unpublished master's thesis (Oakland, Calif.: Mills College, 1996), quoted in Rob Rosenthal and Richard Flacks, *Playing for Change: Music and Musicians in the Service of Social Movements* (Boulder, Colo.: Paradigm Publishers, 2011), p. 128.

There was no sense of performance or judgment, only that the music was breath and food.

Something inside me that was stiff and rotting would feel soft and tender. Somehow the singing wore down all the boundaries and distinctions that kept me so isolated. Sitting there, standing with them to sing, sometimes so shaky and sick that I felt like I might tip over, I felt bigger than myself, like I was being taken care of, tricked into coming back to life.

. . . And one week later, when I went back to church . . . the last song was so deep and raw and pure that I could not escape. It was as if the people were singing in between the notes, weeping and joyful at the same time, and I felt like their voices or *something* was rocking me in its bosom, holding me like a scared kid, and I opened up to that feeling — and it washed over me.[24]

Music Has the Power to Heal One of the most prominent biblical stories of music's power to heal is Saul's asking David to sing and play his harp to ease Saul's mental torment: "And whenever the evil spirit from God came upon Saul, David took the lyre and played it with his hand, and Saul would be relieved and feel better, and the evil spirit would depart from him" (1 Sam. 16:14-23). The healing powers of music (both emotional and physical) have been well-documented in medical research, and there is a subset of music called music therapy, in which music is used in the healing process. Sometimes it involves singing with children in cancer wards; other times it involves singing with mentally ill patients. In a variety of situations, music has the power to alleviate pain and aid in the process of healing.

Music Has the Power to Aid in Transformation As we know from Scripture, music has the power to transform a situation. Such seems to be the case when Paul and Silas were singing in jail in Acts 16:25: "About midnight Paul and Silas were praying and singing hymns to God, and the prisoners were listening to them." We know the rest of the story. There was an earthquake that shook the jail doors open and loosened the chains of the prisoners. Paul and Silas, along with the other prisoners, chose not to escape, and the jailer was so awed by this that he

24. Anne Lamott, *Traveling Mercies: Some Thoughts on Faith* (New York: Anchor Books, 1999), pp. 47-48, 50.

asked the two men how he could be saved. This transforming power that we read about in the Bible and that we know from history still has the power to impact the church today.

The Last Word . . .

Christ Came to Redeem the World,
and Christ Can Redeem Any Music

Whether we like it or not, God can redeem any music, and God can use it for God's glory! Far too often the church has been too intent on the "personal testimony" of the singer or writer or concerned about the "walk of faith" of the composer. However, the Bible is clear that God is the Great Redeemer, and God can redeem any person, any art, or any sermon for God's purposes. We simply must trust God to do that which we are completely incapable of doing.

CHAPTER 7

Community and the Church's Music

"We are food for worms. . . . Each one in this room is going to one day stop breathing, turn cold, and die. . . . Look at these faces of the past. They're not so different from you . . . invincible as you feel. The world is their oyster. They believe they're destined for great things. Their eyes are full of hope, just like you. . . . If you listen real close, you can hear them whisper their legacy to you: Carpe diem . . . seize the day."

From the film *Dead Poets Society*

The music of the church is at its best when it is communally conceived and practiced. Music and community are intricately intertwined: genuine community creates an environment where music flourishes, and enlivened music enhances community. In fact, the two strands of the cord are often indistinguishable, making it difficult to discern whether genuine community produces enlivened music, or enlivened music promotes genuine community. But it is clear that within the inherent commitment of genuine community, music thrives, and when music prospers, community grows.

God designed us to live in community with other believers in which the overarching experience of communal life is our worshiping together. Like music and community, worship and community are interdependent. While worship cannot create genuine community, worship will be richer and fuller when it comes from people who are living in such community. Likewise, living in genuine community may not always result in worship, although it will deepen and strengthen worship.

If it seems to us that worship has created community, then we run the risk of gaining an allegiance to a worship form or a liturgical expression — and without it, we may lose what we mistook for community. Similarly, if it seems to us that community has created worship, then we may have lost sight of God's role in authentic worship; and when we are without this particular community, we may have lost what we mistook for worship.[1] Stanley Hauerwas describes the interdependency of worship and community this way:

> The formation of Christians through the liturgy makes clear that Christians are not simply called to do the right things but rather we are expected to be holy. Such holiness is not an individual achievement but rather comes from being made part of a community in which we discover the truth about our lives. Such "truth" cannot be separated from how such a community worships, since the truth is that we creatures are made for worship.[2]

Exploring Community

According to David McMillan and David Chavis, there are two major meanings of the term "community" when it's used more broadly: the territorial and geographical notion of community — city, town, neighborhood; and the relational notion of community, which has to do with the "quality of human relationship without reference to location."[3] McMillan and Chavis go on to offer their often-quoted definition of community: "[A] sense of community is a feeling that members have of belonging, a feeling that members matter to one another and to the group, and a shared faith that members' needs will be met through their commitment to be together."[4] While this isn't a faith-based defi-

---

1. Selected ideas above are taken from Franklin Segler and Randall Bradley, "Community and Worship," in *Christian Worship: Its Theology and Practice* (Nashville: Broadman & Holman, 2006), pp. 81-89.

2. Stanley Hauerwas, *The Liturgical Shape of the Christian Life: Teaching Christian Ethics as Worship*, ed. David F. Ford and Dennis L. Stamps (Edinburgh: T&T Clark, 1996), p. 39.

3. David W. McMillan and David M. Chavis, "Sense of Community: A Definition and Theory," *Journal of Community Psychology* 14 (1996): 8.

4. McMillan and Chavis, "Sense of Community," p. 9.

nition, it does offer important insight into what constitutes community: belonging, membership, significance, and commitment. Similarly, George Wood and Juan Judikis define community as a group of people "who have a sense of common purpose(s) and/or interest(s) for which they assume mutual responsibility, who acknowledge their interconnectedness, who respect the individual differences among members, and who commit themselves to the well-being of each other and the integrity and well-being of the group."[5] This definition contains six essential elements that determine whether community is present:

1. a sense of common purpose(s) or interest(s) among members;
2. an assuming of mutual responsibility;
3. an acknowledgment (at least among members) of interconnectedness;
4. mutual respect for individual differences;
5. mutual commitment to the well-being of each other; and
6. commitment by the members to the integrity and well-being of the group.[6]

Wood and Judikis go on to name other traits that are important for community but not fundamental to it. These factors involve inclusion, safety, geographic location, beliefs, values, particular practices, decision-making, and community spirit. In addition, communities can be divided into five categories:

1. Nuclear community: Immediate family, extended family, surrogate family, or any group functioning as family. ("Any group functioning as family" means any group having the interdependence and intimacy associated with family.)
2. Tribal community: Racial, ethnic, gender, or social class group. (These are groups which require common physiological or lifetime sociological characteristics; they celebrate their sameness.)
3. Collaborative community: Peer groups, collectives, associations, public/private places of employment, collegial groups, political parties, special interest groups. (The function of this community is

5. George S. Wood Jr. and Juan C. Judikis, *Conversations on Community Theory* (West Lafayette, Ind.: Purdue University Press, 2002), p. 12.
6. Wood and Judikis, *Conversations on Community Theory,* p. 12.

to address the purpose or circumstance that brings them together. Churches and universities belong to this category.)

4. Geopolitical community: Political, educational, social, or economic entities defined by geographic boundaries. (These are the neighborhoods, towns, cities, states, and so on where we live. They provide for the immediate and ongoing living needs of their members/residents/citizens.)

5. Life community: The sum total of family, friends, acquaintances, and other significant individuals directly affecting the member across a lifetime. (One's life community exists in one's own memory and consciousness.)[7]

Many of us belong to most or all of these communities. Although we are influenced by each community we belong to, some communities exert more influence than others.[8] In Western cultures, for instance, communities associated with family (nuclear) and work and religion (collaborative) dominate most often.

Christian Community

Koinonia is the Greek word most often used to describe Christian community. Craig Nessan says, *Koinonia* "comes from the initiative of God in establishing communion with humankind by the power of the Spirit."[9] God's love, incarnated in Christ, came into the world to initiate fellowship with God and with humankind. Jesus gathered a community around him, as exemplified in the group of twelve disciples. Nessan continues, "Jesus was renowned and even notorious for the fellowship he initiated — with sinners, tax collectors, lepers, Gentiles, women, and children. Particularly scandalous was Jesus' practice of open table fellowship. The kingdom of God meant for Jesus a community of egalitarian friendship under God's grace."[10] The early church continued to practice the *koinonia* of Christ by gathering together for worship and the breaking of bread. They shared everything: "All who believed were

7. Wood and Judikis, *Conversations on Community Theory*, pp. 46-51.
8. Wood and Judikis, *Conversations on Community Theory*, pp. 68-69.
9. Craig L. Nessan, *Beyond Maintenance to Mission: A Theology of the Congregation*, 2nd ed. (Minneapolis: Fortress Press, 2010), p. 4.
10. Nessan, *Beyond Maintenance to Mission*, p. 4.

together and had all things in common; they would sell their possessions and goods and distribute the proceeds to all, as any had need" (Acts 2:44-45).

According to Nessan, the quality of life together — the essence of Christian *koinonia* — can be determined by asking the following questions:

> (1) Does a community reflect the spirit of mutual love and concern shown by Jesus to those who followed him? (2) Are all made welcome in the name of Jesus? (3) Is the ultimate source of power that of the crucified Christ, and is that power shared in common? (4) Is special effort made to express concern for "the least" of the sisters and brothers? (5) When there is failure to live up to the ideal, is there readiness to ask for and grant forgiveness for Christ's sake?[11]

These questions are as important today as they were in the past for measuring the quality and genuineness of Christian community.

Nowhere is the Christian concept of community and hospitality more visible than in the ritual of foot-washing. John 13 captures the essence of this act of humility: "I give you a new commandment, that you love one another. Just as I have loved you, you also should love one another. By this everyone will know that you are my disciples, if you have love for one another" (John 13:34-35). The servant act of washing someone's feet demonstrates the immense humility that characterizes genuine community; it also serves as a model for the depth of Christian community.

Christian Community: A Company of Strangers?

Communities exist in many forms. Mark Searle comments, "'Community,' it appears, is above all a feeling; a sense of belonging, of being at home, of knowing and being known. 'Community' is a place where no one feels like a stranger."[12] He also points out that "'community' is less a description of reality than it is an ideal against which the shortcom-

---

11. Nessan, *Beyond Maintenance to Mission*, p. 5.

12. Mark Searle, *Called to Participate: Theological, Ritual, and Social Perspectives* (Collegeville, Minn.: Liturgical Press, 2006), p. 72.

ings of our common life can be measured."[13] In fact, we often find ourselves disappointed that the community that we belong to doesn't seem to measure up to the ideal that we imagine. When we speak of fellow church members as "brothers and sisters" and describe the people with whom we worship as "family," yet we do not feel close to them or share very little in common with them, we can easily become disillusioned with the concept of Christian community. However, as a colony of the kingdom of God on earth, we are already the community of Christ, whether we experience community or not. This may be a consequence of a church trying to establish itself in the wrong way. When the church tries to build community on the same basis as other organizations — through friendship, common interests, shared tastes, and so on — we are unsuccessful. Indeed, Dietrich Bonhoeffer warns against confusing Christian community with any other community:

> Just at this point Christian brotherhood is threatened most often at the very start by the greatest danger of all, the danger of being poisoned at its very root, the danger of confusing Christian brotherhood with some wishful idea of religious fellowship, of confounding the natural desire of the devout heart for community with the spiritual reality of Christian brotherhood. In Christian brotherhood everything depends upon its being clear right from the beginning, *first, that Christian brotherhood is not an ideal, but a divine reality. Second, that Christian brotherhood is a spiritual and not a psychic reality.*[14]

To be sure, we will never have our need for community satisfied fully in this life, for ultimate community is eschatological. While the faith community is the best possibility that we have for fulfilling this need, it will always come up short, because we will never be fully known by all those in our congregation. Are we a "company of strangers," to quote Parker Palmer's phrase?[15] What we need to remember is the miracle of Christian community: the body of Christ is so diverse — male and female, rich and poor, black and white — yet we are one within Christ. And perhaps we need to reconsider what/how we think about a

13. Searle, *Called to Participate*, p. 72.

14. Dietrich Bonhoeffer, *Life Together,* trans. John W. Doberstein (London: Harper & Row, 1954), p. 26.

15. Parker J. Palmer, *The Company of Strangers: Christians and the Renewal of America's Public Life* (New York: Crossroad, 1983).

"company of strangers." Etymologically, "company" comes from the Latin and refers to those who are companions and break bread together.[16] During Jesus' ministry, he welcomed and fed thousands of people. What if Jesus' focus were more on the thousands than on the Twelve of his inner circle? Mark Searle asks, "What difference would it make if we were seriously to consider that it is the people on the fringes of the parish who are normative rather than the core group of church regulars?"[17] What difference would it make if, instead of the strangers being invited to join the liturgy of the regular attenders, the regulars imagined themselves joining the prayers of the company of strangers?

In the spring of 2007 I traveled with a team of students to the remote village of Komolion in the Pokot area of Kenya, which is about eight hours from Nairobi. As we sang for the children in the village school, our Kenyan friend, Zippy, observed that there were no girls beyond the fifth grade. We later discovered that once girls reached puberty, they were subjected to the process of female genital mutilation (FGM) and were married off to men who were sometimes old enough to be their fathers or grandfathers. Often bearing children in their early teens, these girls were caught in a seemingly hopeless cycle. During the days that followed, our team explored how we might help some girls escape this process and the difficult life that it mapped. To assist us, Zippy talked to the parents of some young girls who had not yet been harmed, and the parents agreed to let their daughters leave their community to attend a boarding school where they would be safe and receive an education. Our small team agreed to support these girls.

Four years later I returned to this village with a different team of students, not knowing what we might discover. When we were on our way, Zippy received a call from the mother of Sheila, one of the girls we had been supporting. "Mother Sheila" told Zippy that the community had pooled their meager resources, purchased a goat, and were preparing dinner for us. Later that afternoon, following a torrential rain, we watched as the community gathered to welcome us. Women squatting over small fires cooked rice and fried dozens of pieces of bread; others boiled pans of tea and milk. Eventually, the vat of goat stew was unveiled, and after allowing our hands to be washed by the hands of Kenyan women using water they had carried from miles away, we were in-

16. Searle, *Called to Participate,* pp. 75-76.
17. Searle, *Called to Participate,* p. 76.

vited by this "company of strangers" to the most humbling feast I have ever eaten. The sacrificial meal of goat stew, rice, and bread heaped onto worn metal plates was for us the body of Christ in that place. The company of strangers that God brought together through gifts reciprocally exchanged was a telling picture of God's generous gifts offered in community.

Christian Community and Friendship

Jesus declares, "This is my commandment, that you love one another as I have loved you. No one has greater love than this, to lay down one's life for one's friends. You are my friends if you do what I command you. I do not call you servants any longer, because the servant does not know what the master is doing; but I have called you friends because I have made known to you everything that I have heard from my Father" (John 15:12-15). Choosing the word "friendship" to serve as an apt metaphor for relationships within community is first to acknowledge that Christ names us as his friends. According to Nessan, "To be summoned into friendship with Jesus is to discover ourselves in the company of all those who live as Jesus' disciples. Many of these are people with whom we would never associate by natural inclination."[18] To take the Gospels seriously is to realize that Christ is fully present in the "others" with whom we come into contact each day. To internalize this truth is to begin to grasp the "friendship" of Christ. Christ is among us, mediating our relationships. Nessan continues, "To establish a congregation as an association of the 'like-minded' runs the imminent danger of excluding Christ as the one who meets us in the form of the unlovely. We are summoned to be a church that is radically egalitarian in its composition, inviting exactly those scorned by the world."[19] At the moment we least expect, we encounter one of "the least of these" and encounter Christ himself (Matt. 25:31-46). Nessan concludes, "Jesus is never more present than in those very places where he appears to be most absent. . . . Friendship in the church of Jesus Christ searches for those places of service where no one else dares go — among those most excluded from human company."[20]

18. Nessan, *Beyond Maintenance to Mission*, p. 84.
19. Nessan, *Beyond Maintenance to Mission*, p. 86.
20. Nessan, *Beyond Maintenance to Mission*, p. 86.

Not long ago I served as the interim pastor of music for a church, and recently I had the privilege of accompanying the choir on a weekend trip to sing in four different Texas prisons. In preparation for the trip, I wrote the following piece for our choir's weekly newsletter:

Through the years I've become convinced that we need to make opportunities for music to interact with our world in places and ways other than Sunday morning worship. While we've traditionally treated God as if God lived and resided in church where we gather to worship God, the reality is that God's center of existence is in the world. Therefore, it seems reasonable that we should be joining God where God is working in the world. As we head on this trip this weekend, that's how I see it. I see us traveling to four places where God is at work, where God is showing up for people who have made mistakes just like you and me, people who just like you and me are broken and without hope except for the blood of Christ, people who just like you and me have only the hope of God to hold on to. As we go this weekend, let's acknowledge that we are on a pilgrimage to offer Christ to our brothers and sisters even as we offer Christ to each other. As we look into the faces of God's children this weekend, let's see them as children of God; but, let's also be on the lookout for Christ himself. "I needed clothes and you clothed me, I was sick and you looked after me, I was in prison and you came to visit me" (Matt. 25:36, NIV). Christ promises us that he is there. Let's join with Christ this weekend in doing what it is that Christ wants to do for us and those we encounter.[21]

Christian Community and Ecumenism

The hope of the future church is in its ability to be ecumenical and work together for the kingdom of God. Splintered by theological, political, and ecclesiastical differences, the church finds itself at a broken table, unable to share in the body and blood of Christ. If we believe that there is only one right way to worship, then Jesus is grieved by our divisive spirit, lack of respect, and failure to cooperate. Nowhere are divisions more obvious than in worship and musical style — perhaps worship

21. *The Score*, 23 March 2011, Columbus Avenue Baptist Church, Waco, Texas.

fractures are even more prominent than denominational ones. If we are to take the unity of Christ seriously, we must move toward reconciliation across denominations, within splintered denominations, and among worship styles. Such a movement will surely gladden Christ.

The Christian Community and Music

Making Musical Decisions

While not every musical decision can be made with the involvement of the community, major musical directions should receive community input. However, to receive community input is not to open every musical decision to a majority vote. Involving the community in making musical decisions implies that education, prayer, dialogue, and discernment are integral to decisions regarding the musical direction of the congregation.

While I was a worship leader in a local congregation, our Wednesday-night worship band and vocal rehearsal was a collaborative experience. After we talked through the big picture of the following Sunday's worship, how the songs were chosen, and their intended purpose in worship, we began to rehearse the songs. As we rehearsed, we decided as a group on the number of repetitions, how each song should be introduced and how it should end, and what transitions were needed to connect worship elements. Because of the trust invested in this team and their deep concern for the church's worship, these decisions were communal. The combined wisdom and insight of the group exceeded my expertise, ability to discern, and intuition. Thus the team's preparation and leadership of the community was itself communal.

Involving Others Within many congregations are people who have musical, theological, or liturgical training. These people, as well as others who share a keen interest in the music and worship of the church, are key people for involvement. While involving instrumentalists and singers is a given, engaging others can include enlisting people to help find suitable songs from the Internet and to preview sample CDs and other sources. Likewise, others can assist with physical arrangements, enlistment, set-up and tear-down for a performance, maintenance, copying, worship folder design, and more. To help discover songs that

119

may be suitable for worship, I've enlisted the help of people who are skilled and interested in musical styles and genres where I have minimal expertise. I've also enlisted the help of a woman skilled in musical arrangement to create four-part arrangements of praise songs for the worship ensemble. These are only two examples of the many ways in which others can and should be utilized.

Receiving Input   Feedback regarding the music of worship can be obtained formally or informally, and it should be ongoing. Informally, input is gained through conversations that usually occur following worship, prior to rehearsals, and during regular staff and planning meetings. Receiving formal feedback involves surveys, focus groups, and special dialogue or conversation times. Informal feedback and official times that involve dialogue and conversation are always preferable to surveys. These are problematic because they don't allow for the exchange of ideas, and they're usually anonymous. Anonymity should be avoided because it permits people to express themselves without owning their input — and this violates the spirit of communal practice.

When a planning team is utilized, each member becomes an input receiver (he/she represents a part of the community from which he/she will regularly receive feedback), which allows for much broader input than can occur when one person plans worship. In addition, intuitive leaders get significant feedback from observing the nonverbal cues of others. For instance, when participation is low, feedback has been offered; when body language shows hesitancy and insecurity, input has been given. Learning to interpret nonverbal communication is a key component in learning to listen to the congregation.

Making Planning Effectively Communal   No single person should be responsible for the entire worship planning of a congregation, because all of us have preferences and biases that will influence our planning. However, while planning should be communal, it shouldn't be open to anyone and everyone who wants to participate, because worship planning and music selection require skill and an ability to move beyond one's individual preferences to embrace the perspectives of others. Simply put, not all people possess this capacity. Furthermore, if a person has little knowledge of music, congregational song, or liturgy, his/her input in the process will probably be frustrating to all involved.

Ideally a worship planning team should be comprised of individuals who are primarily responsible for representing a particular entity within the congregation (e.g., children, youth, etc.) or who have expertise with drama, writing worship materials, or some other aspect of corporate worship. Team participants should know the congregation's story and be able to assist in bringing that story to life in worship. They should know the congregation and be able to enlist broad participation in worship leadership. They should be aware of resources and know about worship traditions outside of their own. They should be theologically intuitive in order to sense the theological threads that interweave throughout the worship experience, and they should be committed team players — able to keep confidences and be loyal. For a worship planning team to function well, trust must be established. Since most ideas will not be used in worship as they are initially presented to the group, trust will allow for healthy and productive group critique and evaluation.

Making Music in Community

Becoming Collaborative   All music-making in the context of community should be collaborative. While music-making is rarely effective without leadership, leadership itself can be collaborative. Wise leaders learn to trust other musicians on the team to make both musical and non-musical decisions. For instance, in a choral rehearsal, sometimes the ear of the accompanist is superior to that of the director, and they can work together to correct out-of-tune passages and to remedy errors. Similarly, in a rehearsal with a band, the tempo that the group settles into may be more appropriate than the one that the leader had in mind, and while the leader may be a good guitar player, he may have little skill in helping the drummer establish the best groove.

Of course, there are factors that in some cases indicate that the leader should make the decision — if a decision is controversial, has pre-existing baggage, must be made quickly, or must be made based on information that cannot be shared with the group. But a general rule of thumb is this: If a decision can be made collaboratively and within appropriate time constraints, involve others.

It's true that collaboration can be messy and time-consuming, and sometimes involving others means sacrificing quality in the short term. But eventually the investment of time and training is well worth the initial sacrifices. In a Christian community, if others can be involved, they should be! It is our responsibility to share leadership with others who are qualified or who are perceived to have leadership potential.

Being Parts of the Whole   The goal of music within the community of faith is to combine many individual parts to create a complete picture. Musically, it takes many instruments to create an orchestra and many voices to form a choir. The biblical model of the community's being different parts of the body in order to complete the body of Christ is applicable to music-making. When each person plays a part in the "orchestra" or sings a part in the "choir," the masterpiece that results is much larger and more complete than anything that any of us could create on our own. Therefore, in worship, music speaks textually, musically, and metaphorically as well.

The Singing Community

Expressing Local Flavor   The music of the faith community shouldn't look or sound the same in any two locations. The music of the church is at its best when it is rooted in the local context and it embraces local distinctiveness. In fact, music can never be duplicated from one context to another. Even with the same group of musicians, the variants within the room change, the make-up of the community changes, and the innate musical instincts of the musicians change from one context to another. Thus, because the music of worship is offered fully and completely each time, it can never be wholly used or repeated again. In that sense, all church music is disposable — once the container is opened and its contents are poured out, it is finished. But this shouldn't discourage us. We should be reminded that God is a God of generosity, not scarcity; there is always an endless supply of God's grace.

I grew up in a rural community in southern Alabama and was influenced by the worship of two different congregations — the one where my family worshiped and the one where my grandmother worshiped. Although these congregations were in adjacent rural communities (fewer than five miles apart), were both Baptist, and were both using the 1940 *Broadman Hymnal,* each had a distinctive communal context. One church had hardwood floors and a low ceiling, while the other had carpet and stained glass — and these made for acoustic differences that affected the way the music sounded and the way the preacher's words affected us. Because the pianist in one church could play only in certain keys, the hymn repertoire of that congregation was severely limited, while the repertoire of the other was broader and more inclusive of different styles. One church had both an organ and a piano, and the other had only a piano — hence the mood of worship was often vastly different in the two churches. Since prayers were always led by laypersons, each congregation developed prayer language based on its patriarchs and matriarchs — and thus the words that were chosen for prayers were different, and they were spoken with different levels of urgency. One congregation had more educated people than the other, so the responses of the people to worship were different. In one church, many of the men wore their best work clothes to the Sunday service; in the other, many of the men wore their best suits. So manner of dress also affected the context of worship.

These distinctive qualities shaped everything about the worship of these congregations — the community and its context shaped the worship. As a child, I instinctively recognized these differences, although I couldn't have verbalized them then, nor can I completely understand them today. The worship sounded different, it felt different, and it affected me differently.

My point is that each church has a different ethos — a different DNA — that is community-specific. These differences can be good and should be nurtured. Rather than attempting to duplicate the worship of another congregation, each congregation should carefully assess its distinctive qualities and should capitalize on them while continually adding "new blood," lest the community become inbred and atrophied.[22]

Telling the Local Story   The music of the Christian community should tell stories that are meaningful and understandable to the people within a local context. While songs (and the stories they embody) from other places play an important role in worship, people like to hear the songs that they know and understand. Songs differ from one local context to another, and they are filled with meaning as they are passed from one generation to another. The favorite song of a grandfather becomes meaningful to a grandchild because the child values Grandpa. The songs that portray key moments in faith history are meaningful to those

22. Segler and Bradley, *Christian Worship*, pp. 87-88.

who know the story-song, and once their meaning is revealed, they become meaningful to the next generation.

Songs in a communal context carry meanings that far outstrip the obvious meanings of text and tune. Indeed, certain songs become stories, because they remind us of the times when they took on meaning beyond themselves and became God-stories for us. In my small, rural Southern congregation, Sunday-night worship was often given to singing the favorite songs of the faithful few who gathered. As people announced their favorite song, they often took a moment to share why the song had special meaning for them: "It was sung at my mother's funeral," "It was sung the night I gave my life to Christ," "It was sung the first day I brought my baby to church," "It was sung the Sunday we first worshiped in the new building," "I first heard it at a Billy Graham crusade," "I learned it when I was in the military," "It sustained me through my cancer treatments" — and the list goes on. While some of us may not have the privilege of hearing such intimate and significant stories, we can be sure that the faith stories of those with whom we worship are intricately intertwined with the songs that we sing.

Emphasizing Participation   There is no community without participation. To stand on the sidelines is to give up our place within the local worshiping community and to abdicate a part of our spiritual development. Being participants is the primary way we learn new skills, hone our talent, grow in faith, and deepen our commitment. Community, worship, and singing are all built around participation, and each symbolizes God's participation in our lives and our offering gratitude back to God through hearty involvement.

Standing in for Others   Each of us will have times in our life when we are unable to sing, times when the tears of grief stifle our words and the abruptness of shock silences our vocal cords. As a community of faith, we sing for others when they are unable to sing. When to praise would be to pretend, others sing for us; when anger rises up and short-circuits joy, others sing for us; and when bitterness snuffs out our melody, others sing for us. To "stand in" for others in worship is a sacred task. To become a surrogate worshiper for someone else is to serve as a priest for him or her, to carry that person's concerns directly to the feet of God.

When we cannot sing, we allow others to know us in the deep places which demand our silence and their song. To stand in for others is to "pay it forward," because a time will come when we will not be able to sing for ourselves, and our hope will be in the songs others sing in our stead. As we stand at the graveside of a spouse, others sing for us; when we lose our mind to dementia, others sing for us; and when we experience mental anguish that causes us to forget the words, others sing for us.

Building a Sense of Belonging   All of us desire places where we can belong and find meaning with others. Music can help us to find these authentic experiences. Music entices us to participate, and music is winsome and welcoming. We are attracted to music, and music can help us to connect with others in meaningful ways. When we sing with others, we are vulnerable, and vulnerability creates trust. When we sing with others, we submit our wishes to those of the group: we sing the same song, sing in the same key, and breathe in similar places. Through this process, we become part of something that is larger than ourselves. The music that we sing together sounds better than the music we make on our own. Weaker voices are joined by stronger ones, the sound is larger and fuller, and together we feel a sense of oneness and belonging.

Remaining Authentic   In order for music to function effectively in community, it must be authentic to the group. The texts must be words with which we can identify, and the melodies must be notes and rhythms that are genuine for us. To sing a song that isn't authentic is like being cast in a role in a play that we can't identify with — it's impossible to play the role honestly and authentically. While not all texts that we sing must be true for us, they must be true for others within our community, and we must understand them contextually. For example, to sing a contemporary song that isn't authentically yours on behalf of a younger person in your congregation for whom the song has deep meaning is to remain communally authentic.

Remaining Faithful   Singing in community requires faithfulness to the community. First and foremost, we must be faithful to the group that regularly gathers to worship — that is, we must care deeply for them and be willing to stand beside them even when they frustrate us. Without our commitment to faithfulness, we would abandon them and search for a more compatible community. Musical faithfulness involves singing songs we don't particularly like because we're committed to the community, advocating for music that we wouldn't sing if it weren't important to others in the group, and being willing to sing less meaningful texts and tunes for others' sake. Faithfulness requires us to sacrifice some of what is important to us because of what is important to others. Faithfulness requires maturity.

Offering a Safe Place   Music can be a signal that a place is safe for us. To hear the songs with which we're familiar, to hear tunes that resonate with our past, and to sense the spirit of a group in song can indicate that we are entering sanctuary. Just as babies feel safe and comforted when their parents sing them to sleep, so we are comforted by the music of our faith and know that we are at home. Even though danger surrounds us, we can sing ourselves into a sense of safety by singing the songs that have been sanctuary for us at other times, and we can provide safety for others by singing to them in their fearful times, such as singing in a hospital room or a nursing home. Throughout history people have sung when they faced fearful times. Music helps us to transcend reality, and it calms our fears and steels our nerve.

Extending Welcome   There is nothing more welcoming than the sound of singing. When we hear singing, we know that "community" is in process. Many years ago, I was privileged to travel with a group of musicians for several weeks throughout the Republic of Kazakhstan, then under Soviet control. As we traveled through remote areas in our bus, we stopped in many villages to give impromptu concerts. Invariably, we were greeted by song, and the immediate bond that was forged developed trust and encouraged dialogue. As our group interacted with Kazak singers and musicians, the tremendous hostility that our governments exhibited toward each other dissipated, and both Americans and Kazaks felt safe and welcome in the presence of song. Singing said, "You're welcome here. You're safe in this place. Our differences are suspended." Singing draws people in because the vulnerability that it fosters breaks down barriers and places us on equal footing. Much in the same way that working with someone causes us to forget our differences, singing together allows us to lose our inhibitions and feel welcome even when we're a long way from home.

Singing Ourselves into Belief   While it's important to believe some of the words we sing, it isn't necessary to believe everything we sing. In fact, many of the words we sing are not words that we believe but words that we *want* to believe. We are seldom able to commit our lives at the level that songs such as "I Surrender All" suggest, and we are seldom able to be as grateful as "Great Is Thy Faithfulness" would propose; however, through singing, we are able to believe more — we are engaged in singing ourselves into belief. In the Bible, the father who brings his spirit-possessed child to Jesus says, "I believe; help my unbelief!" (Mark 9:24). We often find ourselves in a similar situation in worship when we want to believe but we are unable. Through singing songs over our lifetimes, we are able to believe them more and more until at last, in the presence of God, we can sing the songs with full honesty and integrity.

My younger brother died on January 20, 1989, just days before my twenty-ninth birthday. Receiving the shocking news on a Friday afternoon, within hours my wife, Brenda, and I were on a jet, making our way to Alabama to be with family. The funeral was held on Monday, and in the days that followed, with everyone gone but my parents and me, we sat beside the fire in the kitchen, warming ourselves and searching for words to express our deepest grief. As we sat and waited, my dad would often break into song, singing the songs of his faith journey and the songs of my childhood. One of them was "Farther Along" by W. A. Fletcher:

> Tempted and tried we're oft' made to wonder,
> Why it should be thus all the day long;
> While there are others living about us,
> Never molested, though in the wrong.
>
> Farther along we'll know all about it.
> Farther along we'll understand why;
> Cheer up, my brothers, live in the sunshine,
> We'll understand it all by and by.

Another was "We'll Understand It Better By and By" by Charles Tindley:

> Trials dark on every hand,
> And we cannot understand
> All the ways of God would lead us
> To that blessed promised land;

But he guides us with his eye,
And we'll follow till we die,
For we'll understand it better by and by.

By and by, when the morning comes,
When the saints of God are gathered home,
We'll tell the story how we've overcome,
For we'll understand it better by and by.

I had suppressed and undervalued these songs as unsophisticated relics of my past. But as my dad and I sang these songs, which are a part of my life's soundtrack, God came to me in my deepest need. These songs returned to me through the comforting voice of my dad and served as balm for my weary soul.

Recognizing Song as Grace   The song of community can be a transmitter of grace. Many of us have had the experience of receiving grace through the medium of song embodied in the community of faith. The combination of text and tune has the ability to wash over us and leave us refreshed in the grace of Christ himself. When we are ill, songs can heal; when we are angry, songs can soothe; when we are depressed, songs can lift us up; when we are discouraged, songs can encourage; when we are grief-stricken, songs can sustain us; and when we are confused, songs can offer perspective. The grace-gift offered to us is reciprocal, for we should in turn offer it to others.

Recognizing Song as Eschatological Connection   Song is the one earthly activity that will accompany us to heaven. When we sing in worship, we are surrounded by a great cloud of witnesses. Furthermore, to sing on earth is to join with the angels themselves as they sing around the throne of God:

Shall we gather at the river, where bright angels' feet have trod,
With its crystal tide forever flowing by the throne of God?
Yes, we'll gather at the river, the beautiful, the beautiful river,
Gather with the saints at the river that flows by the throne of God.[23]

23. Robert Lowry, "Shall We Gather at the River?" (1864).

Voting with Our Voices Singing communities always vote with their voices. If the congregation sings wholeheartedly, it's clear that they like the song; if they sing feebly, they either don't know the song or they don't like it. In a sense, all congregational song is folk music, because it's music supposedly meant to be sung by amateurs. For a folk song to survive, it has to be sung; if it isn't, it's not a song of the "folk," and it loses its distinction as a folk song. If a group doesn't like a song, they have two choices: don't sing it, or alter it. Some scholars believe that folk music is the best music because it has been planed and sanded until its rough edges have been worn away; it has been altered until it sings freely and easily. Hence, in the genre of folk music, there may be many variants of a single melody — which explains why we have a number of versions of many African-American spirituals, as evidenced in denominational hymnbooks. Similarly, much of the music of the "praise and worship" genre is folk music — music learned primarily through oral tradition and meant to be sung as it is heard, not necessarily written.

Encouraging Dialogue Inherent in dialogue is good listening. For healthy dialogue to occur, listening is critical. The music of the church should be distinguished by healthy dialogue in which individual stories are valued and group stories emerge. Once we understand why songs are important to others, we are able to abandon our critical postures and move toward understanding and acceptance.

Connecting Worldwide

Expanding the Community Through singing we expand the community of faith, and we are able to connect to the larger community of faith worldwide. Perhaps nothing personifies a people more than their music. When we sing songs from history, we're connected to people who sang these songs hundreds of year ago; and when we sing the songs of other cultures, we're connected to the people for whom these songs are more familiar. Music enables us to stand alongside someone from a different time or culture and experience God through his/her lens. Since song often spreads more quickly than other worship forms, we are able to travel to many distant places and share their worship as we join with them in their song. When we sing the songs of Christians around the world, their world is brought closer to us.

Being Catholic   Since we regularly sing songs from all over the world and from all faith traditions, the music of the church is the most universal of all worship forms. In the last half of the twentieth century, the song of the church moved from being denominationally specific to being catholic or universal. Songs are now shared among denominations, and songs from remote parts of the world are found in the repertoire of many congregations.

While theological differences characterize the various denominations, the songs that most churches sing are truly ecumenical. In today's worship environment, Baptist churches sing songs written by Catholic composers, Lutherans sing praise and worship songs that originated in non-denominational churches, and Episcopalians sing songs from the Gospel song tradition. While most denominations have always sung some songs from outside their tradition, the cross-pollination of songs today is more widespread than at any other time in history. Also, with the advent of the Internet, the propagation of songs has increased, and this trend will continue. The good news of Christ's death and resurrection is a message for all times and places.

Moving Beyond, Moving Ahead

Resisting Individualism   Individualism took strong root in congregational song in the last half of the previous century. While songs focusing on personal experience and using personal pronouns were prominent among churches that utilized gospel songs, the praise and worship movement has taken individualism to new levels. What distinguishes it from other "personal experience" genres that focus primarily on textual individualism is that praise and worship also utilizes individually expressive body language. While lifting hands to God is both biblical and appropriate, in praise and worship we rarely reach out to each other. Likewise, while closing our eyes can express sincere involvement, closing our eyes and never looking at other worshipers can be non-communal. Non-communal body language used with texts that are often individualistic creates a formidable obstacle to worship in the context of community.

Resisting Autonomy   Acting independently and without the authority of the larger community of faith regarding congregational song works in direct opposition to the rising tide of ecumenism and the free exchange of song that are beginning to pervade the Christian world. While song should be local and contextual, and while all faith communities should make decisions about congregational song based on their local community, autonomy for autonomy's sake is a failure to cooperate with the larger body of the church to which we belong. Likewise, practicing freedom for the sake of being eccentric, novel, or rebellious is to fail to connect to the larger church worldwide.

Resisting Provincialism The church must move beyond acknowledging its regional or provincial story while ignoring the larger narrative of the church, the biblical account, and its historical heritage. Churches are prone to becoming comfortable in their habits of being and can spend decades embracing minimal change. The music of the church is not immune to this sort of stasis; sometimes music is a mainstay of the provincial nature of worship. Getting stuck in a historical time period or in an outdated style is counter to the dynamic nature of the gospel.

Developing a Communal Aesthetic Traditionally, we have often thought of aesthetics as individual; I have my own aesthetics or I determine beauty according to the standards to which I subscribe. But this needs to change. One's aesthetic sense needs to be formed by and informed by various communal understandings of aesthetics. The value that each of us places on art and other sensory media should largely be a result of a developing communal aesthetic.

We need to remember that beauty is relative. While there seem to be universal standards that contribute to our understanding of beauty, those standards are not necessarily cross-cultural. What is beautiful in one culture may not be perceived as beautiful in another. Within our multicultural world, we must relearn our sense of beauty and redefine beauty as contextual. Just as "good food" is defined differently from culture to culture, so are "good art," "good music," and "good dance." Just as one person's trash is another person's treasure, one person's noise is another person's music, and one person's paint splatters are another person's art. Within community, beauty is also influenced by story. When we know the story of the art, we are able to recognize its beauty more readily. Likewise, when we understand a people and know their story, we are able to see them as beautiful.

Practicing Restraint   There is a fine line between appropriate restraint and bottled-up anger. While some communities veer too far toward "withholding" and suppress important issues, others are too free with their critiques and criticisms, and they become individually rather than communally centered. Community is based on our being mature enough to practice Christian restraint. While telling our story and participating in dialogue are important for developing community, restraint is equally important. Bluntly speaking our mind and failing to weigh our words are harmful and destructive. When it comes to music, we all have opinions, and we believe that our opinions matter and should be expressed; however, practicing restraint for the sake of the community is a virtue. We should embrace this virtue in regard to other communities as well. For too long, we have failed to restrain our thoughts about the music practice of other congregations or about their music and worship leadership. Our lack of Christian restraint and charity has been a seedbed for divisiveness, pain, and separation, and the cause of Christ has been damaged as a result.

We need to remember that practicing the virtue of restraint can be more than charitable — it can be joyful too. When we embrace restraint for the sake of our community as well as others, and for the building up of others within the body of Christ, we can experience joy.

Moving beyond Musical Toleration   For too long the church has mistakenly maintained that musical toleration is enough. If I don't like the style or genre of some of my church's music, then I'll simply tolerate it in hopes that it will go away. If it's true that our culture values its music so deeply that it's part of our very identity, then mere toleration isn't enough. Jesus was clear that loves trumps all:

> "You have heard that it was said, 'You shall love your neighbor and hate your enemy.' But I say to you, Love your enemies and pray for those who persecute you, so that you may be children of your Father in heaven; for he makes his sun rise on the evil and on the good, and sends rain on the righteous and on the unrighteous. For if you love those who love you, what reward do you have? Do not even the tax collectors do the same? And if you greet only your brothers and sisters, what more are you doing than others? Do not even the Gentiles do the same?" (Matt. 5:43-47)

If we read these verses and replace the word "love" with the word "toleration," this passage doesn't carry the same punch! While toleration may be the first step in accepting someone or his/her music, we must accept toleration only as the beginning of the journey that leads down the path past acceptance to the love which is our destination.

Conclusion

All music of the church must be characterized by genuine love for God and for others. This music helps to create a community; and to fully realize its purpose, this community must continually renew itself through the inclusion of others. The worshiping community is always at its best when it finds its life and relevance in the Christ model of generous outpouring. While the community of faith nurtured by music experiences trust, safety, and solidarity, these qualities are not to be hoarded; they are gifts to be shared generously with a world that is hungry and thirsty for the proclamation of Christ's redemption.

CHAPTER 8

The Call to Be Missional

The books or the music in which we thought the beauty was located will betray us if we trust to them; it was not in them, it
only came through them, and what came through them was
longing. These things — the beauty, the memory of our own
past — are good images of what we really desire; but if they are
mistaken for the thing itself, they turn into dumb idols, breaking the hearts of their worshipers. For they are not the thing itself; they are only the scent of a flower we have not found, the
echo of a tune we have not heard, news from a country we have
never yet visited.

C. S. Lewis, *The Weight of Glory*

Missiologists seem to agree that the modern missionary movement was
a success.[1] Through the efforts of missionaries of the past several hundred years, many peoples and groups in the world now have access to
the good news of Christ. In North America, however, declining numbers in church membership, cultural shifts, and a loss of cultural significance have called attention to this continent's status as a mission field
itself. As a result, churches are reassessing the theological underpinnings that have long guided their ministries. The modern theology and
methodology of missions so ingrained in the faith formation and devel-

---

1. Darrell L. Guder et al., *Missional Church: A Vision for the Sending of the Church in North America*, ed. Darrell L. Guder (Grand Rapids: Wm. B. Eerdmans, 1998), p. 1.

opment of many Christians (particularly in North America) may take some churches a generation or more to re-imagine.

The term "missional" first began to be explored in America in the late 1980s by a network called The Gospel and Our Culture, first initiated in Great Britain in 1983 by the publication of Bishop Lesslie Newbigin's book *The Other Side of 1984: Questions for the Churches.*[2] Brought into wide usage in 1998 by the seminal volume *Missional Church: A Vision for the Sending of the Church in North America,*[3] the term and its suggested ways of being church have taken deep root. Dozens of additional books and numerous articles have been written on the subject; it has also spawned hundreds of Web sites and discussion groups.

At this point in our discussion, it's time for us to explore the particular role of music in supporting the church's mandate to be missional. However, we must first explore the term "missional" and its many implications.

"Missional" Explored

The term *missio Dei,* "mission of God," is best used to describe the meaning of the term "missional." The church's mission began to be discussed in the early 1980s in light of the concern that Western Christianity, in its attempt to evangelize the rest of the world, had imposed its form of Christianity by shaping the communities it birthed not only in the image of Christ "but in the image of the church of western European culture."[4] Meanwhile, the church in its post-Christian (or anti-Christian) Western context was moving (or being moved) from its privileged place at the center of society to the fringes. Historically, the Western church "has tended to shape and fit the gospel into its cultural context and made the church's institutional extension and survival its priority."[5] But the Western church now finds itself "dislocated from [its] prior social role of chaplain to the culture and society and [has] lost [its] once-privileged position of influence." Religious life has been "relegated to the private spheres of life," and the church's beliefs

---

2. Lesslie Newbigin, *The Other Side of 1984: Questions for the Churches* (Geneva: World Council of Churches, 1983).

3. See footnote 1 for full bibliographic information.

4. Guder et al., *Missional Church,* p. 4.

5. Guder et al., *Missional Church,* p. 5.

and the ministries it actually performs seem at times to be at odds with each other.[6]

A deeper look at the church shows that its mission should be broader, more inclusive, and more transforming. "In particular, we have begun to see that the church of Christ is not the purpose or goal of the gospel, but rather its instrument and witness."[7] The church exists to embody Christ in the world, not to draw people to itself. In the past, many churches had a "missions" approach that viewed missions as one of many programs in which the sending church financed and sent others to proclaim the good news of Christ to "pagans" who needed to hear the good news and gain the benefits of the Western church. By contrast, the missional church is to embody the gospel in its own context. All within the body of Christ are sent forth to embody the living Christ and to impact their communities. Living missionally is for all. It is not a program or a call to which some with unique giftedness participate while others sit on the sidelines and pray, give money, and encourage. Being missional Christians calls us to an active faith — we are called to be the hands and feet of Christ. In the words of Taylor Burton-Edwards, "Mission is not *our* agenda as the church or primarily something *we* either invent or direct. We participate actively in *God's* mission as we discover it already at work in and through the various cultural contexts in which we may find ourselves or to which we may be sent."[8]

Mission is at the heart of all the church does. According to Darrell Guder et al., "mission is the result of God's initiative, rooted in God's purposes to restore and heal creation."[9] "Mission" means sending, and it is at the heart of God's acts in history. It started with "the call of Israel to receive God's blessings in order to be a blessing to the nations." And "it reached its revelatory climax" in the incarnation of Christ, who was the ultimate fulfillment of God's work, and in Christ's death and resurrection. Since then, God has been revealing God's self in order that the church might share this good news with others. The sending of the Holy Spirit at Pentecost further empowered the church as the witness of the good news of Christ's salvific work. As the church lives out its call to

6. Guder et al., *Missional Church*, p. 78.

7. Guder et al., *Missional Church*, p. 5.

8. Taylor W. Burton-Edwards, "The Church as Network in Early Methodism and the Emerging Missional Church: Worship, Mission, and Institutions in Symbiosis." Find this essay on the Web site of the North American Academy of Liturgy: www.naal-liturgy.org.

9. Guder et al., *Missional Church*, p. 4.

share Christ's love with all people, we are continually moving toward the time when we will be with God in the *eschaton,* the final day.[10]

Attractional Church versus Missional Church

In the attractional church model, the church tends to be like "a star or a planet. It seeks to bring people into its orbit," and it encourages them to put their lives in sync with the organizational church.[11] Worship is often the "front door" of this church model, and the music and the preaching are expected to appeal to the musical, technological, and communication preferences of the target audience. Consequently, this worship model is often performance-driven, expecting little from those who attend. It is rarely highly participatory or interactive. It is often spectator-driven and is primarily the work of the leadership instead of the gathered community. Success in this model is based on how many people regularly attend these services and whether the attendance is growing. Attractional congregations typically offer a variety of programs, groups, and ministries either designed to meet the needs of their congregants or to serve people outside the congregation. Even programs and activities that serve those outside the church are usually designed with the goal of eventually bringing them into the institutional life of the church. Ministry effectiveness is determined by how many people are involved in the programs. In this model, time and resources are invested in programming, facilities, and staff. Relatively minimal attention and few resources are invested in local or global initiatives in which direct oversight and immediate supervision are not done by the group paying the bills.[12]

In contrast, the missional church is not focused primarily on the church in a particular location. It sends people into the world to be the presence of Christ and participate in God's work wherever they may find themselves. Recognizing that Christians spend most of their lives in activities related to family, school, work, and leisure, the missional church equips people to be "on a mission" in their regular lives outside

10. Guder et al., *Missional Church,* p. 4.

11. Burton-Edwards, "The Church as Network in Early Methodism and the Emerging Missional Church," p. 145.

12. Burton-Edwards, "The Church as Network in Early Methodism and the Emerging Missional Church," p. 145.

of the institutional structures of any given church. Because the church leaders are not given direct oversight of such a mission, they must invest energy in training and equipping their "missionaries" with the core disciplines of the faith such as biblical teaching, discipleship, and other Christian practices; programs and facilities get relatively little of their attention. The missional church gathers for worship and Bible study, and it provides an administrative structure designed not to serve the institution but to equip the people for service in the world.[13]

The Meaning of Missional Community

The body of Christ is always incarnational; it is always being re-created within a given context. The church is a living organism comprised of real people; therefore, the life of the church is ambiguous and flexible. While the church is the embodiment of Christ, the particular locale in which the body-life is incarnated is always shifting. According to Guder et al., the church "will always be called to express the gospel within the terms, styles, and perspectives of its social context. It will be shaped by that context, just as it will constantly challenge and shape that context."[14] In contrast to the established church, with its goal of offering programs and ministries to its members for their growth and edification, the missional community's focus is always outward. The missional community is called together for worship and sent forth to minister not only to each other but to the larger community within their context. The missional church is not foremost a gathering place but a place from which to be sent.

From Place to People

The modern church (in contrast to the postmodern church) was perceived as a place of action — the place where God showed up and the work of God occurred. This view gives little attention to the church as an organic body of believers whose mission is beyond its organizational

13. Burton-Edwards, "The Church as Network in Early Methodism and the Emerging Missional Church," p. 146.
14. Guder et al., *Missional Church,* p. 14.

structures. According to Guder et al., the church was both *"the place where* a Christianized civilization gather[ed] for worship, and *the place where* the Christian character of the society [was] cultivated." Given these emphases, the church increasingly found its identity in its organizational forms and its professional class, its well-educated and trained clergy.[15] "Popular grammar captures it well: you 'go to church' much the same way you might go to a store. You 'attend' a church, the way you attend a school or theater. You 'belong to a church' as you would a service club with its programs and activities."[16] Gradually, this view of church has begun to give way to "a new understanding of the church as *a body of people sent on a mission. . . .* The church is being reconceived as a community, a gathered people, brought together by a common calling and vocation to be a *sent people."*[17] The church is beginning to find its mission as a part of the mission of God in the world rather than as an effort to extend itself.

In *Missional Church,* Guder et al. explain how the modern church was different. In the past, "both members and those outside the church expected the church to be *a vendor of religious services and goods."*[18] Functioning as a "voluntary" organization within society (alongside other volunteer organizations), the modern church competed for members and their time. It organized itself according to the organizational practices of the day, became highly organized and structured, and functioned in the well-oiled business model prevalent within modernity. Complete with its divisions of labor, departments, efficiency models, growth projections, and CEO, the church functioned like any other organization within society. In *The Churching of America, 1776-1990: Winners and Losers in Our Religious Economy,* Roger Finke and Rodney Stark postulate that America's refusal to have "an established religion" meant that religion in America would function as an economic entity. According to Finke and Stark, "Religious economies are like commercial economies in that they consist of a market made up of a set of current and potential customers and a set of firms seeking to serve that market."[19] With this concept in mind, it is appro-

---

15. Guder et al., *Missional Church,* p. 80.
16. Guder et al., *Missional Church,* p. 80.
17. Guder et al., *Missional Church,* p. 81.
18. Guder et al., *Missional Church,* p. 84.
19. Roger Finke and Rodney Stark, *The Churching of America, 1776-1990: Winners and Losers in Our Religious Economy* (New Brunswick: Rutgers University Press, 1992), p. 17.

priate to use "economic concepts such as markets, firms, market penetration, and segmented markets to analyze the success and failure of religious bodies."[20] In this model of church, "the clergy are the church's sales representatives, religious doctrines its products, and evangelization practices its marketing techniques."[21]

A Theology of the Missional Church

According to Craig Van Gelder, the church is; the church does what it is; and the church organizes what it does.[22] It is crucial to keep this sequence in mind — nature, purpose/ministry/organization — because in the missional church model, God becomes the primary acting subject rather than the church. God acts in the world, and through the Holy Spirit, the church is called, gathered, and sent to participate in God's mission in the world — the "Kingdom of God." God is continually bringing back into right relationship all of creation. This activity of the Holy Spirit is the *missio Dei,* the mission of God. The church, then, is to participate in the redeeming work of God in the world by proclaiming the redemptive work of Christ as the good news for every person everywhere. According to Van Gelder, "Seeing the Triune God as the primary acting subject changes the way we think about both the church and the world. The world becomes the larger horizon of God's activity. This represents a fundamental reframing of God's primary location in relation to the world."[23] Shifting the primary locus of work from the church to the world allows the role of the spirit-led missional church to become primarily that of "discerning and responding to the leading of the Holy Spirit." This shift allows congregations to begin to explore and engage in the communities in which they are located. Leadership begins to focus on discerning the Holy Spirit's direction concerning where the community of faith should focus its ministry.[24] Important questions for the church then become "What is God doing?" (which explores is-

---

20. Finke and Stark, *The Churching of America,* p. 17.

21. Guder et al., *Missional Church,* p. 85.

22. Craig Van Gelder, *The Ministry of the Missional Church: A Community Led by the Spirit* (Grand Rapids: Baker Books, 2007), p. 17.

23. Van Gelder, *The Ministry of the Missional Church,* p. 18.

24. Van Gelder, *The Ministry of the Missional Church,* p. 19.

sues of faith and discernment) and "What does God want us to do?" (which explores issues of wisdom and planning).[25]

Music and the Missional Church

Nothing better carries the gospel than song. Since at least the time of the Reformation, music has been a primary disseminator of the gospel. In fact, Martin Luther's detractors said, "Luther has done us more harm by his songs than his sermons."[26] When the perfect marriage of text and tune is consummated, the bond that is established is strong and can withstand the test of time. When sung often, the text is permanently locked in our memory, and for this reason has the potential for long-term impact. Similarly, a good tune can do more than hold the text with which it was paired when we learned it; it is also capable of holding many more texts in the future, perhaps those that we will remember or conceive in our moments of deepest despair or greatest joy. Furthermore, the emotional impact of tunes and their ability to ignite our memory gives them the power to transport us back to a particular time and place and enliven the original experience. As a result, we can return to our moments of high resolve and recommit our lives to future ministry and service. Music is a primary tool for serving the church, and it seems likely that its future impact on the gospel will be at least as significant as its past impact.

In fact, with the advent of postmodernism and the many cultural shifts that the church is experiencing, song may be the most permanent of our current worship forms. Partially because the song of the church has continued to change and adapt, its gene pool may be better able to withstand future challenges than that of any other primary worship element. While the music of the church has undergone continual change and has been the subject of much congregational discernment, other worship staples such as preaching and praying have remained primarily unchanged in many churches despite the changes in technology, information delivery, learning styles, and more. Once postmodernity begins to deconstruct other worship elements, one has to wonder how they will withstand this painful and rigorous unraveling process.

---

25. For a fuller discussion, see Van Gelder, *The Ministry of the Missional Church,* pp. 59-61.

26. T. Harwood Pattison, *Public Worship* (Philadelphia: American Baptist Publication Society, 1900), p. 161.

Another strength of music is its ability to respond readily to contextualization. Because it can be absorbed quickly in different cultures, it is portable and easily transportable within and among cultures. Adaptability is at the heart of the church's song, as seen in the ability for stalwarts within the hymnic repertory to cross musical genres, cultural boundaries, and stylistic barriers. Likewise, songs conceived within the popular music vein of church music have become standards in major hymnals, and they are frequently used in traditional contexts. It may be that the intense scrutiny to which the music of the church has been subjected since the 1960s has prepared the music of the church to serve the missional church in a postmodern world in a way that only God could have imagined. The fact that there is music with a Christian worldview written in every conceivable style certainly gives the church's music an advantage as we move toward the future.

Music's Missional Qualities

Long before we knew the term "missional" or we imagined joining God at work within the world, the church's music was faithfully serving the church and sometimes the community outside the church. Throughout history, the people of God have sung their praises and their laments, and this singing has impacted their daily lives. Music has embodied their beliefs (their lived-out, practical theology), and it has served as a conduit for expressing many of the Bible's most important moments: the song of Miriam after the crossing of the Red Sea; the song of Hannah upon learning of her pregnancy; the praises and laments of David; the song of the Levites, who sang the song of Zion in a strange land; the song of Mary at the Annunciation; the song of the shepherds in their fields outside Bethlehem; the song of Simeon at the fulfillment of Jesus' birth in Simeon's old age; and the song of the angels and the redeemed in the final revelation. Song, with its ability to hold even the most important news, has served the people of God throughout history, and it will continue to do so.

The song of the church is uniquely qualified to serve the missional church of the future, because, as I've noted, it was serving the church in a missional way long before the term was coined. As a near-equal partner with preaching in evangelistic campaigns of the past two centuries, the power of music to carry the gospel and to provide an entree for the gospel was fully realized. It is no surprise that every spiritual awakening in history has its corollary in a body of congregational song. Out of every revival movement and every widely recognized deepening of the faith, a body of song has emerged. From George Whitefield and Charles Wesley, to John Henry Newman and John Keble, to Ira Sankey and Dwight Moody, to George Beverly Shea and Billy Graham, every spiritual awakening has produced songs that have fueled the movement's fire. Interestingly, the songs born out of these movements have often continued to serve the church long after the movements' impact was diminished or forgotten. It seems that throughout history, the song of the people of God has always been eager to be in the world — in the chief domain of God — where the work of God has always occurred!

A few summers ago, I participated in one of our church's Neighborhood Bible Clubs in a transitioning area where some friends lived. As the music leader, my job was to involve the children in singing. As I used my trusted boom box as accompaniment to the singing on the first night, I realized that among our team we had a cadre of different musicians. I asked these friends to bring their instruments the second night, and they agreed. Arriving early, we found that our guitars, djembe, and portable keyboard began to draw a crowd, and by the time we were singing, a large group of community folks had gathered. As the week progressed, we added more musicians, and many more people came to listen and participate. The strains of live music wafting down Ethel Avenue drew people together. By taking music outside the church, lives were impacted, relationships were established, and God's love was communicated.

Music as Agent for the Missional Church

Music Is a Primary Shaper of the Worshiper's Theology

Most of us remember much more about God from the songs we sing than from the sermons we hear or the Bible studies we attend. As Martin Luther noted, "Music is a gift of God. . . . Next after theology I give music the highest place and greatest honor."[27] In his *Nine Lectures on Preaching*

---

27. Luther, quoted in Roland Bainton, *Here I Stand* (New York: Abingdon Press, 1950), p. 341.

Delivered at Yale, R. W. Dale states, "Let me write the hymns and the music of the church, and I care very little who writes the theology."[28] Music's ability to shape us theologically has been well-documented over time. And it still has that power today: "Through music we recognize God's presence among us, offer our praise, confess our sin, accept forgiveness, hear God's word, respond with offerings, and move into the world to live lives that reflect the power of Christ's resurrection. In the divine-human dialogue that shapes worship, music functions as our voice to God, God's word to us, and our witness to the world of the power of Christ in our lives."[29] Marva Dawn says that music in worship will "instruct, educate, nurture, cultivate, rebuke, exhort, discipline, warn, delight, enlighten, edify, [and] develop."[30] Congregational song can function in any part of any service as the primary communicative tool of worship's many forms, moods, and elements; it can also play a supportive role to the spoken word, to prayer, and to the Eucharist.

Important to worship's shaping of our theological perspectives are the elements of repetition and memory. In the free church tradition, where worshipers do not regularly read prayers, recite the Creed, or speak other liturgies, music is the only element that benefits from frequent repetition, and it is the only element besides Scripture that is frequently memorized. While liturgical churches do recite components of the liturgy regularly, they, like the free church, repeat hymns and songs, so song texts are likely to be committed to memory.

In the same way that music helps to shape us theologically, music will shape us missionally. As songs are written that are more missional in concept and priority, they will impact the church.

Music Is Adaptable

The missional church, under the guidance of the Holy Spirit, needs to be adaptable to the many cultures and contexts of our world, and music's natural adaptability makes it a ready tool for proclaiming the reign of

28. R. W. Dale, *Nine Lectures on Preaching Delivered at Yale* (London: Hodder & Stoughton, 1953), p. 271.

29. C. Randall Bradley, "Congregational Song as Shaper of Theology: A Contemporary Assessment," *Review and Expositer* 100 (2003): 358.

30. Marva Dawn, *A Royal "Waste" of Time: The Splendor of Worshiping God and Being Church for the World* (Grand Rapids: Wm. B. Eerdmans, 1999), p. 16.

God in the world. Many of the great tunes of the church have shown their adaptability throughout history. Some of the best tunes of the Renaissance found themselves the subjects of masses and cantatas in succeeding periods; tunes of the Baroque period found themselves embedded in future symphonic works. Even to this day, some tunes are compositional rites of passage for composers to arrange and use cross-historically and cross-culturally. Similarly, popular song classics find themselves absorbed in the jazz standards of our time, quoted in classical works, and retreaded as popular songs time and again. The great hymns of history serve as *cantus firmi* for masses, cantatas, and symphonic works. They also surface as movie themes, as fodder for popular songs, and, with additional stanzas and refrains, "re-gifted" music for current generations of worshipers. In fact, one of the signs of music's greatness is its ability to be adapted among different genres, contexts, and historical periods.

Music Breaks Down Barriers

It's true that the many different styles and genres of music do not necessarily speak universally. Still, all cultures have music, and in that sense, music is universal. It has the ability to unite and to break down barriers of race, economic status, class, social standing, and national identity. It is readily apparent, for example, how popular music transcends many of these barriers. Interestingly, most people pay little attention to the identity of a "pop" performer if they like the music. Historically, this allowed music to break down racial barriers in places like Johannesburg and Selma. Music transcended social barriers as jazz moved into the mainstream in the early decades of the previous century. More recently, music has transcended social standing when singers from humble upbringings have become household names among the wealthy and have been received by worldwide dignitaries. Music has transcended national identity when singers from one country have become well-known in another.

In some cultures, music and work are inseparable. Where there is work, there will be song, because music makes the load lighter and the distance shorter, and offers dignity to the mundane. One of the best ways to break down barriers is to work together for a common goal, whether by working alongside someone with whom you have differences or by working together on a project as simple as moving a pile of stones from one location to another. When we work together, we put aside our differences and focus on our ability to use our bodies — muscle, sweat, and endurance — to accomplish an agreed-upon task. This process strips away what divides us — class, education, status, and more — and highlights what many of us have in common: a body capable of work. In the process, we're stripped down to our core selves, and our need for others with whom to share our task becomes greater. Music accomplishes a similar function, because music, like work, requires us to be vulnerable. For example, when we sing, we expose our voices (about which many of us are insecure), we usually move our bodies in time to the music, and we risk being uncomfortable. Still, singing together forces us to get our breathing patterns in sync with those around us, which creates a remarkable sense of communal dependence. Furthermore, when we sing together, we mutually agree on a text and tune, which may require us to yield our wants to the wants of others. So it seems that nothing further reduces barriers than work and song combined. And, since *liturgy* literally means "work of the people," worship with its full component of song seems to have the potential to be transformative in our world.

When I've coordinated teams of college students to travel to Kenya and share their music, I've discovered music's ability to break down barriers and build bridges. Realizing that music in Kenya is not performance-oriented but communal, our group has memorized a wide variety of unaccompanied songs that we are able to sing in any setting. Rather than depending on offering our music only in prearranged performances, we offer our music to people wherever we are — in restaurants and schools, during service projects, while touring, and even when stopping for travel breaks. Whenever we encounter people, we offer them a song. Usually we are offered a song in return, which creates an instant bond between the two cultures, and more music and conversation follows. Whenever we sing, people gather, and music's ability to engender trust begins the process of building community.

Music Is Found in All Cultures and All People Groups

All cultures and people groups employ music in their daily lives — in their work, their rituals, and their celebrations. While the forms are as diverse as the people, music is a foundational component of all the world's cultures. In all societies, music travels with us and marks all the rites of passage in our lives — births, baptisms, weddings, graduations, and funerals.

Primary distinctions in music come from differences in accompaniment, vocal quality, and movement. While the music of Africa is primarily a cappella, with some percussion used, the music of South America usually involves various stringed instruments and percussion. Even within cultures, the diversity of music often runs the gamut. For instance, in African-American church culture, the pendulum swings from unaccompanied spirituals to highly instrumentally infused versions of gospel songs. This variety can easily be found within a single worship event; it is at the heart of the African-American experience.

A primary point of departure for many Western cultures is the noticeable lack of movement utilized in their indigenous song. In Africa, music and movement are inseparable, and all music is communal. As a consequence, the lack of bodily involvement of many Western worshipers, coupled with their idea that music is performance by the "gifted" for the novice, can make Western music seem unapproachable and cold to Africans. In addition, music in Africa and many other countries is portable: you need only your voice and perhaps some instruments that can be carried in your hand or backpack to fully create the music of the culture. African Christians are also free to use the full range of their emotions as they participate in worship. Contrast this with the "non-portability" of much Western music, and its often limited emotional range. If the music of Western churches is to be more fully missional and have the potential to shift more freely within various contexts, Western Christians must begin to use their bodies, emotions, and voices more freely and expressively in order to participate in a full-bodied, multisensory worship experience.

Music Is Easily Shared

Since music is present throughout the world, it is easily shared from culture to culture. Since it fervently affects our theological development and our worship of God, the sharing of music among Christian cultures is one of the most important ways to foster an awareness of the vastness of God's kingdom in the world. To encounter the music of our friends around the world and to vicariously participate in their music-making is to personify the body of Christ more fully and completely. According to educator Bennett Reimer, "We cannot suddenly be members of a foreign culture, experiencing music as natives of that culture can, but we can share something of what they are experiencing while at the same time retaining our reality as persons."[31] For an affluent community to sing the heart songs of brothers and sisters from the Two-Thirds World is to unite with them in their suffering and eventually to share empathetically in the suffering of Christ in the world as well.

Music Appeals to All Ages

We have to learn *not* to like music. If we say we don't like to sing or don't like music, we're probably lying! As we observe young children listening to music, it's interesting to watch how they respond — singing along as best they can, smiling, sometimes laughing. They show us how natural it is for us to enjoy music. Since we're all eager to participate in singing as young children, it seems apparent that music intrinsically appeals to all of us, and we all would enjoy musical participation if our culture valued participation more than performance and if we were willing to view music skills as teachable rather than as mysterious gifts reserved for those lucky enough to be endowed with musical talent. While it is true that some people are naturally gifted singers, all people can learn to sing in tune with acceptable quality.[32] If people have musical experiences early and often, they are able to sing and joyfully participate in communal music experiences regardless of musical aptitude. From our earliest history, music has been integral to our worship and faith development, so the church has a serious stake in teaching both children and adults to sing, for when we instill confidence in singers, we are equipping them for a lifetime of uninhibited worship through music. While music isn't necessary for worship, it is nevertheless a primary component of our worship, and if history, biblical revelation, and current practice are any indication, our singing can be imagined as a dramatic upbeat to a heavenly anthem.

31. Bennett Reimer, "Education in Our Multimusical Culture," *Music Educators Journal* 79 (1993): 25.

32. As a music educator, I have worked with many children, young people, and adults who were un-tuned singers. I've been able to help all of them sing in tune with the exception of a young girl who had undiagnosed hearing deficiencies.

Music with a Christian Worldview Already Exists in Most Known Styles and Genres

There is likely not a musical genre or style in which Christian songs are not already written. Wherever the gospel is present, a likely corollary to this gospel encounter is Christian music in some form — whether it be in the many musical genres of Western music or in the indigenous styles of more remote cultures. I often wonder if God has been in the process of preparing our culture for a new day — perhaps the advent of the missional church — as God has allowed the music of Christendom to be transmitted into every imaginable style. For instance, in today's music marketplace, one can easily access Christian music in rock, reggae, country, jazz, bebop, and a myriad of world music genres. Since a primary component of the missional church is contextualization, it seems that the music of the Christian faith may be poised to serve God in the world.

Christian music is also accessible in most countries and people groups. Particularly in the last quarter-century, Christian musicians and ethnomusicologists have been collecting the indigenous music from many cultures, and although some churches rarely use this music as a part of their regular worship, it is nevertheless easily accessible. This body of music and its continually expanding repertoire create immense possibilities for the gospel of Christ to engage with most of the world's people in ways that are understandable and hospitable. Furthermore, this body of Christian global song gives churches the opportunity not only to sing about our brothers and sisters in other places but also to sing their songs. Perhaps there is no better way (other than being there) for us to stand in solidarity with Christians in other parts of our vast planet than to join them in singing their songs.

A Worldwide Body of Christian Song Is Developing

Historically, every culture had its own various musical styles and genres; there was no common body of Christian song that transcended their differences.[33] However, praise and worship songs seem to be progressing toward becoming universal songs with the potential to unite Christians

---

33. One might make the case that the gospel song, which was transmitted via missionaries to many places in the world, provided a common song repertoire.

throughout the world in an unprecedented manner. Through the traditional marketing of these recordings, as well as their marketing on the Internet and, later, through YouTube, iTunes, iCloud, and various social media, praise and worship music is taking root in most parts of the world in a way that no other music has.

Perhaps one reason why praise and worship music has propagated so quickly is because it became popular on several continents simultaneously; it generated an immense outpouring of song from Australia and New Zealand (Darlene Zschech, Reuben Morgan, and all of Hillsong), Great Britain (Matt Redman, Tim Hughes, and others), and North America (Chris Tomlin, David Crowder, and others). This movement took root early on, and it has feverishly spread to other places. As early as 2005 I attended chapel at a university near Nairobi, Kenya, fully expecting to hear the finest indigenous Christian music led by college students. To my surprise, the songs we sang were songs I knew — ones by such songwriters and artists as those just mentioned. When I went back to Nairobi in 2007, I visited a children's home where I heard dozens of children singing praise and worship songs, although the children had acculturated the songs by adding movement, percussion instruments, and harmonies that came from their own experience. Recently I worked with young Christians in an extremely remote part of Malaysia. Even there the teenagers had learned the latest praise and worship songs.

While we may be losing the unique voice of God through the languages of God's people and the indigenous music of many cultures, we may be gaining a universal song that has the potential to unite most of the world's Christians through a single shared experience.

Music Can Move Us to Action

Music has the power to move the church to action, and it seems that music is also an ideal tool for the church to use to interact with the wider culture. Historically, the power of music has often inspired us to attempt to change our present circumstances both within the church and outside of it. For example, music played a primary role in launching Luther's Reformation in Germany, and it has played a primary role in every significant time of spiritual renewal since. Music's ability to foster unity through text and tune moves beyond the power of rhetoric, technology, and other persuasive forms. If music weren't so powerful, it wouldn't be one of the first forms that is restricted or banned by would-be dictators around the world.

While the power of music is often distorted through advertising, it nevertheless contributes to many of the purchases we make, the decisions we contemplate, and the feelings we act upon. While there is a solid historical record of music's moving the church to take action in God's world, much of the potential for music to be rightly used for God's glory remains untapped. With the assurance that God's creative powers will be unleashed through humankind, the church should realize that its best songs are likely yet to be written. These new songs could launch the missional church into participating more actively with the Triune God working in the world.

Music Has a Strong Association with the Holy Spirit

With the missional church's strong dependence on the Holy Spirit as a guide to where and how God is working in the world coupled with music's strong alliance with the person of the Holy Spirit, there is a real possibility for music to be uniquely yoked with the missional church. Traditionally, when we explore the work of the Holy Spirit, we imagine creativity, innovation, freedom, spontaneity, and more. It seems likely that the arts in their various forms stand ready to recognize a greater reliance on the Holy Spirit. Furthermore, in faith expressions that are more Spirit-influenced, music plays an enhanced role in worship. Perhaps it's time to ask if the Holy Spirit seems to favor music, or if this historical pairing has been happenstance. If part of the role of the Holy Spirit is to express "groans too deep for words" and to serve as "comforter and friend," then surely the Holy Spirit plays a pivotal role in our emotional expression, thus making the Spirit's pairing with music all the more fit and likely intentional.

Music May Have the Greatest Power to Impact the Church

The church of the future needs to be strategic. Since the church has lost its privileged position as the center of society and culture, the new reality is that the church now finds itself on the margins. Guder et al. observe that "while modern missions have led to an expansion of world Christianity, Christianity in North America has moved (or has been moved) away from its position of dominance as it has experienced the loss not only of numbers but of power and influence within society."[34] Summing up Lesslie Newbigin's commentary on the issue, they add, "What had once been a Christendom society [Western society] was now clearly post-Christian, and in many ways, anti-Christian."[35] Without the capital of political clout, unlimited resources, and formidable structures, the church will be forced to use its best strategies to make a significant impact in its context. Music may very well have the greatest power to impact the missional church of the future. Appropriately harnessed, the power of music may be unrivaled in its ability to join in God's work in the world, and in fact, we will likely find that music has been toiling for the sake of the gospel in places that many of us have yet to visit or acknowledge. While many Christians have been holed up in the fortresses of our churchly kingdoms, many artists have already been taking the gospel of Christ to the streets. The missional church may do well to find out where they are, and in so doing may discover where God is as well.

Music Has Been More Fully Scrutinized than Some Other Worship Elements

The preponderance of discussions about music from the last quarter-century to the present may have benefited the music of the church in ways yet to be realized. Having moved through the period that some have labeled the "worship wars," music has been more fully discussed than any other worship element, and the scrutiny to which it has been subjected may have helped it to be a more fit tool for the missional church.

The fact that music continues to be a topic of discussion and interest within the church attests to its importance and power. The church's musicians are accustomed to discussing their craft with others, and some have learned to talk about music in terms that are accessible to other musicians as well as to laypersons and the theological community. This ongoing interest will ultimately serve the church as future discussions within the missional church turn from style to issues such as

34. Guder et al., *Missional Church*, p. 1.
35. Guder et al., *Missional Church*, p. 3.

texts, tunes, appropriateness, and more. Additionally, topics such as cross-cultural appropriateness will likely dominate music conversations of the future.

Music Plays a Significant Part in Changing the Cultural Identity of a Congregation

In a blind experiment, one could probably listen to the music of a certain congregation and discern its cultural identity. Music is linked with style, and style is linked with culture. Different cultures are often attracted to different kinds of music, and they seek to use the music with which they are familiar both in their worship and as a corollary to their faith development. As churches seek to become more contextual and to go where they perceive God to be rather than expecting God to come to where they are — cloistered in church — music will be an important implement through which the church will become a vibrant means of grace within its particular locale. As the missional church seeks to identify with the reign of God in the world more than with a specific church or organization, the church will become more diverse in the music it utilizes when it gathers for worship. This more inclusive stance will assist the congregants in understanding, identifying with, and serving their neighbors in more meaningful ways.

Music Impacts Us at a Deeper Level than Words Alone

Music's ability to impact us more deeply than we realize is at the heart of its power. Long after the experience of worship, we are often transported again to that experience through hearing the melody of a song, even if it's out of context. Music is an important part of our memory, and it helps us revisit important moments in our lives and recommit to the tenets of our faith that we may have forsaken or forgotten.

When trying to analyze music's impact objectively, we always fall short because music's power can never be fully realized or quantified. As a musician who has served the church for many years, I continue to be astonished when I hear people in congregations I serve attempt to put into words the inexpressible capacity of music to impact their lives. Our best attempts to illustrate the indescribable qualities of music are always deficient. While we may discuss texts and analyze them poetically, textually, and theologically, to converse about the power of music that goes beyond text usually leaves us wanting. To be sure, music can be discussed theoretically in terms of melodic contour, harmonic structures, tessitura, and more; however, these discussions fail to capture the qualities of music that are too deep for words.

Serving the Missional Church: What Music Needs to Do

As we contemplate how the music of our faith can best serve the missional church, we discover that music is a powerful tool. Music has much to offer the church of the future, and music will continue to be a primary means of disseminating God's grace in our world. But, as we consider the church's music in light of the call for the church to be missional, we discover areas in which the song of the church can be strengthened.

Songs Need to Be Written that Employ More Fully Orbed Texts that Are More Likely to Impact Our Lives

The church needs songs with texts that move beyond themes of God's reign, God's greatness, God's kingship, our standing in awe of God, our need to praise God, and others. Pete Ward observes that "the spiritual high of the praise and worship experience may leave worshipers unsatisfied with the relative mundaneness of the rest of life, causing a disconnect between faith and life altogether."[36] The church needs texts that challenge the core of our Christian living and move us to reflect more deeply on our need to serve the world. While many of these songs are already written, they often don't find their way into broad circulation — perhaps a casualty of marketing or of style.

Likewise, there is a need for easily singable and folk-like tunes which use the meters that hymn texts usually employ. Helpful in this regard are the texts and tunes of Stuart Townend (England) and Keith

---

36. Pete Ward, *Selling Worship: How What We Sing Has Changed the Church* (Waynesboro, Ga.: Paternoster, 2005), p. 206, quoted in Sarah Koenig, "This Is My Daily Bread: Toward a Sacramental Theology of Evangelical Praise and Worship," *Worship,* Journal of the North American Academy of Liturgy 82 (2008): 156.

Getty (Ireland) and the texts and tunes of John Bell (Scotland). Without songs that are more theologically well-rounded and that contain language which challenges us, the church of the future is likely to experience theological atrophy and historical amnesia. We must encourage the church's artists to compose music that is winsome and singable and to write texts that pique our theological imagination and challenge our Christian living.

The Texts of Our Songs Need to Engage More Fully with the Human Condition and Our Day-to-Day Lives

The songs of worship shouldn't be sung in a vacuum. The worship of the church must intersect with the world — its problems, its pain, and its needs. If the book of Psalms were to be the model for the songbook of the contemporary church, I would say that we have spent far too much time with the Psalms of Ascent while neglecting the Psalms of Lament and the Imprecatory Psalms. For too long we've sung texts that speak only of the joyful aspects of God's nature without acknowledging God's role in the pain of our world and God's ability to offer hope in any situation. We must move through the themes of worship highlighted above and deal with the rubber-meets-the-road issues that affect all people in the world. Our songs must acknowledge that God is sometimes silent, that we are often unable to understand God, and that our hope in God is the core of our existence.

We Must Pay Careful Attention to the Contextual Nature of Our Music

In order for the missional church to function effectively, it must seek to impact the world in which it lives; we must use music that connects with our local context. In order to communicate effectively among various contexts, we need music that can speak to a range of contexts and music that is unique to a particular context. As Christ followers, we must move past the narcissism of "The music that I like is good enough for others" and "If they don't like it, that's their problem." The heart of the gospel and the Christian commitment to community would be grossly misrepresented by such an attitude.

Our Songs Must Move from Worship to Home to Workplace

When music becomes a part of our work, it has fully integrated into our lives. Once, in a music education class, an instructor said, "You know that children have made the songs that you've taught them their own when they sing them on the playground." I've often thought of this statement in relation to the church. Just as children can internalize the songs they've been taught and sing them at play, so the congregation can internalize the songs that we've taught them — and we know they've done that when they sing these songs in their homes and their workplaces. For the music of worship to reach its fullest impact, it must move from worship to home to workplace. The highest compliment a worship leader can receive isn't "I love the songs we sang this morning" but "I've sung the song we sang last Sunday all week. It's been in my mind, and I just can't stop singing it."

I grew up with my paternal grandmother living with us most of the time, and my granny knew the importance of music in daily living. There was rarely a time during the day that she couldn't be heard singing, whistling, or humming, and I distinctly remember her helping me to learn to hum as a preschooler and whistle as a young grade-schooler. Many years later, when I was in my late twenties, she was blind and unable to fully care for herself. One day I asked her, "Granny, how do you stay so positive? You're no longer able to read, write letters, or do handiwork. How do you do it?" She replied, "Honey, when I get discouraged, I start praying, and before long I'm shoutin', and then I'm able to sing again. Me and the Lord have a good time." This story came from a woman who spent her daily life singing the songs she learned in church. The "singing habit" served her faith for her entire life, even to her last days. Interestingly, my father, who is now nearly eighty, is just like his mother. He continually sings as he goes about his daily chores.

The Music of Worship Must Become a Shared Communal Song

Far too much of our worship is privatized worship within a communal setting. We often spend too much time singing songs in the first person, encouraging a relationship with a personal rather than a corporate and communal God. According to Sarah Koenig, "Despite the potential for praise and worship to be a shared liturgical event, . . . there is also potential for it to become a plurality of singular worshipers disconnected from one another in their intense desire to focus on God alone."[37] If the community of God in the world is to be fully realized and on mission, we must continually emphasize the communal nature of our worship. If the church is to be the redeemed community of God in the world, then we must be countercultural as we encourage each other to move out of the privacy of individual faith. Without a greater emphasis on living in community, every Christian will struggle more than she has to, and her faith will be only as strong as she is. The church must be built on the combined strength of the community of faith.

Conclusion

At the end of the day, what we think about the church and its music will be of little consequence, for God will accomplish what God wants to do with the church and its music. In essence, God will do exactly what God chooses, and it is our role to try to discern where God is working in the music of the church and to join God in that pursuit. In the past, God has used the church's music to assist in accomplishing God's purpose in the world, and it is likely that music will continue to be a significant component of God's plan. What if the immense changes that have occurred in music over the last quarter-century might be preparing the church's music for its finest hour? What if God were to use the brokenness that the church has experienced over its music as a seedbed for renewed creativity and the development of a new song yet to be imagined?

---

37. Koenig, "This Is My Daily Bread," p. 159.

CHAPTER 9

Embracing Hospitality

As long as you notice, and have to count the steps, you are not yet dancing but only learning to dance. A good shoe is a shoe you don't have to notice. Good reading becomes possible when you need not consciously think about eyes, or light, or print, or spelling. The perfect church service would be one we were almost unaware of; our attention would have been on God.

C. S. Lewis, *Letters to Malcolm: Chiefly on Prayer*

The release of the *Constitution on the Sacred Liturgy* by Vatican II in 1963 launched Catholic Christians into discussions related to hospitality and worship. Protestants, however, are just coming to consider the issues regarding hospitality and the life of the church. While many churches have explored "user friendliness" and "church growth," most congregations have not fully looked at the theological and liturgical implications of hospitality. Many in our culture consider hospitality a lost art, and hospitality is often equated with entertainment, as we shall discover. Hospitality as a discipline is firmly rooted in the church's tradition, and its reintroduction will significantly impact the church's future.

True worship involves our practicing hospitality as host, stranger, and guest. Worship is hospitality, and the way we welcome new people is a hallmark of our Christ following. In worship, we are sometimes the host, showing hospitality to someone who is our guest. At other times, we are the stranger, the one in need of hospitality, the one who does not yet understand or know his or her way around. Yet at other times, we are the guest, the one being hosted, the one who comes from afar and needs a temporary home. Hospitality, according to Karen Ward, "deals with how a community receives, welcomes, 'blesses,' and sends forth guests."[1] Yet the roles of host, stranger, and guest are interchangeable; as we will see, we will play more than one role in any holy encounter.

I have been to the house of CuCu (Kikuyu for "grandmother") three times, and it feels like home. CuCu lives in Nakuru, Kenya, and this eighty-six-year-old great-grandmother first hosted over two dozen Americans in her rural country home in 2005. After singing at her church for morning worship, we went to her house, where she and her friends had prepared their best dishes of beans, potatoes, bananas, greens, ugali (a polenta-like dish), corn, goat stew, and chapatti (fried bread). After enjoying this meal, we spent the afternoon singing and dancing around the kitchen table, sharing stories, playing games, eating fruit and desserts, and sipping porridge and tea. We loved the food they shared, and they relished our enjoyment of their food gifts. Americans and Kenyans shared songs and dances and taught them to each other. We talked about our families, our dreams, our memories, and our visions for a better world. Through the process of sharing and receiving gifts, we became the family of God in that sacred place.

Catholic theologian Henri Nouwen has defined hospitality this way:

> [Hospitality is] primarily the creation of a free space where the stranger can enter and become a friend instead of an enemy. Hospitality is not to change people, but to offer them space where change can take place. . . . The paradox of hospitality is that it wants to create emptiness, not a fearful emptiness, but a friendly emptiness where strangers can enter and discover themselves as created free — free to sing their own songs, speak their own languages, dance their own dances; free also to leave and follow their own vocations. Hospitality is not a subtle invitation to adopt the lifestyle of the host, but the gift of a chance for the guest to find his own.[2]

Similarly, Ana Maria Pineda defines hospitality as "the practice of providing a space where the stranger is taken in and known as the one who

---

1. Ward, in Thomas Schattauer, Karen Ward, and Mark Bangert, "What Does 'Multicultural' Worship Look Like?" *Open Questions in Worship,* 7, ed. Gordon Lathrop (Minneapolis: Augsburg Fortress Press, 1996), p. 19.

2. Henri Nouwen, *Reaching Out: The Three Movements of the Spiritual Life* (Garden City, N.Y.: Doubleday, 1975), p. 51.

bears gifts."[3] Both of these definitions emphasize the importance of a space where hospitality can occur. In a worshiping community, worship provides the space where the host (the church on behalf of Jesus) opens up its community for the stranger or guest who wants to bring his/her gifts and offer them to the hosting community. But the stranger/guest is also a gift recipient in that he/she is the recipient of the gift of space offered by the hosting community. Space matters because a space, whether literal or metaphorical, has to be created/opened for the gifts of hospitality to be exchanged.

Also prominent in both Nouwen's and Pineda's definitions is the importance of gifts. There is no hospitality without the exchange of gifts. The host offers the gift of space, preparation, community, and comfort, and the guest reciprocates with many of the same gifts as he/she interacts with the host. In essence, all have gifts to offer, and all are in need of gifts. As Christ followers, we are on a pilgrimage to offer Christ to our brothers and sisters even as they offer Christ to us. As we look into the faces of the strangers and guests, we see them as children of God. At the same time, we are also to be on the lookout for Christ himself, as that well-known text from Matthew reminds us: "I was hungry and you gave me food, I was thirsty and you gave me something to drink, I was a stranger and you welcomed me" (Matt. 25:35). To extend hospitality to the stranger is to participate in the reciprocal gift-giving of Christ himself.

Reconsidering Hospitality

Reconceiving Hospitality as Communal Practice

Our culture tends to see a practice as something that's done by an individual; for example, spiritual practices such as meditation, Bible reading, and prayer are often viewed as private spiritual exercises done by oneself. But according to Elizabeth Newman, "It is a mistake to imagine hospitality as an insolated activity done by an individual. To learn a practice is to learn a tradition, one sustained by many people over a

---

3. Ana Maria Pineda, "Hospitality," in *Practicing Our Faith,* ed. Dorothy C. Bass (San Francisco: Jossey-Bass, 1997), p. 31.

long stretch of time."[4] When we participate in hospitality, we are participating in a communal activity that is much larger than ourselves. Newman continues, "Our practices are flawed, halting, and at times unfaithful. If they were only 'ours,' this would be a serious setback."[5] However, by the graceful participation in the community of Christ, we join a work that transcends our individual shortcomings and is a part of God's redeeming work in the world. If hospitality is a "practice," then it must be "practiced"; we must participate in the regimen to develop the necessary expertise. Because Christ is best seen through the church that he has established, the practice of hospitality is best lived out in the body of Christ.

Transcending Sentimentality

People sometimes remark, "I just don't have the gift of hospitality," as if it were an inborn quality that one has no chance of developing. Hospitality is a practice that everyone can embrace. Unfortunately, for some, hospitality is limited to dinner parties, luncheons, and receptions with the obligatory polite conversation, appropriate pleasantries, and fadeless smiles. Over time, hospitality seems to have taken on sentimental baggage and become more like the hospitality of a bygone era than the activity of the contemporary church. Sentimental hospitality is inherently flawed, because it acts out of wrong feeling for the stranger/guest, is dependent on the power of the host, and fails to recognize the reciprocity of gift-giving that true hospitality embodies. Furthermore, sentimental hospitality risks being practiced only when accompanied by feelings — perhaps even feelings of pity or guilt — and it fails to recognize the importance of transcending the will of the individual. True hospitality moves beyond being "nice" and is often courageous and costly. It requires us to do that which we are capable of doing only through the grace of Christ.

4. Elizabeth Newman, *Untamed Hospitality: Welcoming God and Other Strangers* (Grand Rapids: Brazos Press, 2007), p. 19.

5. Newman, *Untamed Hospitality*, p. 20.

Hospitality: Going Deeper

Seeing the Church as Home

In order for hospitality to be extended, a home or place in which to offer it is necessary. Postmodernity has left us with a gnawing sense of homelessness and lack of place. In contrast to our forebears, many of us have lived in numerous places, and when someone asks, "Where are you from?" we might reply, "No place at all." Even within the places that we call home, much of our activity isn't anchored by "place." We live in a world that seems to make no distinction between home and hotel, even though they are very different places. A hotel is a temporary place where lodging and a basic breakfast are for sale, whereas a home is a place of memory, a place from which our stories are launched and nurtured and to which we can return when we feel weary and wounded. Although this definition of "home" is as it used to be and should be, many postmoderns have no such homes. Today many of us see home as a place only to sleep — hence the phrase "bedroom community." Even our neighborhoods, which we often call "subdivisions," are neatly lined with houses of near-identical design. Furthermore, some studies have shown that many people actually prefer to remain at work instead of going home.[6] The fragmentation or loss of place is connected to our diminishing meta-narrative and our struggle to find ourselves within the larger story. However, Newman observes, "Christians believe that our salvation and freedom reside in God's acting in history, in the people of Israel, Jesus Christ, and the church for the sake of the world. To the extent that we allow ourselves to be bound to this history, this story, our fragmentation and modern homelessness are overcome."[7]

God's house on earth can give us a sense of place, a sense of home, which Newman describes this way: "Home relies on a concrete sense of place, a location that I can call 'mine' because I identify with it in particular ways. It has formed part of my identity and the identity of those who are from the same place."[8] If hospitality is to catch hold in the church, the church must re-establish itself as a home; "hospitality with-

6. Arlie Russell Hochschild, cited in Newman, *Untamed Hospitality*, p. 34.
7. Newman, *Untamed Hospitality*, p. 39.
8. Newman, *Untamed Hospitality*, p. 51.

out a home is an oxymoron," Newman remarks.[9] The church must become a place where the homeless find safety, orphans find family, and outcasts find acceptance. The church must become a harbor from the storm, a lighthouse for the lost, and a buoy for the drowning.

Drawing a Wider Circle

> He drew a circle that shut me out —
>   Heretic, a rebel, a thing to flout.
> But love and I had the wit to win:
>   We drew a circle that took him in!
>
> Edwin Markham, "Outwitted" (1915)[10]

In a sense, all hospitality is about creating a wider circle that includes rather than excludes, and as the poem suggests, our choosing to include can supersede another's choice to exclude or to be excluded. Juan Sosa cites Jesus as the model for hospitality, noting that "for him there were no foreigners or strangers, no favorite friends or special dignitaries. . . . He was available to others, even when he grew tired and preferred to retire by the seashore or to the desert. . . . Jesus challenged others to become hospitable to him. He wanted to go into their homes."[11] Jesus extended the circle as he invited children, outcasts, the infirm, people with questionable reputations, and the disenfranchised into his circle. Many of our churches have signs that boast "All Are Welcome" when, in reality, they may extend only minimal hospitality. We may sing songs of welcome while failing to extend welcome beyond the confines of the song. We would do well to take seriously the words of the song "All Are Welcome" by Marty Haugen:

> Let us build a house where love can dwell
> And all can safely live,
> A place where saints and children tell
> How hearts learn to forgive.

9. Newman, *Untamed Hospitality*, p. 53.

10. Markham, in Hazel Felleman, *The Best-Loved Poems of the American People* (New York: Doubleday, 1936), p. 67.

11. Juan J. Sosa, "Hospitality for and by Musicians: Melody and Text," *Pastoral Music* 17 (1993): 18.

Built of hopes and dreams and visions,
Rock of faith and vault of grace;
Here the love of Christ shall end divisions.

Let us build a house where prophets speak,
And words are strong and true,
Where all God's children dare to seek
To dream God's reign anew.

Here the cross shall stand as witness
And a symbol of God's grace;
Here as one we claim the faith of Jesus.

Let us build a house where love is found
In water, wine, and wheat:
A banquet hall on holy ground,
Where peace and justice meet.

Here the love of God, through Jesus,
Is revealed in time and space;
As we share in Christ the feast that frees us.

All are welcome, all are welcome,
All are welcome in this place.[12]

Making Gift-Giving Reciprocal

All hospitality involves reciprocal gift-giving; we all have gifts that we may offer to others. Persons with severe physical and mental handicaps can teach us patience, gratitude, and value for life; the aged can teach us to measure our days; the infirm can offer us a sense of immediacy and the importance of the moment — all people have gifts to offer if we are able to accept them. When the system of gift-giving inherent in hospitality becomes distorted through power, prestige, or lack of gratitude, hospitality fails to flow freely from host to guest and guest to host.

All involved in the free flow of hospitality must be responsible par-

12. Marty Haugen, "All Are Welcome" (Chicago: GIA Publications, 1994). Text © 1994 by GIA Publications, Inc.

ticipants. For hospitality to proceed, the host must initiate the process by offering a place in which an exchange can occur. In return, the guest/stranger must be willing to accept the host's initial overture. Hospitality is short-circuited when the guest/stranger resists this overture. A teenager, for example, might attend a family reunion but refuse to remove his headphones. A man might visit a different country and refuse to attempt to reciprocate overtures of native speakers because he doesn't speak the language.

In worship, there is always a gift because God initiates worship and offers us the gift of Jesus. God richly gives us all that we need to live in God's abundance, and through worship, God repositions us into who we are meant to be. Worship is the closest we come to God's reality, and in worship we are re-oriented so that we allow God to be God and we get our perspective straight once again: we confront the *reality* that God is God and we are not! In a sense, worship re-orients our compass so that we are able to find our true direction; it resets our clock so that we are in sync with God's timing; it empties our cache so that we are free from the clutter that we have accumulated. The gift of worship offered through God's grace restores the perspective that is continually being distorted through our fallen nature.

Giving Thanks

Gratitude is at the heart of all hospitality — both gratitude for God's good gifts to us which are shared through hospitality and gratitude to each other for willingness to participate in freely offering gifts to each other as host and guest. In her book *Untamed Hospitality,* Elizabeth Newman highlights a conversation about gratitude and hospitality from the Isak Dinesen story "The Roads Round Pisa." A young woman and a count discuss in some detail the desires of a typical guest — to be "regaled," to be "diverted," to "shine," to "impress," and to "expand." However, in the closing lines of the exchange, the count asks the young woman, "What does a hostess want?" The simple response provides cause for reflection: "The hostess," says the young lady, "wants to be thanked."[13] This poignant exchange points to the host's desire for a response of gratitude in

13. Isak Dinesen, "The Roads Round Pisa," in *Seven Gothic Tales* (New York: Vintage Books, 1972), p. 185; cited in Newman, *Untamed Hospitality,* p. 38.

the exchange of hospitality. Newman goes on to use the exchange as a secular parable pointing to God's desire to be thanked, not because God is in need of our gratitude but because God desires communion with us. In our thanksgiving, we are able to acknowledge our lives as gifts and to offer them freely to God in gratitude. When we find our worth in God's gifts to us, we are able to offer our gifts to others, as broken as they may be, thus becoming an embodiment of God's gifts to us.

This cycle — the dialogue of God's giving and our response — is at the heart of all worship, and it is the core of the model of hospitality initiated through the Holy Spirit and imitated and multiplied in the lives of Christians.

Remembering and Being Remembered

Closely connected to giving thanks is the Eucharistic idea of remembering: "Do this in remembrance of me." A remembrance of God's work throughout history is implied in the act of hospitality, for we offer gifts to others out of the abundance of God's gifts to us in the past and the promise of God's continual gifts to us in the present and the future, culminating in the eschatological fulfillment of God's promise to us. Failure to remember God's work in our lives results in our inability to offer ourselves as host or guest in the exchange of hospitality.

Fortunately, "remembering" is not all up to us, for God never forgets us in spite of our forgetfulness. Just as we once had the nightmare of forgetting everything we studied just before sitting for a final exam, we now find ourselves continually forgetting the most important God-news at the most crucial times. However, Newman reminds us that "worship does not depend upon our remembrance of God but upon God's remembrance of us."[14] God initiates worship, and worship is possible only through God's grace inviting us into communion with God. In worship, we are always responding to God's revelation of God's Son through the incarnation of Christ. God can be trusted with remembering. Because God's revelation is dynamic, God will never cease to persistently remind us that memory is ultimately a God act rather than a human responsibility. The following lines from a Robert Browning text are a poignant reminder of God's faithfulness in remembering us:

14. Newman, *Untamed Hospitality*, p. 152.

If I forget, yet God remembers.
If these hands of mine cease from their clinging,
Yet the hands divine hold me so firmly I cannot fall.
And if sometimes I am too tired to call for him to help me,
Then he reads the prayer unspoken in my heart and lifts my care.

I dare not fear since certainly I know that I am in God's keeping,
Shielded so, from all that else would harm,
And in the hour of stern temptation, strengthened by his power.

I tread no path in life to him unknown.
I lift no burden, bear no pain, alone.
My soul a calm, sure hiding place has found:
The everlasting arms my life surround, my life surround.

God, thou art love! I build my faith on that.
I know thee who has kept my path.
And made light for me in the darkness,
Tempering sorrow so that it reached me like a solemn joy.

It were too strange that I should doubt thy love.[15]

Always Remaining Humble

Since hospitality is a gift offered in response to God's ongoing generosity, it is always offered out of a sincere sense of humility. Gratitude and

---

15. Although commonly attributed to Robert Browning, the first three stanzas, beginning with "If I forget" and ending with "my life surround," are themselves a separate poem entitled "God's Remembrance," copyrighted by the author Edith Hickman Divall. The last five lines (only) are by Browning; they come from Act V of his dramatic poem *Paracelsus* (1835). However, they do not appear together as they do in this excerpt. It is not known when the "poem" as quoted above was "assembled" and began to be attributed to Browning. However, curiously, it was somewhat foretold by the editors of *The Expository Times*. The following entry appears in Volume 17 (October 1905-September 1906): "The Secretaries of the Sunday School Union have published a series of Christmas booklets and cards, wonderful for beauty of workmanship. The verses are all Miss Edith Hickman Divall's. Is Miss Divall to take the place of Frances Ridley Havergal? She has less simplicity of expression but more variety of experience; she is less like Tennyson and more like Browning."

humility are our responses to God's unceasing gifts, and hospitality comes from this unending spring of God's grace. An important biblical image of hospitality — a model for our offering of hospitality — is found in the story of Jesus' washing the disciples' feet (John 13:2-15). Jesus exhibited ultimate humility as he stooped and individually washed the feet of his friends. The disciples experienced a sort of embarrassment (humility) at Jesus' extravagant action, and Peter overtly resisted allowing Jesus to wash his feet. However, Peter eventually moved beyond initial embarrassment, and he assumed a posture of humility in allowing Christ to become servant and slave to him; thus, this event exemplifies the humility of both Christ (the host) and the disciples (the guests).

Like Peter, we are conditioned to conceal our weaknesses behind a facade of strength and self-reliance. In an enlightening discussion concerning the lessons that we can learn from children and from the mentally handicapped, Elizabeth Newman reminds us that "while the larger society would have us hide our vulnerability and weaknesses, those with mental handicaps simply cannot."[16] Jean Vanier, founder of the L'Arche community for people with disabilities, writes, "It is precisely their vulnerability that is their gift to the church and the world. In their vulnerability and poverty, they can teach all of us not to hide our own weaknesses but rather to see these as places of grace, where we see our need for others and for the grace of God."[17] The recognition of our own poverty and brokenness allows us to be vulnerable to others. To risk disclosing our faults and failures ultimately opens us to the work of Christ, and it schools us in offering the hospitality of Christ to others. Anything that we offer to God that is not broken and flawed is idolatry, for all that we are and shall ever hope to be is broken and distorted. God's grace offers us wholeness, and through this grace-gift, we may participate in the hospitality of Christ both as guest and as host.

Hindrances to Music's Hospitality

Music is a fit receptacle for embodying the hospitality of Christ. When we offer music to someone, we are serving as host; when we receive mu-

---

16. Newman, *Untamed Hospitality,* p. 181.

17. Jean Vanier, *Our Journey Home* (Maryknoll, N.Y.: Orbis Books, 1997), p. 35, cited in Newman, *Untamed Hospitality,* p. 181.

sic, we as guests accept it as a gift. Ideally, music functions in the reciprocal gift-giving roles of host and guest, and it readily serves as welcome to the stranger. However, music's ability to serve freely can easily be encumbered. In the following section we explore hindrances that can inhibit music's ability to engage in free-flowing hospitality.

Spectator Music

Because it isn't meant for sharing except in a passive manner, music that is designed for performance with little or no congregational involvement is inherently inhospitable. Music that encourages the congregation to remain in a spectator role, which doesn't invite them to fully participate, lacks the possibility for gifts to be exchanged, and it fails to facilitate dialogue. When worship ceases to include participation and congregants are thrust into a position of "cheering for" the worship leaders, or when worshipers are allowed to assume the role of evaluators (what spectators at concerts and sporting events are), worship loses its ability to reach out and draw others into dialogue, which is the essence of hospitality. Hospitable worship welcomes participation, encourages dialogue, and discourages hierarchical relationships. Spectator worship, on the other hand, encourages soloism, elitism, and monolithic messages.

Sentimental Music

When music relies excessively on sentimentality for its appeal, its ability to be hospitable is significantly diminished. Sentimental music — music that relies heavily on feelings of tenderness, sadness, or nostalgia — excludes those who don't share the story of those for whom the music evokes these exaggerated feelings. Sentimental music is often associated with a particular experience that, due to its high emotional impact, significantly marked certain participants. It assumes particular feelings and emotions, and consequently excludes those who don't identify with the experience that the music recalls. To them the music is subjective and burdensome. According to Sarah Koenig, "The more the worship service is founded solely on subjective experience, the more it will exclude people for whom that subjective experience is inaccessible.

People who are grieving, doubting, or otherwise in a state where they cannot engage in celebratory emotionalism will be marginalized. Such marginalizing both undermines the community and makes the church an unwelcoming, inward-focused body."[18]

It is common for overly sentimental music to be hopelessly stuck in memory and have little chance of progressing toward imagination. It can be confining and stifling to those who are stuck in this quagmire. A particular danger is that, due to the length of time they have been in this slough, they may be unaware of their predicament.

Privatized Music

When music becomes overly individualistic, it loses its communal appeal, and its ability to be hospitable is compromised. While private worship is possible and sometimes important, we were created to worship in community, and music is a crucial component of corporate worship. When we privatize our worship music — either through exclusionary texts or actions — we shut others out and forfeit the ability of music to encourage mutual exchange and edification. Regarding praise and worship music, Koenig observes, "there is a potential for it to become a plurality of singular worshipers disconnected from one another in their intense desire to focus on God alone."[19] Sometimes communal worship is mistaken for individual worship that happens to take place in the company of others. Communal worship implies that there is mutual exchange, mutual dependence, and a synergy that results in "the sum being greater than its parts." While texts that utilize personal pronouns exclusively are sometimes responsible for individualistic worship, movements, gestures, and facial expressions that indicate private moments can also exclude. By contrast, gestures and movements that reach out to others and invite their participation in a process involving group dynamics can encourage community. Learning something new together — something we all need to know or practice together, such as singing in a round, in another language, or with clapping or movement — breeds communal worship, group process, and group vulnerability.

18. Sarah Koenig, "This Is My Daily Bread: Toward a Sacramental Theology of Evangelical Praise and Worship," *Worship* 82 (2008): 159.

19. Koenig, "This Is My Daily Bread," p. 159.

Confined/Defined Space and Music

In order for music to be embodied, it, like hospitality in general, must have space; it must be anchored within a given location or environment. The effectiveness of music's hospitality is related to the space in which the music occurs. For instance, music's ability to invite participation can be affected by the proximity of the leader to those who are gathered and to the space available for instrumentalists, singers, and other leaders. If the music is intended to be intimate, a leader who is forced by space constraints to stand far from the congregants will not be perceived as hospitable. Furthermore, hospitality can take many forms and speak in varied voices. While a pipe organ might seem ostentatious and pretentious to some, it can be welcoming to others who have good memories of organ music. Similarly, a trap set and a keyboard could appear informal and unfit for worship to some, while it may be inviting and hospitable to others. Clearly, music's ability to be hospitable is closely related to the message sent by the space and its furnishings.

A worship space may be inhospitable to the music or the message of its worship. For instance, a room with a live acoustical environment will be friendly to *a cappella* choral music and the music of a pipe organ; however, it will be less acoustically conducive to electric guitars and technologically dependent instruments. In addition, when the message of a space is diametrically opposed to the message that is intended, the space will often outwit the message. The space may be more dominant or prominent than the message of the music, and some messages — verbal or musical — are not powerful enough to transcend some spaces.

Music as Agent for the Church's Hospitality

Music Is Welcome

While the text of a song can overtly speak "welcome," as in the earlier example by Marty Haugen, music's ability to establish common ground makes it especially hospitable. Music can move us from stranger to guest, from outcast to family. To enter a space and hear a familiar melody, text, or musical style is to be assured that this space could become "home." When music connects to shared memory, we find ourselves within a common story, and bonds of trust can be formed. Since music is intricately connected to emotion, music can calm our anxious spirits and offer us repose in the midst of the otherwise unfamiliar. Perhaps you recall having been in a threatening environment and then hearing a familiar melody or song, one that connected in some way to your memory. Instantly you felt calm and assured that safety is near.

Welcome is about helping the "other" to feel at home. When we welcome others into our home, we want them to feel as if our home is their home. We try to help them feel at home by offering possible ways in which our story connects with theirs — through sharing food that we both enjoy, through discovering mutual friends and relationships, through recognizing places that we've both visited or lived, through realizing that we have common interests, and through discovering points at which the musical soundtracks of our lives converge.

Often the musical connection is one of the first to be established, for in the church, music is often the first element that we hear. Many songs that we sing and play in worship serve the function of "welcome"; their primary purpose is to establish rapport with newcomers and to assure regular attendees that they are "home." Furthermore, the role of host implies vulnerability, and when we risk being vulnerable through offering ourselves through music, we create a space where our willingness to be vulnerable inspires guests to take similar risks.

Music Is Multilingual

Music's ability to speak multi-musical languages offers incalculable points at which hospitality can occur. Creating threads of connection between one person or group and another is innate in hospitality, and music's ability to function multi-musically makes it particularly effective in spinning threads that become conduits for relationship and involvement in shared stories. Just as the text of songs can be translated into any language, so music can speak the language of any imaginable musical style, and it can travel easily among musical genres. Even if the particular song or music that the church's guests are hearing isn't familiar to them, often the "feel," style, or musical elements remind them of other music which resonates with their experience or through which they make positive associations. Similarly, just as attempts at speaking the language of another create avenues of communication even if our linguistic abilities are limited, so attempting to speak/sing/perform musical language that is familiar to another also facilitates dialogue.

In order for hospitality to occur, "gifts" must be exchanged between host and guest, and music serves as an ideal facilitator of gift exchange. For instance, if I (the host) introduce a song in worship and you (the guest) participate, you are gratified that I've offered you a song that is either familiar, accessible, or learnable for you, and I am gratified that you've accepted my gift by participating and reciprocating my act of hospitality; your acceptance and attempts to participate are acts of gratitude for my gift, and they demonstrate your trust in me as the host. In future encounters, perhaps I learn a song from you; then you become the host and I the guest, making the circle wider and more complete.

Music Is Inclusive

Music is inclusive of all people, and all people have the ability to interact with music. However, inclusivity isn't the same as accessibility, and we need to remember that music should be accessible to all, and that we are responsible for helping it to be accessible to those for whom accommodations may be necessary. With music's power to affect us beyond cognition, people with limitations are often able to connect with music in ways that they might not connect with other worship media. For instance, Alzheimer's patients who have access to music often continue to exhibit emotional responses and to connect with their former selves and those who care for them long after nothing else seems to reach them. Similarly, people with some forms of mental illness may continue to retreat to music for safety when they are unable to trust others. Children who have intellectual disabilities are often responsive to music, and they may have musical aptitudes that outstrip other intelligences. Faith communities must seek to discover ways to make music more accessible to all people, regardless of their needs.

The responsibility of accessibility reaches into other areas too. The church must find ways to serve those who lack mobility and are unable to be transported to places where others typically worship. Additionally, as the church offers music education classes, it must accommodate the needs of special learners.

The music of the church — like all other ministries and functions — must serve everyone, not just those with easy physical, intellectual, and emotional access to it. If the church is to be the church in the truest sense, it must serve those who may be ignored by the world's standards. Elizabeth Newman reminds us that we are not called to be normal (however "normal" may be defined); we are called to holiness. Jean Vanier writes, "For people with handicaps, even more important than 'normalization' is their growth in love, openness, service, and holiness, which is the ultimate purpose of each human person."[20]

Music Is Embodied

In addition to having the ability to affect us emotionally and cognitively, music is embodied — music is physical. The singing instrument is the human body itself. Therefore, singing is the most intimate, vulnerable, and personal of all musical offerings. The movement that often accompanies singing engages the body even further.

When we sing with a group, we are joining our vocal instrument with those of others; it is another act of intimacy. Our breathing becomes synchronized with the breathing of others, and a physical conformity ensues that is unlike that of any other human activity. The sheer power of dozens or hundreds of human bodies forgoing their own preferred breathing patterns to reconcile with others is in itself a striking picture of community and of the power of group singing. With the added strength of merging our pitches to a single set of tones that work well together, the power of singing increases exponentially.

Elizabeth Newman points out that when our bodies respond before our minds do, we are "remembering with our bodies."[21] This is a phenomenon particularly prominent in music: our hands, once conditioned through years of practice, can remember songs and play them on the piano far beyond our mental recall. Similarly, once we begin to sing a song, we can often sing the entire song, although if we're called upon to recite the words alone, we can't remember it. Through repeated engagement of our sensory learning process, worship becomes literally embodied as our body-memory responds to God's initiative.

Like other theological concepts, hospitality becomes reality when it

20. Jean Vanier, *An Ark for the Poor: The Story of L'Arche* (Toronto: Novalis, 1995), pp. 59-60; quoted in Newman, *Untamed Hospitality*, p. 179.
21. Newman, *Untamed Hospitality*, pp. 62-63.

is lived out or embodied. Therefore, when we sing and music takes on the role of host or guest, it becomes embodied theology. It is theology incarnate — hospitality in the flesh. Stated differently, singing is not only a tool through which hospitality can occur; since singing is full-bodied — requiring voice and breath, visible and audible — it is incarnational hospitality.

Music Is Intergenerational

Music appeals to all ages, and it should function intergenerationally within the church. However, just as individuals often have specific musical preferences, age groups often have particular affinities as well.

In order for the church to function at its best, it should be intergenerational. In contrast to many of our society's systems and organizations which segregate people according to age, the church must recognize the importance of relating across generational lines, and it must promote genuine community, which involves people of different ages living life together. Far too often, the church has taken the path of least resistance by having separate worship services for each age group. In many churches, children attend children's church, youth attend youth worship, college students attend college worship, and adults are segregated into services with other labels such as "contemporary" and "traditional." As has often been the church's pattern in its tendency toward expediency, it fails to consider carefully the future consequences of its present action. While we wonder why young adults abandon the church, we fail to recognize the connection between our promoting age-specific worship and losing our young adults. When segregated by age from birth through college, they're accustomed to worship designed for them alone. When this cycle ends and the church ceases to acknowledge their needs as most important, they have no context for understanding the benefits of intergenerational worship.

Musically speaking, intergenerational worship can often be messy and require significant sacrifices on the parts of all. That said, it does model the true body of Christ, and there is no known substitute for the impact that it can offer. The model of community that leads a grandparent to sacrifice his/her particular needs for those of a grandchild and vice versa is much too neglected. Nowhere is this sacrifice more obvious than in music, but the rewards for all are worth the ongoing costs.

Music Is Abundance

Hospitality is extravagant. It goes beyond what is necessary or required and offers itself sacrificially. Hospitality attempts to empty itself only to discover that the source is endless. By worldly standards, Christian hospitality is viewed as wasteful because it is rooted in God's never-ending grace rather than the scarcity model of commerce. To be sure, we are unable to offer others anything of lasting significance from our own human finitude. However, through the generosity of Christ, we embody Christ himself, and our small deeds and meager offerings become significant and valuable because they are *not* ours — they belong to Christ himself. Hospitality flows from this great body of abundant grace. Newman concludes, "God's hospitality does not operate on assumptions of scarcity and savings but rests on the assumption of superabundance where there is no need to hoard and save."[22]

Musically, our gifts are also abundant and free-flowing. When we offer ourselves as host (representing Christ himself) in worship, the music that we lead and embody should portray the extravagance of Christ's endless self-giving. To hold back our best musical offerings for a bigger crowd or a more elite gathering, to fail to practice and offer our best, or to reduce musical offerings lest they bring attention to us is to fail to see Christ's abundance for what it really is. While we are capable of showing glimpses of the Christ whom we are called to embody, we can never do so by withholding what God has implanted in us. On the contrary, showing too little of God's work in us is where the short-circuiting can occur. The music of worship can be like a potluck meal for which many people bring gifts of food that combine with each other to create an abundance where all are fed and nourished regardless of whether all were able to contribute. The extravagance of this potluck is a metaphor for the extravagance of worship that is not dependent on us but instead relies on Christ's work within and through the entire community. Musically, the different "dishes" that we bring combine to produce an offering that is beyond our individual gifts or imaginations.

---

22. Newman, *Untamed Hospitality*, p. 115.

Hospitable Songs

Why Familiar Songs Are Important

We all like the music that we know and understand, and familiar music is often most hospitable. Just as a home-cooked meal is a welcome change after a long trip that involved eating the food of an unfamiliar culture, music that resonates with our memory and our story is a welcome reprieve from the alienation that we experience even within our regular routines. While away from home, many of us have found our way to a local church and experienced the comfort of familiar texts and tunes. As our story-through-music connected with the story of others, we found a home away from home, and we relished the safety and assurance that we experienced.

While familiar music offers the most easily accessible hospitable possibilities, unfamiliar music can be hospitable as well. The text of a new song often connects with our experience in a way that allows us to engage fully with this new song instantly. Or we may find that a new tune resonates with our memory bank of tunes in such a way that the new tune readily finds a home on our playlist. Context also plays an important role in our receptivity to newer songs, since we're most open to new songs when they're woven into the patchwork of other tunes and texts with which we are familiar. Learning a new song in the context of our community of faith makes it more likely that we'll appreciate that song; learning a new song during a time when it resonates with our deepest need assures that it will find a way into our memory; and learning a new song during a time when we're most spiritually open and available makes us more receptive to it. In fact, most new music to which we are drawn connects with us in one of these ways. Either through text, tune, or context, a new song echoes with an existing melody that is already lodged in our hearts.

Why Short Songs Are Hospitable

Short songs are usually more hospitable because they are easily accessed musically and contain minimal texts, and because their repetitive nature makes them easy to memorize. These cyclic songs[23] (songs

23. Michael Hawn uses the term "cyclic songs" to describe songs that are intended to

that repeat) build instant rapport and are ideal for creating opportunities for greeting and interaction. Since they're easily memorized, they create options for movement and for interspersing Scriptures and other readings with them. They're often most valuable when paired with other shorter songs to form a unit, and when used to form a liturgical framework for longer songs and lengthier spoken worship elements.

As hospitality, music seeks to minimize barriers to communication and vulnerability. Music wants to create venues through which interaction can occur and ongoing dialogue can be spawned. In much the same way that most initial conversation contains shorter ideas with minimal monologuing, shorter songs facilitate briefer exchanges with less musical and textual content. Thus they help to create welcoming environments that longer songs, introduced too hastily, might easily short-circuit. The longer and richer texts of some songs also might inhibit rather than encourage continued dialogue. As we will see, longer songs are equally valuable, but worship can be guilty of introducing too much content before a relationship is developed at a level that will sustain it.

Why Longer Songs Matter

Just as shorter songs play an important role in hospitality, longer songs are also important. As seen above, shorter songs build rapport, facilitate initial conversation among worshipers and between worshipers and God, and ease the process of using bodily movement in music. However, as in any relationship, introductory conversation must lead to more fully orbed expressions. My experience with small groups can serve as an example. Initial conversation — "small talk" — is an important component of the first stages of the group's dynamics. But if the group is going to establish genuine community, eventually longer stories must be shared, pain and grief must be recognized, and weightier theological issues must be introduced and discussed.

When we associate hospitality exclusively with introductory worship elements such as welcoming, and we liken hospitality to being out-

---

be sung more than once. He also says that in order for these songs to reach their full impact, they need to be sung in combination with other cyclic songs. See C. Michael Hawn, *Gather into One: Praying and Singing Globally* (Grand Rapids: Wm. B. Eerdmans, 2003).

going and friendly, we fail to recognize hospitality's real worth. For, as we've already discovered in this chapter, hospitality is a practice, a way of life, and a spiritual discipline. Accordingly, the depth of hospitality related to music comes to fuller fruition through longer and richer texts. The extended texts of many hymns and songs are afforded more space to explore theological ideas, to deal with difficult and hard-to-understand life issues, to tell a more complete story, and to more fully employ poetic elements. These longer song forms are vital to the long-term health of a congregation. If it is true that we learn most of our theology through the music we sing, the contemporary church must begin to integrate more fully orbed song forms if future generations of worshipers are to avoid spiritual malnutrition. Our current obsession with musical and textual immediacy will eventually leave us spiritually weak. Although we may feel "full" and satisfied, we will lack the strength and vigor necessary for spiritual functioning, and we will find ourselves unable to share the good news with the world.

Making Hospitable Musical Connections

Remaining Authentic

When we offer music as hospitality, our offering must be shared from our own experience, always with the view of the receiver in mind. If the music is to be authentic and capable of true exchange, it must embody our story and connect at a mutual point with the other person's story. When I offer a gift to you, you receive the gift, and I receive a gift from your glad acceptance. The failure of our gifts can happen on either side of the exchange. If I fail to consider your needs as I offer the gift, the gift will be poorly received because it will reveal that I don't really know you. On the other hand, if you don't receive the well-intentioned gift that I offer, the gift breaks down because you fail to understand me well enough to comprehend fully the perspective from which I offer the gift; you aren't able to understand the thought, motivation, and perspective behind my gift.

Remaining authentic is one of the chief ways that we can offer true hospitality to others. Authentic music is a true gift.

Presenting Our Music as Well as Possible

Gifts that embody the person presenting them are the most valuable and are always the most authentically received. The most valuable gifts are those that show time invested in imagining, preparing, and presenting. Although quality is contextual, and it can be interpreted differently from one context to another, most of us have some sense of quality even in areas that are beyond the normal boundaries of our expertise. We can sense when music is well-presented, whether or not we understand the particular style. We instinctively know whether or not a gift reflects an investment of time and imagination.

Including as Many Connection Points as Possible

Where are the places where the story of the host connects with that of the guest? How can these connection points be maximized? How can they be embodied through the music? In order to identify connection points, we must spend time reflecting on what it's like to be the other person and live in his/her world and become a part of his/her story. Much like finding the perfect gift for a person whom we love, choosing appropriate gifts of music requires us to invest time in imagining what the other values. Choosing the best music also draws on our previous experience of what we know has worked in the past. Making good choices requires research and invites us to consult the community to receive their input.

Presenting Music of Quality

Resist offering cheaply produced imitations. It is almost always better to give a smaller, authentic gift than a large imitation. Give a small diamond instead of a large rhinestone. Offer a small group of live instruments instead of a full orchestra that is recorded. Quality can rarely be defined, but it can almost always be recognized.

During a recent choir outreach event, our church's choir spent a weekend singing for people who were incarcerated. As the weekend progressed, one of the choir members shared his initial apprehension about the music that I had selected for the trip. "When I saw the music that we were singing," he told me, "I thought 'Oh, my! These folks will never appreciate or understand this music.' But I was completely wrong." While the program was broad in the many styles that it included, it presented the highest-quality music in many different genres. The music was well-received by the prison audiences, who came from different cultures, different races, and varied educational and economic backgrounds. In the final analysis, I'm convinced that the quality of the musical presentation and the musical selections was the key factor in the music's ability to reach a widely varied audience.

Offering the Gift Repeatedly

In order for hospitality to be genuine, it needs to be offered more than once. Repeated hospitality shows that it is intentional. Much of the genuineness that we perceive in our world is the result of an act that is repeated enough times so that we're convinced that the story it represents is authentic. Just as we earn trust from those closest to us by showing our love day after day and in many different contexts, so we must earn the trust of church guests by offering our musical gifts multiple times, so that they will be received as they were intended. People desire gifts that last, and many are cynical about motives and intentions. Recognizing this, we must use music as a conduit to establish genuine relationships with others. Once relationships are developed, the real gift-giving begins.

After returning from my third trip to Kenya, I was reminded that people begin to trust you when you care enough to return. There is no substitute for returning and building on relationships that are already in place.

Remembering that Presence Is Always a Gift

Often we minimize the importance of showing up — yet sometimes our presence may be the only gift we can offer. The simple act of being there offers embodied space through which God can be present. Those familiar with grief acknowledge that in times of anguish, having others show up for them is everything. Still, we can fail to make similar connections in other life situations. Since Christian hospitality involves exchanging

God-gifts with others, presence (whether you are host or guest) is the first step in being fully engaged.

In order for music to be hospitable, it must be offered through the presence of a gift-giver, and it must be accepted in the spirit in which it is offered. Often we are unaware of how and when our gifts of music might be needed, how they might be offered, or what form they might take. Recently I was visiting a family whose loved one was in the final stages of life, and they asked me to sing to him. I didn't know beforehand that I would be asked to sing and lead others in singing, but my presence allowed me to offer this gift both to the dying man and to his family. My presence and the song I offered also enabled the others who were present to offer their gifts of music. Sometimes we're invited somewhere to offer our song-gifts of hospitality. But this recent experience shows how sometimes our chance presence itself allows the hospitable gift of song to be presented and received in situations we could never have imagined.

Conclusion

In the final analysis, we must not discount the mystery of God and our innate failure to comprehend fully the drama of worship in which we participate. Fortunately, worship is not dependent on our ability to understand cognitively or on our ability to conjure up the right emotions, feelings, or images. No matter how hard we work at thinking the right thoughts, concentrating more intensely on God, or focusing more passionately on *our* desire to commune with God, our efforts will always fall short and leave us feeling inadequate, because we are. We are incapable of worship without the grace of Christ, and our best efforts, deepest concentration, and hardest work will not assure deep communion with God. Worship is possible only through God's initial reaching out to us through the grace of Christ, and our response can only be humble acceptance and participation.

As we participate in the hospitality of Christ in worship, we offer it to others. Christ stands as the gentle host in offering us the gift of worship even as we stand in Christ's stead as his surrogate in offering worship to others. Likewise, as Christ's guests, we accept his gifts with deepest gratitude even as we accept the gifts of others who are also Christ's understudy. The dramatic hospitality of Christ's generosity and our participation with Christ are beyond our ability to comprehend. Perhaps the writer of 1 Corinthians 13:12 expresses it best when he says, "For now we see through a glass, darkly; but then face to face: now I know in part; but then shall I know even as also I am known" (KJV).

CHAPTER 10

Becoming Multi-Musical

I've decided to stop pitying myself. Other than my eye, two things aren't paralyzed — my imagination and my memory. They're the only two ways I can escape from my diving bell. I can imagine anything, anybody, anywhere . . .

From *The Diving Bell and the Butterfly* (2007), a film about the life of Jean-Dominique Bauby

As church musicians in a multi-musical world, we must strive to become multi-musical. We must cultivate the ability to speak multiple musical languages with fluency. While we will likely never speak two linguistic languages equally well, it is possible to become bilingual, and some people can even become multilingual. Although most of us will have a preference for our first language, and it will likely always be the preferred language of our prayer, of our dreams, and of our emotions, we can learn to communicate effectively in a second language. Similarly, we — musicians and worshipers — typically have a preference for the musical language(s) that have provided the soundtrack for the significant moments in our faith journey, and because this musical language becomes a key component of *our* story, we easily forget that it isn't *the* story of the community. Although most worshipers prefer to worship in what they come to know as their native musical language, living in a musically and liturgically multilingual world makes it unlikely that our individual preferences will always — or even often — be reflected in the music of our worship community. And we should recognize that worshiping only in our first language keeps us from experiencing the rich diversity that the rest of the musical world has to offer.

In Defense of Musicians

Musicians are usually perfectionists, which explains their high levels of technical proficiency. In order to master an instrument or the voice, musicians spend inordinate amounts of time practicing alone and in groups where they hone their art. Their perfectionistic tendencies inspire them to make this costly investment of time and energy; however, perfectionist tendencies have a dark underbelly. Perfectionism generates evaluation and critique both internally and externally, and it also produces high levels of insecurity. Being a perfectionist also means that you are exceptionally aware of your flaws and foibles. And being a musician means that your skill — flaws and all — is always public; there's no way to hide. Understandably, the vulnerable lives that musicians lead often come with high personal costs.

I remember my first teaching job as a high school band director in my hometown. The principal reminded teachers in our weekly faculty meeting that he would be stopping by our classes to observe our teaching. As the second semester wore on, Mr. Stevenson still hadn't visited my classes. Concerned, I asked him about it. He responded, "Mr. Bradley, I observed your teaching at every Friday night football game last fall, as did the rest of the town. We all know what kind of teacher you are." When we're involved in music, our work is always public. As worship leaders, our musical skills are on display, and our spiritual lives are visible too. The pressures of living so publicly can be difficult to shoulder.

Too often, the humanness and limitations of musicians are overlooked. Most musicians have significant limitations, and while they may excel in a particular musical style, they are rarely comfortable negotiating multiple musical styles. For instance, I have a doctoral degree in the field of church music, but it can be distressing when people who aren't musicians assume that I have a doctorate in *all* music. They expect me to *know* and *do* all things musical. They seem to forget that music is a specialized area of study and performance. If you're a singer, it doesn't mean that you're also a pianist or an organist or that you can play a guitar or a cello. If you're a classically trained pianist, it doesn't mean that you can play a well-embellished hymn. If you're a jazz-trained vocalist, it doesn't mean that you can sing a convincing rendition of "The Lord's Prayer." If you're a classical guitarist, it doesn't mean that you understand jazz comping or rock riffs. The public often views musicians as being something like iTunes or Pandora — with a small click they can change the style and genre of what they sing or play. In reality, however, musicians are probably more like the old-fashioned jukebox in a restaurant — all the songs contained therein are likely similar in style and function!

It's also important to remember that musicians have preferences, too. Musicians care deeply about different styles and musical genres, and they're sure to dislike some types of music. In order for them to perform and lead in styles that are unfamiliar or distasteful to them, they must prepare with extra diligence, and they have to be convinced that doing so is worth sacrificing their personal tastes and often what feels like their integrity. Asking a musician to perform/lead in a style that is foreign or unfamiliar could be similar to asking a person to wear someone else's clothes in public. All music can be visually stereotyped, and imagining a musical style's clothing and accessories can help us comprehend how frightened a musician might become when asked to cross the lines of his/her musical style, how inauthentic that could feel. Musicians find that their musical preferences are intricately linked to their personhood, yet church musicians must face the challenge of thinking outside themselves and into the faith community that surrounds them. Church musicians continually offer their musical tastes, preferences, and opinions as a sacrifice for the sake of the gospel. This sacrifice often comes out of immense struggle, and it is often costly.

This struggle can be very real for an academic musician who is also called to serve the church. Because of my commitment to serve the church and its people and my commitment to all types of music, I have sometimes been misperceived as "selling out" to what some would call "second-rate music." Because of my commitment to not being stereotyped as belonging to one musical camp or another, I have often found myself in a lonely middle ground. But this is often the lot of church musicians. We are called to serve God in our particular context, and that means that we can't be all things to all people. It's impossible to develop or maintain skills in all types of music, it's impossible to equally advocate for all styles and genres of music within the church, and it's impossible to speak all musical languages with equal fluency or to enjoy all of them equally.

Music Appreciation for Church Musicians — A Word about Snobbery

The stereotype is that musical snobbery exists primarily among the classically trained. But experience teaches us otherwise. Snobs come in all types, and no church is without them. Music seems to attract snobbery, probably because we're always trying to one-up each other with our music (or at least it seems that way). According to David Peterson, "You can either be a classical snob, or a rock snob, or a folky snob. Basically, what we do with our music is say, 'I love this kind of music; this is what really excites me, and I can't bear that other stuff.'"[1] We become so partial to a particular style or musical preference that, according to Peterson, we escalate from refusing to tolerate someone else's music to calling it false: "We say, 'I'm not willing to listen to your kind of music. I'm not willing to sing one of your silly songs.' We get even more intense than that. We say, 'Your music isn't true worship. Your music isn't honoring to God.'"[2]

When we participate in such selfish behavior, we fail to recognize our place within the larger body of Christ, and we ignore the voice of the community in favor of our own preferences and ego. Just as there is space within the body of Christ for all of us, there is also space for all of the music that we can bring. Just as Christ redeems each of us and makes us a part of his body, Christ is also up to the task of redeeming our music, for all of it is as broken as we are. Our musical knowledge, skills, and offerings are acceptable only because of the redeeming power of Christ. Yes, there is even room for our snobbish attitudes, our over-sized egos, and our narcissistic tendencies if we are willing to bring them to the feet of the Redeemer of all brokenness.

A Pastoral Perspective

In our culture, which is immensely infatuated with music, and in which people often identify themselves through their musical tastes, not ac-

---

1. This quotation came from an e-mail message sent to the author on 25 August 2009 by Carl Stam. Stam quoted from David Peterson's lecture presented at the Southern Baptist Theological Seminary, Louisville, Kentucky, April 2005.

2. Peterson, lecture presented at the Southern Baptist Theological Seminary.

cepting someone's music is not accepting him or her. In *The Closing of the American Mind,* Allan Bloom recognizes the importance of music in contemporary culture when he says,

> Nothing is more singular about this generation than its addiction to music. Today, a large proportion of young people between the ages of ten and twenty live for music. It is their passion. Nothing else excites them as it does. They cannot take seriously anything alien to music. When they are in school and with their families, they are longing to plug themselves into their music.[3]

Michael Hamilton amplifies Bloom's point: "When one chooses a musical style today, one is making a statement about whom one identifies with, what one's values are, and ultimately, who one is."[4] When we don't accept the music of others, it can easily be taken as a personal rejection, and they likely won't accept our preferred music or us. Accordingly, becoming multi-musical is a way that we build bridges with people both inside the church and outside it. As leaders, we must earn the right to expand the musical boundaries of our faith community by gaining long-term trust. Since music is integrally intertwined with everyone's personal and faith journey, we must try to understand and value a person's music before we attempt to encourage musical exploration. Ultimately, all church music is pastoral, because it is a tool for connecting us more intimately to God and to each other.

On many fronts the church is struggling to prove its relevance. People are posing hard questions to the church about its priorities, its ministries, and its relevance to their lives. People want evidence — through the actions of the church and the lives of those committed to the community of faith — that God is active in their world and that the God of the ages remains pertinent for them and their brokenness. Given the great importance of music in this context, failure to establish connections between the music of the church and the music of the culture will be a nail in the coffin of the church's relevance.

In addition, we must recognize that the music of the church must

---

3. Allan Bloom, *The Closing of the American Mind* (New York: Simon & Schuster, 1987), p. 68.

4. Michael S. Hamilton, "The Triumph of the Praise Songs: How Guitars Beat Out the Organ in the Worship Wars," *Christianity Today,* 12 July 1999, p. 30.

be connected to musical experiences outside the church for it to be contextual and relevant. If the church is to be missional, its music must be noticeably linked to the music of the surrounding culture, its context.

Our Musical Native Tongue

Most of us have a musical native tongue, a musical language that we spoke (or heard) early in our lives and one through which we are able to connect at a profound level. For the Christian, this native musical language is often related to the music surrounding early spiritual formation or to times of spiritual renewal. This musical language can in some ways be compared to the linguistic language of prayer. For example, people who use their second language to function in a society other than that of their origin usually prefer to pray in their first language. Music functions similarly, and it is important to recognize and authenticate our musical "heart language," because sometimes it is only in doing so that we can proceed to embrace other musical languages and allow them to speak to us as well. Some of us have a tendency to diminish early experiences and to view them as naïve and uninformed. However, in times of crisis, we may find ourselves singing the songs that served us early on, and often during these times we are able to acknowledge a significant component of our musical faith formation. On the other hand, some of us become calcified in the music that accompanied earlier times, and we resist authenticating other genres and styles while also continuing to acknowledge the gift to our lives of the music we prefer. Just as reconciling our past with our present is vital to mental and emotional health, so reconciling our musical past with our present reality is a central aspect of our spiritual and theological well-being. Music can be a catalyst for acknowledging God as fully present in our faith memory and for launching us forward as we discover the music of God's imagination.

Several years ago, the beloved pastor of our church moved to a new church. In the depths of grief over this loss, our worship planning team struggled over what songs to sing the first Sunday after her departure. Finally, we decided to sing several of the church's most beloved "heart songs," even some directly associated with the pastor. When the congregation gathered together, we gained strength from the memories associated with these songs, which had become lynchpins in our faith story. Rather than avoiding our grief by singing neutral songs, we decided to sing songs that spoke directly from our spiritual native language, and they bolstered us to face the days ahead.

Our Musical Soundtrack — and What It Reveals about Us

All of us have a musical soundtrack[5] that is a part of the footage of our lives. Without a musical soundtrack, we may have difficulty telling our story accurately. I was reminded of a soundtrack's importance when, a few years back, I put together a slideshow for my parents' fiftieth wedding anniversary. Once the photos of their life were scanned and on the computer screen, the frayed edges, the faces blurred by too many handprints, and the colorless black-and-white images began to sparkle. And, once the photos were set against a background of songs from my parents' fifty years together, the presentation began to live and breathe. The flat photos became multidimensional, and this chronicle of their time together lived! Without a soundtrack, their story would have been dull and perhaps misunderstood. The music was integral to understanding their story.

Music is usually intertwined with our personal and faith stories; we can frequently track our faith development through the songs we have chosen to call our own over time. For this reason, it's always worth considering how the music we choose for worship will be telling the faith stories of generations to come. Since music helps to form our faith, profoundly influences our theology, impacts our faith memory, and provides a soundtrack for our stories, we must assign the highest priority to music choice in the church's corporate life.

What do our musical choices reveal about us? Three things in particular.

We Love What We Know

Over the many years that I have been a worship leader in various churches, parishioners have often begun conversations with me with the sentence, "I don't know much about music, but I know what I like

---

5. Randy Edwards uses this image to describe the role of youth choirs; he says they provide a soundtrack for the lives of young people. See Randy Edwards, *Revealing Riches and Building Lives: Youth Choir Ministry in the New Millennium* (St. Louis: MorningStar Music Publishers, 2000).

when I hear it." Often, after we exchange a few pleasantries, they move on to the real purpose of their conversation, which is this: "But I haven't heard that music in a while." This simple illustration reinforces the point that we love what we know. Familiarity is safe, comfortable, sentimental, and reassuring. The challenge for the church and its leadership is to acknowledge, authenticate, and value the familiar while also continuing to challenge with the yet-to-be-familiar. This process is ultimately a pastoral act, and it is accomplished only through genuine love — and persistence. In my work with choirs, I have observed repeatedly that while there may be some resistance to taking on a very difficult piece at the outset, the group will invariably love the hard piece once they've memorized it. We love what we know!

Further complicating the issue is the fact that music is tied to our emotions, so many of the "musical" judgments that we make are actually emotional observations rather than textual, musical, or theological ones. Again, approaching each of these issues pastorally is important. Since we normally engage with our worshiping community weekly, we must be especially patient when introducing new music, because the community won't "know" a song until it's had repeated experiences with it. Therefore, frequent repetition is the key to a community's knowing and eventually loving new songs.

We Value What We Understand

Often we don't value a song because we don't understand it. Frequently, congregations aren't sure why a song (of any style, any genre) is sung; for whom (if for anyone) it's important; if and why it has historical significance; how and if it relates to the church year; what the text (whether antiquated or modern) means, and why it matters; why the song is repeated numerous times — and so on. While these questions aren't easily answered within the worship experience, leaders should make an effort to contextualize worship songs. Prefacing a song with a statement about its importance, connecting it with its history during the sermon, telling a story that provides background for it, enlisting someone who highly values the song to present it, framing the song with scriptures that more fully develop its text — any and all of these things aid in the contextualizing process. Furthermore, if we value the person who wrote or who sings the song, we begin to value the song itself.

The point is that a worshiping congregation should never experience music in a vacuum. If we as worship leaders fail to connect songs to meaningful experience, we lose opportunities for new songs to become familiar. On the other hand, we don't want to put the music of worship on a pedestal. Songs are a *part* of the story, not *the* story. They must be intertwined with the meta-narrative of God's redeeming work and the narrative of God's work locally.

We Have Always Had Style Preferences

If people hadn't always had style preferences, music history wouldn't have produced more or less coherent stylistic periods — Renaissance, Baroque, Classical, Romantic, and Impressionistic. At some level, people who lived during the Renaissance preferred sixteenth-century counterpoint, madrigals, and church modes, and those who lived during the Baroque period preferred eighteenth-century counterpoint, terraced dynamics, cantatas, and fugues. It seems logical that Bach and his contemporaries, who wrote in the popular styles of the Baroque period, must have perceived that their forms and compositional techniques were the most God-honoring for their time. Yet, while Bach built on the historical precedents of his era, we have little evidence that his choir at the St. Thomas Church in Leipzig regularly incorporated the music of the Renaissance into their worship. They seem to have sung primarily what Bach wrote for them; that may explain why he wrote a different cantata for every liturgical season of the entire Christian year. Furthermore, they used the organ because it was in vogue, and they didn't use the hurdy-gurdy because its popular usage had declined by this time.

The above comments are not meant to discredit the importance of utilizing the music of history. This music attests to God's continual work in the church, and we should regularly employ the vetted song of history in worship. My point here is that it's reassuring to realize that the church has tended to create and re-create its music with every generation. The church has always gravitated toward a new song, and it will likely continue to do so.

Several years ago, I became the minister of music in a church that was in the process of transitioning to a more contemporary style. Because I had only served in congregations that used traditional music, I accepted this position reluctantly. Leading a congregation in a new musical direction meant leading people to places that I had never been, and I was forced to live out the musical inclusivity that I had claimed only verbally. It meant that I often had to give up my personal preferences, my "heart language," and my training in order to value others and speak their language. I had to learn musical languages that were new for me. As a result of this adventure, I learned dozens of new songs, became more creative, grew spiritually, and began the journey toward learning new musical languages. By learning to sing new songs, I grew to understand fellow worshipers in new ways, and I learned to relate to God in fresh ways.

Having examined the role of personal preference and historical development in Western worship music, let us broaden our examination to consider the role of worldwide cultural diversity in the enrichment of worship.

The Value of Many Musical Languages

Linguistically, the world is a more aesthetically pleasing aural environment because of its many languages. The differences in languages around the world help to differentiate the people who speak them, and they offer yet another glimpse into the vastness of God's creation. Because of the myriad of languages and dialects, the entire world experiences a more expansive vocabulary. If we were to remove the words from any particular language that are borrowed from another language — say, remove all French words from the English language — it would be readily apparent how we are all the richer for the linguistic resonances that fill our world. Closely related is the greater nuance that we gain from each other. Our multilingual world gives us the ability, through borrowing, to come closer to the exact meaning we wish to convey. Often we discover that one language has a better expression for a particular idea or concept than another language, and engaging with that alternate word or phrase offers us added meaning and greater clarity.

Similarly, the many languages of music also enrich our world through their various melodies, rhythms, and harmonies. And, just as using a word or phrase from a different language can help us say what we mean, so using a different musical "language" can help us better portray a particular mood, idea, or concept. This is particularly helpful in worship as we seek to progress through the liturgy of a given worship experience. Lastly, as we discover the music of different cultures and as we sing and play music of different styles, we are able to see God more clearly. Since all of these soundscapes were created by God's creatures, we are reminded of the varied voices through which God has chosen to express God's self throughout history and in the present.

How Musical Languages Grow

Through Cross-pollination

One of the ways in which musical style is expanded and enriched is through the process of cross-pollination. For instance, when one style borrows recognizable elements from another style, both styles can be enhanced. Cross-pollination has been used in most forms of music; classical music in particular offers many explicit examples. In fact, the immense cross-pollination of American art music of the twentieth century influenced some of the greatest composers and resulted in some of their most significant output. Particularly notable is the influence of folk music styles in the works of composers such as Aaron Copland, Zoltán Kodály, Béla Bartók, Ralph Vaughan Williams, and George Gershwin. Each of these composers borrowed from folk idioms and used them to spawn new ideas in Western art music. Copland's use of the "Shaker Song" in *Appalachian Spring* and his use of Western folk idioms in *Rodeo* are notable. Likewise, Kodály and Bartók's use of Hungarian folk melodies in their compositions greatly enriched their legacies. Gershwin's use of blues and jazz clearly distinguishes many of his works, including *Porgy and Bess* and *Rhapsody in Blue.* English composer Vaughan Williams employs folk music in his use of the tune "Greensleeves" in *Fantasia on "Greensleeves."*

For decades these composers and their works have influenced the church, but it's important to remember that this compositional technique has fertile ground still left to plow. One effective example of cross-pollination in the church's music is the music of Keith Getty and Stuart Townend. The texts and tunes that they write combine expanded texts of traditional hymns with newly composed tunes that often sound like folk tunes. Instrumentally, the songs easily take root in both contemporary and traditional settings, and they have been used successfully for choral and organ arrangements. Given these examples, we can see that it may be time to take down some of the fences that separate the music of the church from the music of the culture and to focus on sharing our strengths.

Through Creating Hybrids

Similar to cross-pollination is the process of creating hybrids. Generally speaking, a hybrid is a cross of two similar elements which creates a third element that is distinctive. The terms "fusion," "mix," and "cross-breed" capture the idea. Musically speaking, there's a need for the church to create not A or B but C. Instead of my music or your music, let's create a third way which we both can support and appreciate. While hybrids can result in blandness when they lose the distinctiveness of both originals, a successful hybridization can produce new life and revived energy for both. Examples from other fields include farming and farm products. Actually, many of the foods we eat are a result of taking the best qualities from two different but similar plants and creating a hybrid that serves both the farmer and the world more effectively. Similarly, in the field of dog breeding, new varieties are developed by combining the gene pools of two different breeds, creating pets that have some of the best qualities of both. Recent examples include Labradoodles, Bulladors, and Peagles.

The Diversity of Musical Languages

In thinking about music and learning to speak/perform its many languages, respected music educator Bennett Reimer reminds us that music is, in certain respects, *like all other music,* in certain respects, *like some other music,* and in other respects, *not like any other music.*[6] The fact that most music shares certain basic qualities — rhythm, melody, dynamics, pitch, tone color, texture, and form — gives music a common vocabulary, regardless of culture or style. Still, not all of these elements are shared among all kinds of music. For instance, some music may not employ harmony or dynamic contrasts. Furthermore, there are

---

6. Bennett Reimer, "Education in Our Multimusical Culture," *Music Educators Journal* 79 (1993): 24.

musical elements that distinguish one type of music from another. These subtle qualities are what make no two songs sound the same, what make styles distinctive, and what differentiate one song within a style from others. Even within a style and genre, no two songs sound the same. Additionally, because all musical performance occurs within a given time and place, no performance can ever be exactly duplicated, not even by the same performers.

Musical Dialects

Each genre of music has many dialects. In much the same way that language has dialects, music within a genre also has dialects that themselves may be further divided into subdialects. For instance, there are many types of gospel music: black gospel, Southern gospel, white gospel, gospel hymnody, and more. Similarly, there are many forms of rock (hard rock, soft rock, heavy metal, indie rock, punk rock, etc.), various kinds of country (classic, urban, bluegrass, honky-tonk, Western swing, etc.), and several varieties of jazz (cool, fusion, big band, swing, bebop, etc.). Additionally, there are numerous periods of music history, each with many genres and subsets, and hundreds of kinds of ethnic music representing all countries around the world, each kind with its individual subcategories. Even within American ethnic music there are many varieties and subsets. For instance, the category of Southern white Christian folk music could include Sacred Harp, Stamps Baxter, Southern Gospel Hymnody, White Gospel, and more. All of these kinds of music are from the same region and the same people group. Similarly, African-American music of the South might include spirituals, black gospel, blues, work songs, call and response, and more. What this means for the church is that the varieties of music are endless, and even the best local group of musicians will be able to master only a few styles well while roughly approximating several others.

Ways of Traveling through Musical Languages

If musical style is viewed through the metaphor of travel, there are a number of ways in which musicians can travel among the many musical languages of the world. Ideally, we would all become fluent in every language in the world. However, since we've concluded that this isn't possible, what can we do? While we can likely speak/perform a limited number of musical languages fluently, we must find other ways to travel among other styles. One such option is to attempt to speak/perform even if we don't do very well. In this model, our efforts are usually highly appreciated by those to whom the music belongs, and our attempts help build bridges and create conversation and community among us and native speakers. Consequently, along the way, we will develop greater fluency, a broader vocabulary, and more confidence. When in doubt, we refer to a phrase book (a published arrangement or a transcription), which helps us to negotiate the style/musical language well enough to function as a leader in worship.

Another option is to depend on interpreters. With this model, we utilize others within our community to speak/perform within the language/style with which we are unfamiliar. For instance, if we're unable to play piano in a gospel style, we may ask someone else to play the song in question. Likewise, if we're unable to play guitar and we don't have the facility to play or lead the popular styles prevalent in praise and worship music, we can enlist others in our community and empower them to be our interpreters — they will guide us to places that we couldn't visit without assistance.

In essence, not speaking the musical language isn't an excuse for us or for the congregations we serve to be musically homebound. The more we are all engaged as learners and not experts, the more those less confident will feel invited to truly participate.

Becoming Musically Diverse

Since the body of Christ is a diverse group comprised of people from all walks of life, from all over the world, and from all times and places, it is worth considering the need for the musicians of the church to move toward becoming diverse as well. If the church is to join God in God's work in the world, then God needs our diverse musical gifts and our willingness to offer them for the cause of Christ. When we show value and love for all of the music that God has allowed to be created, we model the bigness of God and the vastness of God's creation. When we approach the music of the church as freeing rather than entangling, we reflect a God who accepts all people and values all the gifts that they bring to worship.

When we prize the diverse music of God's people throughout the world, we begin to actualize the profound imagery of the final heavenly gathering of all God's children. Lastly, participating in the eclectic music of God is ethically right. It is right and good to value all that God values, which includes the music of all the people of the world — including those closest to us.

The Motivation to Speak New Musical Languages

When we're called upon to learn to speak/perform new musical languages, what motivates us to invest the time and energy that helps us add to our musical palette? The motivation to make changes in our skills requires deliberate thought and careful consideration. The following lists several possible personal motivations:

Your commitment to continued growth motivates you. You've probably been successful in your past musical endeavors, and your dedication to continued growth spurs you forward.

Your commitment to Christ motivates you. Your desire to follow Christ and to serve the church prompts your service. Your desire to serve others and to lead them in worship causes you to make the necessary sacrifices.

Your commitment to the local community motivates you. You serve among a group of people who are intent on following Christ, and you're committed to them and their goals. Their desire to see you grow stimulates your willingness to attempt new ventures on their behalf.

Your love for your neighbor motivates you. Your desire to see the church in God's world is important to you, and it prompts you to gain new skills in order to reach out to others.

Your desire to know God more fully motivates you. You're inspired by the possibility that through learning new music and sharpening your skills you will see new aspects of God. You have a profound desire to know God more fully, and you're willing to take risks that might make your relationship with God more complete.

Our individual motivations may vary, but as musicians who serve the church, we are always driven by love — love for God, love for our community of faith, and love for those in the world whom we have yet to encounter. Love motivates all that we do, and because of love, we can attempt what we would never attempt otherwise.

Individual Learning Differences

As learners we are all different, and we respond to challenges in different ways. Following are some of the variables that affect how we learn and grow:

Aptitude: Our aptitude can be described as our capacity to learn.[7] The particular skills required for mastery are based on the complexity of the musical competency we are seeking to achieve, on our previous experience, and on our individual ability. People have different aptitudes for different skills, and our aptitude will partially determine how quickly and effectively we master new skills.

Motivation: Motivation can be defined as "wanting to learn."[8] Our motivation correlates with how far we progress. Motivation can be external or internal. Our motivation for learning new skills in worship is likely twofold. The community probably gives us the external motivation to assist it in reaching its shared goals. We may be internally motivated to learn new skills and expand our horizons.

Learning Styles: This term refers to different ways in which learners perceive, process, absorb, and recall new information and skills. They indicate preferences about how people interact with their world, learn, and acquire new skills.[9] An example of two different learning styles is concrete versus abstract thinking. Concrete thinkers are drawn toward experiences and emphasize feeling over thinking. Conversely, abstract thinkers are drawn toward logic, ideas, and concepts. Another distinction is field dependence versus field independence. Field-dependent learners have difficulty distinguishing the detail from other information around it. In contrast, thinkers who are field-independent sepa-

7. Bill Van Patten and Alessandro G. Benati, *Key Terms in Second Language Acquisition* (New York: Continuum International Publishing Group, 2010), p. 63.

8. Van Patten and Benati, *Key Terms in Second Language Acquisition,* p. 111.

9. Van Patten and Benati, *Key Terms in Second Language Acquisition,* p. 102.

rate details and subtleties from the surrounding context. Closely associated with learning styles is the area of learning preferences. Some learners prefer to learn through seeing (visual learners), some through hearing (aural learners), some through reading or writing, and some through physical activity (tactile or kinesthetic learners).

Learning Strategies: These are efforts by the learner to learn more effectively. This is a broad and inclusive field; however, some of the key learning strategies are these: (1) metacognitive strategies, which involve organizing, focusing, and evaluating one's learning; (2) affective strategies, which involve handling emotions or attitudes; (3) social strategies, which involve cooperating with others in the learning process; (4) cognitive strategies, which involve linking new information with existing information and analyzing and classifying it; and (5) memory strategies, which involve entering new information into memory storage and then retrieving it when it's needed.[10]

Considering Multimodality

Generally, the term "multimodality" refers to the practice of using multiple modes (methods or means) to accomplish a task. When related to learning theory and particularly to our discussion of becoming multimusical, multimodality explores the various means through which we may acquire knowledge or skill. The ways in which we gain and process information continue to evolve. According to Gunther Kress, "The screen has replaced the book as the dominant medium of communication. This dramatic change has made the image, rather than writing, the center of communication."[11] Moreover, James Gee has argued that "children are learning more about what it means to be literate outside of school than they are learning inside school."[12] As a case in point, consider how learning has evolved through the introduction of smartphones and other similar devices. The smartphone allows its owner to send, receive, and for-

10. Van Patten and Benati, *Key Terms in Second Language Acquisition,* p. 102.

11. Gunther Kress, quoted in *Literacies, the Arts, and Multimodality,* ed. Peggy Albers and Jennifer Sanders (Urbana, Ill.: National Council of Teachers of English, 2010), p. 28.

12. James Gee, quoted in Albers and Sanders, *Literacies, the Arts, and Multimodality,* p. 28.

ward messages in various media (text, photo, video). These messages are aural, spatial, and/or dramatic. With the Global Positioning System (GPS) and social media such as Facebook, Twitter, and Myspace at our disposal, the possibilities seem endless. Peggy Albers and Jennifer Sanders agree: "In sum, social networking sites and modern tools of communication offer us a range of ways in which we can create simple messages or complex texts and have brought about cultural shifts in communication."[13] Indeed, our communication has become multimodal.

Learning is technical as well as relational. Albers and Sanders point out that "each sign system (language, art, music, mathematics, dance, and drama) has a technical component as well as a relational component."[14] It is common to teach the technical components while ignoring the relational. While every discipline or study has a technical side, mastery also entails "ethos," or new ways of belonging, as a result. Different cultural groups have different ways of knowing and being in this world, and while linguistics may be the dominant way for children in a Western European context to understand and interact with their world, "art and dance may be the dominant way of knowing for children raised in other cultural traditions."[15] Multiple studies have shown that children around the world learn differently — and indeed, children in Western contexts are shifting in their ways of learning primarily as a result of technology and its emphasis on the visual, the spatial, and the dramatic. For instance, studies show that visual arts are important for bilingual children, and that Hawaiian children learned better through a "talk story" (an informal conversation) rather than through traditional instruction.[16]

How does multimodality affect learning a second musical language? Since we all learn differently and our learning is becoming increasingly multimodal, we must keenly observe our own ways of responding to our learning environment as well as the ways in which others respond to theirs. In the final analysis, learning is learning, and mastery is mastery. It doesn't matter whether we learn traditionally or non-traditionally. Learning a second musical language is likely very different from learning our first musical language; therefore, we must be attuned to the various media and ways of imagining that are available to us.

13. Albers and Sanders, *Literacies, the Arts, and Multimodality*, p. 12.
14. Albers and Sanders, *Literacies, the Arts, and Multimodality*, p. 28.
15. Albers and Sanders, *Literacies, the Arts, and Multimodality*, p. 29.
16. Albers and Sanders, *Literacies, the Arts, and Multimodality*, p. 30.

Considering Multiple Intelligences

Each of us has intelligences that function within our own minds and that interact with the intelligences of others and within the larger culture to achieve common goals. According to Seana Moran, while "intelligences are often thought about as an individual property, . . . they are less a property or end in themselves and more a tool to achieve cultural goals."[17] While mathematical and linguistic intelligences are traditionally valued across cultures, other types of intelligences have been posited by psychologists, neuroscientists, and educators, including spatial intelligence, musical intelligence, relational intelligence, and so on.[18] These are increasingly acknowledged as important. However, most tasks depend not on a single intelligence but on multiple intelligences to achieve a purpose.[19] Similarly, most performances are not accomplished by one person but represent a collaboration of intelligences from one or more others. The outcome may be greater than the sum of its parts. Following are some of the ways that intelligences interact with each other:

> *Bottlenecking:* In this process, one intelligence can restrict another. For instance, if a student in a musicianship class has strong aural musical skills but is being evaluated only for visual musical skills, a bottleneck may occur.
>
> *Compensation:* Compensation occurs when a strength offsets the effects of a weakness. Let's take the example above to illustrate. The student may compensate for poor evaluations of his visual music skills by scoring nearly perfectly on aural-based assessments. With this ability to compensate, the student will pass the class.
>
> *Catalysis:* This occurs when one intelligence stimulates growth in other intelligences. Let's further expand the example above to

17. Seana Moran, "Why Multiple Intelligences?" in *Multiple Intelligences Around the World,* ed. Jie-Qi Chen, Seana Moran, and Howard Gardner (Hoboken, N.J.: Jossey-Bass, 2009), p. 365.

18. Howard Gardner is a leading thinker in this field and has developed an extensive theory of multiple intelligences that includes nine different types of intelligences: linguistic, logical/mathematical, musical/rhythmic, bodily/kinesthetic, spatial, naturalist, intrapersonal, interpersonal, and existential. See Howard Gardner, *Frames of Mind: The Theory of Multiple Intelligences* (New York: Basic Books, 1983).

19. Moran, "Why Multiple Intelligences?" p. 366.

illustrate. The student's aural success may encourage him to participate in exercises to increase his visual musical acuity; in this way his aural strength is a catalyst for growth and further development.[20]

When intelligences work together in groups of people, the process might easily be compared to a jigsaw puzzle in which different shapes and images fit together to form an overall image. Collaborative musical endeavors fit this image perfectly, since most of our work within the church is dependent on the individual musical skills and strengths (intelligences) among the team that combine to create the larger, more complete presentation.

In learning to speak new and expanded musical languages, our multiple intelligences are at our disposal. For instance, once we are able to internalize the style and understand the work cognitively, our existing technical skills might allow us to perform the piece. Similarly, our analytical intelligence may help us to understand the style theoretically, which allows us to understand the chord structures, rhythmic challenges, and melodic contour; our relational intelligence may connect us to others who can mentor us; and our strategic intelligence may help us to set up a practice schedule that fits within our family and work commitments. Furthermore, in most instances, we are required to fill in only one piece of the larger performance picture. When our individual intelligences work in tandem with the various intelligences of others, the task at hand soon becomes achievable.

Learning from Second Language Acquisition Studies

The broad field of Second Language Acquisition is an independent research area with decades of qualitative and quantitative studies to its credit. One of its discoveries is that, although we can become proficient in a new language, we aren't likely to pick up the nuances that native speakers know. So it's possible to sound like a native speaker, but it's not probable. Applying the following terms[21] to the acquisition of a sec-

---

20. Moran, "Why Multiple Intelligences?" pp. 367-68.

21. The terms in this section are taken from Van Patten and Benati, *Key Terms in Second Language Acquisition*.

ond musical language will offer insight for the music of the church and for the musician seeking to learn new musical languages.

Aptitude

Aptitude refers to the cognitive abilities that learners bring to the task of acquisition. The training and experiences that we bring to a task largely determine the ease with which we're able to master it. Because these factors vary among individuals, some will master musical skills and concepts more easily than others.

Acculturation

The process of acculturation (adapting to a new culture) is directly linked to acquisition — and social and psychological factors have a direct effect on success. When we adapt to the culture around us, the possibility of learning a new skill that serves the culture gains purpose and meaning. Consequently, it becomes easier to attain. For example, if your child marries a person who speaks a different language and lives in a different country, you will be highly motivated to speak the language and understand the culture in order to communicate more effectively with your child's spouse and your prospective grandchildren. The same thing is essentially true for musical acculturation. We find ourselves more motivated to learn a new musical language that reflects the culture to which we are adapting.

Avoidance

In linguistic pursuits, "avoidance" applies to situations where speakers are hesitant to attempt difficult grammatical constructions. In musical pursuits, this might mean that you're willing to play slower songs in a rock style on your guitar but that you avoid songs with faster chord changes and faster strumming patterns.

Adapted Speech

Adapted speech is used by native speakers to help learners comprehend. This kind of speech involves using a simpler vocabulary, words that have meaning in both languages, gestures, and so on. Musically, we often need to use partial components of a new style until we're able to master more skills and vocabulary. For instance, we might teach the congregation a song from Africa by keeping the musical text the same but using English instead of Swahili.

Bilingualism

Even people who are bilingual are usually more fluent in one language than the other. This is also usually true in music. Musically, we will likely never be equally proficient in multiple styles.

Connectivism

Connectivism has to do with learning to connect disparate parts. Linguistically, that means being able to connect an aspect of one language to an aspect of another. Connectivism occurs musically when we're able to take technical skills and knowledge from one genre or style and relate it to another genre or style. In both cases it allows people to save time and learn more quickly.

Critical Period

There is likely a time (probably before the age of sixteen) when the potential to sound like a native speaker is possible. This means that the earlier we learn to speak a second language, the better. Musically, the earlier we are exposed to sounds and skills from all types of music, the better.

Fossilization

Fossilization refers to the point at which the learner ceases to develop. This term could also refer to a time when a learner has reached his/her maximum potential. Sometimes we reach a plateau in our study and performance of a given musical style. When this happens, we need to step back and carefully analyze why our progress has stopped.

Initial State

This concept is a theory of language study which suggests that the beginner assumes that all the rules of the original language are applicable to the new language. Musically, we can transfer all the properties from our first musical language to the new musical language. Over time, however, we'll discard those properties (techniques and knowledge) that aren't applicable to the new style or genre.

Motivation

Motivation is key to learning new musical skills. As a veteran teacher, I've discovered that the highly motivated student with lesser aptitude nearly always outpaces the highly gifted student who has less motivation. Many times we don't master new musical skills and materials because we lack the motivation either to begin or to continue the process.

Overgeneralization

Applied linguistically, overgeneralization could describe using subject-verb constructions in all situations when the new language frequently calls for other constructions. In learning a new musical style, we may tend to take one concept and apply it too broadly. For instance, we may swing all eighth notes in gospel music, or we may add our own improvisation to a classical piece.

Restructuring

When we learn new information, it restructures what we already know. Adding new knowledge shifts the ways in which we categorize and systematize our existing knowledge. Learning a new musical style alters a musician's existing style — usually it opens up more possibilities in what he/she knows. For example, if a classically trained musician studies jazz structures, that will help him/her to learn Western European music more quickly because he/she has developed a heightened awareness of harmonic structures.

Silent Period

The silent period describes the time when we're listening and processing but are still unwilling to speak in the language we're learning. Musically, we're often able to play and perform long before we're confident and willing to do so. How long the silent period lasts will vary from person to person.

Transfer

Transfer refers to relying on the first language system to construct the second language system. Linguistically, we use the first language to provide the scaffolding for the new language. This concept is invaluable for the musician since, according to Bennett Reimer, all music is in some ways like all other music.[22]

U-Shaped Acquisition

This refers to the process in which the learner produces something correctly but then reverts to producing the same thing incorrectly — most likely due to new learning. Our musical learning is usually uneven and occurs in starts and spurts. Often in an attempt to correct one problem area, we regress in another. Our success comes as the overall average of our performance ascends.

Practical Beginnings

As we near the close of this chapter, it's time to consider some ways to begin the process of learning new and expanded musical skills. Following are suggestions for starting the journey:

22. Reimer, "Education in Our Multimusical Culture," p. 24.

Listen, listen, listen. There's no substitute for listening to music, particularly music of a style that we're exploring. Listening is the all-important first step, for only then can our minds begin the sometimes subconscious process of unraveling the musical data that is introduced. Once we're aurally familiar with a new style or genre, our subsequent study will progress more quickly.

Associate with people who have different musical skills than yours. Spending time with people who have different musical skills provides the possibility for collaboration, experimentation, and exchange. Vicariously and intentionally, we'll begin to piece together ideas and concepts that will aid our learning. Also spend time with people whose musical skills aren't as strong as yours. This will help you to become a better teacher, since the vast majority of people in any congregation aren't confident singers, don't play a musical instrument, and don't consider themselves "musical." Those who most need to learn aren't those who are already highly skilled.

Begin where you are. Recognize your current abilities and skills. Start by finding ways to enhance the competencies you already have, and allow those successes to launch you toward further musical development.

Design a growth plan. A well-conceived and strategic plan is your best assurance of change and growth. The process of gaining a few new skills every year results in long-term change.

Take it slowly. Mastering new skills doesn't have to be accomplished rapidly. Often we fail to attempt new ventures because we believe we have to achieve quickly, when in fact what we need to do is practice steadily.

Create a laboratory. Find a safe place for experimentation. Try out your new skills in a low-risk environment. Use your new knowledge in a place where the stakes are low. Taking this approach will allow you to gain confidence.

Listen to your context (learn what has meaning). Base what you decide to attempt on what has the most meaning for your particular context. Since using your skills for the church will provide added meaning to your life, decide what is most helpful for the community and focus on these skills first. Working thoughtfully and intentionally within your context will motivate you and will serve others as well.

Learning to Compensate

Lastly, when we believe our skills are substandard, we can learn to compensate. I have often asked my students if the axiom "Anything worth doing is worth doing well" is true. At first they usually say yes. But after further thought they usually come to realize that "well" is relative, and that if we only participate in the activities that we do "well," we'll miss out on much. They also come to realize that we're not always capable of doing everything well in all times in our lives. For instance, in the process of writing this book, I've had to do some of the other responsibilities of my job "adequately" in order to spend extra time with this manuscript. This illustrates that one of the ways that we learn to move through life is by learning to compensate in the areas in which we are less gifted and capable or are unable to invest significant time. Following are some suggestions for ways to compensate in areas where our skills are modest.

Depend on written materials at first. Written-out music is available in nearly every imaginable style and genre. Until you're more familiar with styles that are aurally conceived or highly improvisatory, depend on transcriptions and the notated works of others.

Change the frame. When dealing with unfamiliar music, think about how the frame for the picture can be altered to change the look of the photo. In other words, how can you alter the surroundings, the most obvious trappings, in order for the music to put its best foot forward? For example, in order to enhance music from another culture, purchase percussion and other incidental instruments related to the culture so that you're able to create the correct ambiance for the musical presentation, even if the style, language, and other aspects of the music may not be culture-specific. If singing a standard hymn in a room without an organ, consider adding brass or other instruments in order to give the hymn the sense of grandeur that makes it more historically grounded.

Depend on others. We are called to live in community with others because we are stronger as a result. We aren't designed to live in isolation, and nowhere is this more apparent and important to recognize than within the musical community. Christians must function in community, and musicians must function within musical and faith communities. As individuals we're not capable of doing all things musical in an excellent manner. We must depend on others to compensate for us in areas where we are weaker. In return, we can compensate for them.

Develop others. Resist the temptation to do everything yourself. Always be looking for others whose dormant skills need to be developed. Invest in the lives of others.

Considering Music Learned Aurally

Much of the world's music is transmitted aurally. While music in the Western European art music tradition is transmitted through written notation, and many other types of music have been transcribed as well, many of the world's musicians depend on their ears to learn the music of their culture. Closer to home, much of the music that we sing in church, particularly the music of the praise and worship movement, seems meant to be learned by listening rather than from notation. I discovered this firsthand several years ago when working regularly with our church's band and vocal ensemble. Even this group of classically trained musicians was often challenged to read the score as written, and when they did, it often sounded contrived. I would often ask, "Does anyone know how this song is usually sung in worship settings?" Eventually we adopted the pattern of listening to recordings and relying on the score in tandem. While notation is readily available, praise and worship music is often more akin to folk music in that it is often performed differently than it is notated. Also, in praise and worship music, as in folk music, variants of most songs have emerged. According to Carol Richardson, musicians who are trained to rely more on their eyes than their ears find learning music by ear to be "challenging, difficult, and sometimes impossible, particularly when learning songs in a language foreign to [them]."[23] Well-trained musicians who are accustomed to a symbol-based, visual translation process can seriously question their musicianship when they have to rely solely on their aural acuity and aural memory. Richardson goes on to observe that independent musicianship is not valued in an aural tradition, since mimicry and repetition are the means of mastering these styles.[24]

It is worth noting that one of the most significant points of resistance among some regarding praise and worship music is related to the

23. Carol P. Richardson, "Multimusical Competency for Music Educators: Problems and Possibilities," *College Music Symposium* 44 (2004): 70.
24. Richardson, "Multimusical Competency for Music Educators," p. 70.

lack of music scores available for the congregation. Being deprived of a musical score in the hymnal significantly handicaps worshipers who are accustomed to worshiping in a visual musical tradition. Here it should be acknowledged that, in terms of rhythm, much of the music in this genre is too difficult and challenging for most lay musicians; however, I have found that providing a melody line with notes and text usually gives hesitant worshipers the confidence they need to attempt new musical forms. Most musicians trained in classical visual traditions are deeply appreciative as well.

Final Words

We must learn to accept the fact that some people in our congregation may have greater expertise in a particular genre than we do. Do we then cease making any evaluations of music that is beyond our first language? No, we simply depend on others to help us with our discernment. We must listen to others who understand the various complexities of the music of the church and are able to provide information that isn't readily apparent to us. Because music is continually evolving, we must continue to learn. Of course, we'll never know all that we'd like to know or be able to master all the instruments we wish we could play. Nevertheless, we must be willing to offer what we have in the time and place to which we are called.

Even though our musical preference may not match some of the preferences of our congregation, accepting their preferences will model genuine Christian community, and our grace-giving attempts at understanding their music will likely assure reciprocal grace. We are always to be agents of grace, and when in doubt, we should always err on the side of grace. Grace offered is grace received.

We will never move past our personal musical preferences, nor should we. We are unique musical creations, and God created us with preferences. God wants to use all that we have been given — our training, our early experiences, our creativity, our intellect, our perceptions, our skills, and much more. Offered to God, all that we are is enough.

CHAPTER 11

From Memory to Imagination:
Finding Our Way Forward

Let us build a house where prophets speak,
And words are strong and true,
Where all God's children dare to seek
To dream God's reign anew.

Here the cross shall stand as witness
And a symbol of God's grace;
Here as one we claim the faith of Jesus:

All are welcome, all are welcome,
All are welcome in this place.

Marty Haugen, "All Are Welcome"

As we approach the conclusion of this exploration of the church's music, how do we find our way forward? Where do we go from here? What do we do with what we have uncovered? How do we leverage this discussion and dialogue to serve the church better and extend the gospel of Christ?

Once our experiences are expanded, we can never fully return to where we were. While we can always return to a memory, the places we've visited in the meantime and the contexts that the places, people, and experiences offer always alter the original memory. Similarly, your having read this book and interacted with its ideas forfeits the option of returning to where you began. Interactions, new knowledge, and exposure to different contexts change us. We can deny change, but once the kernel of transformation has been planted, it is permanently imbed-

212

ded. Either we let it lie dormant from neglect, or we decide to water and fertilize the seed.

In what follows, I'll revisit some of the themes we've explored and offer possibilities for taking steps into the future. God is still with us in this journey. Although we may become fatigued and travel-weary, God never tires. God will not forsake us or the church's music to which we are committed.

Toward Inclusivity

For the music of the church to move forward in its fullness, it must continue toward hearing all voices, perspectives, stories, and histories in order to discern new directions. We often have difficulty with this. Rather than receiving the message that was intended, we are conditioned to hear what we expect to hear — we often hear what we have predecided. Arjun Appadurai makes this point more specific: "We find in what we hear some of what we have been taught to expect by our own training, reading, and cultural backgrounds."[1] While these things should contextualize the messages that we receive and send, moving toward an understanding rooted in the context of the "other" better positions us for genuine dialogue. When differences are treated as proper and expected rather than as novel and non-essential, our hearing will be improved and our communication enhanced.

Also inhibiting open and honest dialogue is our tendency to privilege our own training and experience while diminishing that of others. Marilyn Strathern and George Marcus comment, "[We are] concerned with avoiding the illusion of the panopticon, whereby our own histories and situation are exempt from examination as we gaze across the landscape of our 'others.'"[2] In reality, neither our stories nor those of others are fully "accurate," but our tendency to accept our own stories and experiences as "true" while viewing those of others as "possible" skews our ability to fully engage. Too often, "the appearance of dialogue conceals the reality of monologue."[3] While we give the impression of being

---

1. Arjun Appadurai, "Place and Voice in Anthropological Theory," *Cultural Anthropology* 3 (February 1988): 17.

2. Strathern and Marcus, cited in Appadurai, "Place and Voice in Anthropological Theory," p. 20.

3. Appadurai, "Place and Voice in Anthropological Theory," p. 20.

engaged in discourse, our long-rehearsed monologue may be the only voice we're really hearing. In what Appadurai calls "ventriloquism," we often speak for others, verbally or silently, instead of allowing them to speak for themselves. The music of the church is many-faceted, and its DNA is as gene-specific as that of the millions who lead and participate in it each week. Local voices need to be heard in their communities, and collective voices must join together in imagining the music of the church throughout the world.

Establishing Commons

A commons is a place where people meet, interact, and share ideas. Popular within some university settings, a commons offers an open space for relationships to be established and dialogue to occur. Dwight Friesen describes a commons as a "connective space like a village square, a plaza, a forum, the Internet, or any open meeting place."[4] Friesen goes on to describe a "Christ-Commons" where people gather to connect around their common allegiance to Christ. Friesen explains,

> A Christ-Commons is a visible structure, institution, denomination, building, worship service, or small group that is formally created with the hope that the structure will provide an environment or space where people are more likely to experience life in connection with God and one another. Christ-Commons exist primarily to provide elaborate systems of support that promote and equip people to cluster together in Christ's service as blessing to others.[5]

Those invested in the future of the music of the church — both locally and globally — need to establish music commons which are hospitable places that encourage and facilitate dialogue about the church and its music. If we don't intentionally establish such places, dialogue is not likely to occur, and we will continue to serve Christ faithfully in our own context and within our individual sphere of influence. While this individual model is noble and God-honoring, it will likely not lead us to-

---

4. Dwight J. Friesen, *Thy Kingdom Connected: What the Church Can Learn from Facebook, the Internet, and Other Networks* (Grand Rapids: Baker Books, 2009), p. 106.

5. Friesen, *Thy Kingdom Connected*, p. 107.

ward the imagination of God to which we aspire. Many of the world's greatest re-formations have found traction where imaginative people met with other imaginative people and the synthesis of their thoughts found a synergy that began to impact those closest to them and eventually others as well.

The Need for Catalysts

Change most often occurs through a burst of energy that serves as a catalyst for creating change among others. When one person or a small group of people offer leadership, renewed energy, and passion to a task or calling, their energy can become contagious, and it can ignite a reaction among others which creates the possibility of transforming an existing situation into one that is quite different. Just as a catalytic converter in a car provides the "environment for a chemical reaction wherein toxic combustion by products are converted to less toxic substances,"[6] a person or group serving as a catalyst can contribute to an environment in which the process of change is accelerated, negative energy is converted to productivity, and new dreams can replace worn-out paradigms. The music of the church is in need of leaders who through their passion and commitment are willing to allow their energy to function as a catalyst for renewal of the church's music.

Ethnomusicology as a Model

Since all music is particular to a group of people, all music can in one respect be considered ethnic music. However, we tend to distinguish between music that is more broadly accepted among many cultures — for example, Western art music — and music that is from minority cultures and hasn't been as widely disseminated — which we call ethnic music. When we seek to understand the music of a culture different from our own, we should first consider the context of the music. How is music used in ceremonies such as weddings and funerals? What music is used for play and recreation? How is music utilized in worship and ritual practice? What instrumentation is prevalent? Is the music pri-

6. Friesen, *Thy Kingdom Connected,* p. 110.

215

marily vocal or instrumental? Do the people move to the music? What music is being currently created within this context? What music speaks across different age groups and demographics? How is the music disseminated? These and other questions help us to determine the context for music-making within a culture.

According to Marcia Herndon and Norma McLeod, "Ethnomusicology is the study of the music, either past or present, of all who participate in music as creators, performers, or hearers of sound patterns, taking into account all factors which lead to a better understanding of this particular type of creative, human display."[7] Ethnomusicologists do not study music as an entity separate from its context — the people who create, perform, and listen are equally important. The work of an ethnomusicologist involves the following:

1. Studying human behaviors that produce music. How is music related to the people that produce it? How is music used to enhance the lives of its creators, performers, and listeners?
2. Studying cultural factors that determine musical behavior. What are the cultural traditions that produce music? How do people within this culture respond to music, and under what circumstances do people produce music?
3. Doing fieldwork, which is the centerpiece of this kind of study. Ethnomusicologists go where the people are. They live among the people for a time, interview them, listen to their stories, and learn about their lives. This fieldwork becomes the basis for their findings.
4. Undertaking application and analysis, making interpretations, and drawing conclusions following field study. All conclusions are drawn from the work that happens among the people.
5. Validating the music of other cultures. Through understanding different types of music, the ethnomusicologist is able to understand the music and its context and validate it.
6. Preserving oral tradition. Much of the world's music is yet to be notated or recorded. By studying the music, the oral tradition is preserved for others.
7. Fostering communication among musicians. Well-trained and

7. Marcia Herndon and Norma McLeod, *Music as Culture* (Darby, Pa.: Norwood Editions, 1981), p. 8.

highly artistic musicians exist in every culture. Ethnomusicology facilitates free-flowing dialogue among musicians.

The ethnomusicologist asks two basic questions: "Why do people
behave as they do?" and "How do behaviors result in music?" By observing the behavior, the day-to-day actions of people, and discerning how
music is integrated into their lives, the ethnomusicologist learns how
music takes on meaning within a particular cultural context.

In this kind of study, it's important to consider the hallmarks of almost every kind of music:

1. All cultures have music.
2. All cultures have singing, ways of using the human voice that differ
   from ordinary speech.
3. Practically all cultures have musical instruments.
4. Music is used for worship or for religious rituals in all cultures.
5. Music acts as an emblem or identity in all cultures.
6. Music transforms everyday experience.
7. In most cultures, music is closely associated with dance or movement.
8. Most cultures also combine music and narrative.[8]

With these hallmarks in mind, it is easy to see how the study of music within a culture offers a window into people's interior lives. While
there are other common components among different cultures, music
is unique in that it plays a part in many of the other areas that cultures
often share — story-telling, dancing, playing games, observing religious rituals, and so on. If the music of a culture is dealt with in a cur-
sory manner, important aspects of that culture can easily be ignored.
However, when one carefully studies and analyzes a culture's music,
one is able to more easily understand every aspect of the culture that
gave birth to that music.

Ethnomusicology can be a valuable paradigm for the music of the
church. It shows us how important it is not to draw musical conclusions
until we've participated in meaningful dialogue with the community,

8. Bruno Nettl, *The Study of Ethnomusicology: Twenty-Nine Issues and Concepts*
(Champaign-Urbana: University of Illinois Press, 2005). Statements 1-7 are from Nettl's
work, and statement 8 was added by my Baylor colleague Laurel Zeiss.

observed the role of music in their lives, and begun to understand the people and engage with their culture. In the context of Western art music, it seems there has been a tendency to make critical decisions about music based on one's own experiences and training, with little concern given to the story, situation, context, and purposes of other kinds of music. Similarly, those in popular music genres have seemed to assume that mass appeal assures that people from the primary culture as well as people from other world cultures should also share their aesthetics. In either case, assumptions and premature critical judgments assure misunderstandings, and they fail to create avenues for cross-cultural dialogue and understanding. Such assumptions are hindrances for musical dialogue in general — but they are debilitating for the church. They may very well have fostered much of the church's misunderstanding about its music in recent decades.

A Community of Memory

In his book *Habits of the Heart,* Robert Bellah calls the "community of faith" the "community of memory." Mark Searle believes that what he means by that is a community "that does not forget its past."[9] Remembering the past is the key to building the future, for however the music of the church is shaped in times to come, it should somehow reference the past and the rich history on whose shoulders it stands. Bellah expounds upon this idea when he says, "In order not to forget [its] past, a community is involved in retelling its story, its constitutive narrative, and in so doing, it offers examples of the men and women who have embodied and exemplified the meaning of the community."[10] He goes on to describe the range of these stories:

> The stories that make up a tradition contain conceptions of character, of what a good person is like, of the virtues that define such character; but the stories are not all exemplary, not all about successes and achievements. A genuine community of memory will also tell

9. Mark Searle, *Called to Participate: Theological, Ritual, and Social Perspectives* (Collegeville, Minn.: Liturgical Press, 2006), p. 77.

10. Robert Bellah et al., *Habits of the Heart: Individualism and Commitment in American Life* (Berkeley and Los Angeles: University of California Press, 1984), p. 153.

painful stories of shared suffering that sometimes creates deeper identities than success. . . . And if the community is completely honest, it will remember stories not only of suffering received but suffering inflicted — dangerous memories, for they call the community to alter ancient evils. The communities of memory that tie us to the past also turn us to the future as communities of hope. They carry a context of meaning that can allow us to connect our aspirations for ourselves and those closest to us with the aspirations of a larger whole and see our own efforts as being, in part, contributions to a common good.[11]

Bellah could easily have had the music of the church in mind when he wrote these words. The stories of church music's past are not all pretty, nor do they describe people who were always kind. In an effort to protect ourselves and what we knew and believed, we have sometimes acted out of self-preservation and failed to see the common good. While some of our church music stories will not likely inspire our future, they are our stories, and their lessons must not be overlooked. As we reflect on stories of the church reacting too harshly against other Christ-followers, we must learn; as we reflect on stories of individuals speaking disparagingly about others and the music they employ to worship God, we must learn; and as we reflect on the times we have used music as a weapon to fight any sort of battle, we must repent and learn. While music can serve many functions, it must never serve as a weapon in any sort of war, no matter how holy we may perceive our cause! If we fail to learn from our checkered past *and* our moments of highest resolve, the future we construct on the shoulders of the past will be unbalanced and may easily tumble. If the music of the church is for anything, it is for the common good. It is to serve all of the world's people as we offer ourselves to God in fresh ways. When the music of one community thrives, we all thrive; when the music of one community suffers, we all suffer. A community with musical memory remembers both the exhilaration of unhindered worship and the grief of actions too painful to share with those who were not there. Still, both make up the musical community, and both enlighten us on our way forward.

Could it be that the artists in the church and the art they foster in the faith community could in some way lead the way forward for the church

11. Bellah et al., *Habits of the Heart*, p. 155.

of the future? Regarding art's importance in building community, David McMillan observes, "Song and dance show a community's heart and passion. Art represents the transcendent values of the community. But the basic foundation of art is experience. To have experience, the community's members must have contact with one another. Contact is essential for a sense of community to develop."[12] Genuine work that moves us beyond our individual agendas can bind a community together as we strive toward a common goal. As I start each fall with a new group of men who choose to sing in the Baylor Men's Choir, I am captivated by the community that develops as the guys surrender their individual musical gifts to the group's goals. Although sometimes unbalanced by ability and by the number of men assigned to each part, individual singers learn to compensate for each other. Bigger voices step up in fortissimo sections, while lyric voices shine during soft, sensitive passages. Well-developed falsettos compensate when the parts become too high for the top tenors, and more refined voices compensate for the rough edges of voices that are still learning to function in adult bodies. Working toward a performance goal that cannot be accomplished by any individual or small group, the guys lose themselves as they rehearse their way toward something bigger than their combined selves. The sheer act of participating shoulder-to-shoulder each day creates a formidable team, and the results are sometimes amazing. McMillan comments on the kind of contact that creates this kind of artistic community and memory:

> The contact must have a certain quality for it to become a collected memory that is art; the community must share in the fate of their common experience in the same way. In effect, it conveys the sense of "all for one and one for all." If it was a success for one, it was, in some way, a success for all members. In addition to being shared, an event must have a dramatic impact. What makes a moment dramatic is that something is at risk for the community or its representative. Dramatic moments may create a collective memory, but this does not make that memory worthy of becoming art that will be passed from one generation to the next. Unresolved ambiguity or cruelty can destroy a sense of community. Events that represent these experiences rarely become art. Dramatic moments of tragedy redeemed by cour-

12. David W. McMillan, "Sense of Community," *Journal of Community Psychology* 24 (1996): 322.

age are events worthy of becoming community stories. These stories represent the community's values and traditions.[13]

The church's musicians must reclaim the power of art to create community, and they must inspire other artists to take the lead in establishing communities that use music's transformative power to share the love of Christ with others and lead them to offer their gifts to God in worship. God is fully present in the making of music and the creation of art, but the church has long failed to empower art to its fullest potential. Imaginative leaders must step forward to inspire the music and art of the church to reclaim its intended role.

An Ecumenical Age

The postmodern situation calls for a crossing of boundaries and a blurring of roles. With lines erased or more lightly drawn, postmodernism will usher in an ecumenical age. Gerald Schlabach observes, "One long-time religious journalist and friend suggests that we might better name this 'postmodern' situation the Ecumenical Age. His point is that more and more people recognize their need for insights and practices that other traditions embody. Whatever we call it, the postmodern or ecumenical situation offers individuals and communities the freedom to appropriate the wisdom of others to enrich their identities, or even to reinvent their identities altogether."[14] Often when visiting with parents and prospective students about the possibility of studying church music as a major, I am asked, "Do you teach Baptist church music at Baylor?" I carefully explain to them that defining the church's music from a denominational perspective is virtually impossible, for in many ways we are already living in an ecumenical age. Without exception, they always nod in agreement — inside, they already know what I verbalize.

Yet, even though the ecumenical age is here, and ecumenism is being practiced particularly as it relates to music, true ecumenicity is yet to be fully developed. While some churches have borrowed from their different-denomination neighbors, many have feared that borrowing

13. McMillan, "Sense of Community," p. 323.
14. Gerald W. Schlabach, *Unlearning Protestantism: Sustaining Christian Community in an Unstable Age* (Grand Rapids: Brazos Press, 2010), p. 23.

might in some way sacrifice their own identity or create a debt that they could not repay. As a consequence, nets are still intact, and the butterflies that could allow cross-pollination have not yet been freed. What might happen if a contemporary church worshiped with the sound of a pipe organ and a traditional hymn, or a liturgical church sang a praise song as a response to the gospel? What might happen if a contemporary church prayed a written liturgy, or a liturgical church participated in spontaneous prayer?

The days ahead will be rich in ecumenism, and in a few short generations, we will find ourselves with only minimal memory of the lines that once divided the body of Christ into easily distinguishable units. As the butterflies are freed one by one, the crossbreeds and hybrids that will grow in the gardens of faith around our cities and across our world will be stronger and more virile than the purebreds of the past. These new varieties of Christ-followers may resemble their long-lost relatives, but their beauty and worth will be in their resemblance to Christ instead of their resemblance to historical mothers and fathers.

Always Re-forming

The church's process of re-forming has only begun, and it will continue indefinitely. During a time when the culture dances along at an unimaginable speed, the church has often appeared heavy-footed and uncoordinated. However, the postmodern church will respond to change much more nimbly. In much the same way that small companies respond to market changes within hours and days, the church will learn to reposition and re-form with greater dexterity. Likewise, the music of the church will continue to re-form and reshape itself while remaining open to scrutiny; according to Paul Tillich, it must be "always subject to prophetic critique."[15] Tillich explains what the church needs to remain unified despite challenges:

> What all of us need are the practices and virtues that make it possible to reform, protest, and even dissent out of love for one's Christian community — even while sustaining a doggedly loyal commitment to "hang in there" with those among whom we disagree. To develop

15. Paul Tillich, quoted in Schlabach, *Unlearning Protestantism*, p. 22.

these practices and grow in those virtues within our respective Protestant and Catholic communities may yet mean to find ourselves growing together. Whether or not official church unity eventually results, and however it may happen, all Christian communities need such virtues to sustain their lives together.[16]

Too often in an effort to be "nice," the church has shied away from honest and open dialogue, and as a result, we have sometimes failed to experience the growth that dissent can eventually engender. Schlabach comments, "Faithful Christian life and practice must always be open and indeed vulnerable to the challenge of prophets, to the voice of conscience, to the work of reform — to protest."[17] However, while we acknowledge the ongoing re-forming of the church's life and music and embrace new things, it is important not to hold all tradition as suspect. In the midst of change and transition, the church must carefully hold on to the traditions which enliven and inform its future.

Re-imagining Institutions

While institutions, like those who form them, are always flawed, they are still what we have to work with, and institutions in their re-imagined state will provide the glue that secures the puzzle that is the body of Christ. As a friend of mine often says, "The church is still the best hope we have for the world." In speaking of the church and its dependence on institutions, Schlabach observes,

> If God in Christ has entered into human history and culture and then entrusted the gospel to sinful human messengers, God has deemed imperfect human ways good enough to carry revelation forward. If Christ has dwelt among us and shared our flesh over time, then God's own work has revealed that our limited fleshly lives through time are good enough to bear the imprint of grace, however imperfectly. If God can reconcile human beings, then human social relationships can enjoy a durability that participates in eternity. . . . Our God is one who never gives up on God's people. But to be a people at all — hu-

16. Tillich, quoted in Schlabach, *Unlearning Protestantism*, p. 32.
17. Schlabach, *Unlearning Protestantism*, p. 34.

man and not an angelic people — we must live together through those structured social relationships we call institutions. No more than manna ought we to think of institutions as ends in themselves, as self-sustaining or incorruptible — yet we do need them too in order to sustain our reconciled life together.[18]

As we look at institutions and their ability to serve the music of the church, we must continue to critique the church, the academic community, the role of commerce, and others who have a direct stake in the role of music in the community of faith. To discover ways in which an institution can serve the music of the church and the gospel of Christ without our becoming beholden to the institution is the challenge of the future. Historically, institutions have been created for the function of serving the church. However, over time, these institutions have often lost sight of their mission, and the money, energy, and passion that should serve the world and its people have been siphoned off to hold up the institutions themselves.

Sticking Together

If those who serve the church through music would learn to stick together, then many of the challenges facing the church could be resolved. If we would decide once and for all that we are all part of the body of Christ despite our differences, many of the problems surrounding the church and its music could be alleviated. However, since the stake that Protestants hold in the music of the church is significant, that music has tended to follow the Protestant principle of focusing on the individual instead of the whole. Throughout Protestant history, when dissension has arisen, Protestants have tended to part ways and form new groups rather than work out their differences and find a better way. While this model has served the church well at times, it is also problematic, for often we have halted the dialogue just before the sun came up and a new day dawned. Schlabach points out the critical difference between Protestants and Catholics, who have had to learn to stick together: "It is simply that Catholics have had to develop this virtue (like it or not) because their faith requires them to stick together

18. Schlabach, *Unlearning Protestantism*, p. 40.

(like one another or not) at those very sorts of junctures where Protestantism would allow or even propose the easier route of splitting and starting over."[19] If we are to become an ecumenical community of faith, this is a lesson that we need to learn.

Let's think back to the 1970s, when younger people were initially creating songs in folk styles and exploring the use of guitars, drums, and other (then) non-traditional instruments in church. Imagine for a moment that the established church, instead of categorically rejecting this music, had instead allowed this new and different form to have a voice in the standard worship of the day. What might have happened? Would the existing worship of the day have been re-formed rather than splintered? Would a generation of younger worshipers have continued to worship with the sound of the organ while adding the sounds of guitars and drums, thus having their worship palette broadened? Would an older generation have expanded their worship and (perhaps their view of God) by adding freshness and new winds of the Spirit? How might the years since that time have been different? What might have transpired if — instead of allowing musical preference and styles to divide parents from children and children from grandparents — we had established dialogue and submitted our power to Christ and the work of the Holy Spirit?

While we will never know the answer to these and many other questions, we can influence the way we move forward from here. We can continue conversations past the point of ease. We can attempt to look forward to see both what we will gain and what we will lose in the decisions regarding the church's music — decisions that are often made hastily and without prayer and submission of ego. With the gift of hindsight, future mistakes can be avoided, and some past mistakes can actually be patched. The Thomas Troeger hymn "When There Is No Star to Guide You" offers a model for sticking together on our journey:

> When there is no star to guide you
> and you cannot wait for day,
> and your ancient maps provide you
> only hints to find the way,
> keep within each other's calling,
> mark each time you make a turn,

---

19. Schlabach, *Unlearning Protestantism*, p. 45.

shout for help if you are falling,
tell each other all you learn.

Be alert to shifts in weather:
if it turns to cold and frost,
huddle closely all together;
check if any have been lost.
Listen for a river flowing,
feel for damper, moving air,
trace from where the wind is blowing,
move on bravely but with care.

If you think you have discovered
with your lantern in the night
some clear path the dark has covered,
let the others bring their light.
Test your single lone perception
in their gathered shining beams;
what you saw may be projection
fed by shadows, fears, and dreams.

You may sometimes trip and stumble
on a hidden root or stone,
but remember as you grumble
that you do not fall alone.
And in risking dark expanses
never marked on map or chart,
you will find that faith advances
through the landscape of your heart.[20]

A Bigger God

One of the problems with the music of the church and the controversy
that has sometimes surrounded it is the notion that God is most
pleased with this music or that music. For years, Christians have used

20. "When There Is No Star to Guide You," in Thomas H. Troeger, *Borrowed Light: Hymn Texts, Prayers, and Poems* (New York: Oxford University Press, 1994).

this God-weapon against each other, every musical camp claiming to know what God prefers and what God doesn't. The real problem with this argument is the mistaken belief that we can decipher what it is that God most enjoys and prefers. When we pit our preferred music or preferred worship form against others, and when we spend lots of time and energy claiming that our preference is in fact God's, we have made our preference our idol and embraced a God that is too small. Kenneth Pargament observes, "Of course, it could be said that all representations of God are too small because the human is incapable of fully grasping the character of the divine. Even so, some spiritual understandings are more encompassing than others. Smaller gods represent a problem because they fail to shed light on the profound dilemmas of life."[21]

When the God that we embrace is not capable of understanding that different people need and prefer different music, that different contexts and understandings call for different music, and that just as we speak varied languages, we also interpret the music of our faith in varied ways, our God is too small. When we think that our God isn't capable of speaking to all the problems, concerns, and needs of the entire world, our God is too small. When our God is too small, we are prone to speak harmful words in order to protect that God from others. We summon our best arguments to defend the One who made us, and we offer our best rational thinking to explain a God who is above and beyond all that we can think or imagine.

If the church's music is to move forward, the God of the church's music must be bigger than those of us who serve God. God must be bigger than the stylistic boxes that our finite musical abilities have constructed. God must be bigger than the limits of our voices, our instrumental abilities, and the surest technique we can muster. God must be bigger than any argument, apologetic, or case study we can construct. In the final analysis, what may be most likely to allow the size of our God to increase is the full release of our imagination. Allowing the size of our God to grow makes us open to others, gives us space to think creatively, and allows us to imagine a world that is yet to be fully realized.

---

21. Kenneth I. Pargament, "The Sacred Character of Community Life," *American Journal of Community Psychology* 41 (2008): 29.

Transforming Narcissism

Narcissism, so rampant in our culture today, is an overwhelming obsession with self. It is unhealthy and doesn't allow a Christ-follower to care appropriately for others. However, if group narcissism (believing that a class or group is superior) were turned on its head, it could serve the church and its music. Instead of maintaining that our group was the most important, the smartest, or the most privileged, we could believe in the good of the entire human race and the ability of all to learn, grow, and succeed. This idea is well-articulated by William Sadler:

> If mankind, the entire human family, could become the object of group narcissism instead of one nation, one race, or one political system being this object, much might be gained. If the individual could experience himself primarily as a citizen of the world and if he could feel pride in mankind and in its achievements, his narcissism would turn toward the human race as an object, rather than to its conflicting components. If the educational systems of all countries stressed the achievements of the human race instead of the achievements of an individual nation, a more convincing and moving case could be made for the pride in being man.[22]

What would happen if we could obliterate the group narcissism of believing that "our" music is superior while putting down the musical preferences of others and learn to value the music of the entire human family? We would be moving closer to a stance that God could bless and use to move us forward. Too much of the posturing in the Christian music community is akin to the group narcissism of those who use shallow defenses to justify their feelings of inferiority and their fear of loss of power. Learning to embrace all the music of the church could allow all Christ-followers to take pride in belonging to the greater body of Christ and to embrace the music that our worldwide brothers and sisters choose to express themselves in worship. Instead of seeing our differences as problematic, we could choose instead to express joy in our differences, which are all redeemed through Christ.

In order for such a dream to be realized, we must be willing to sur-

---

22. William A. Sadler Jr., *Personality and Religion: The Role of Religion in Personality Development* (New York: Harper & Row, 1970), p. 131.

render our individual and group sovereignty in favor of valuing all people as beings created in the likeness of God. Sadler comments,

> As people of faith, we must recognize and be willing to live in the reality that nothing human is alien to any other human. In essence, "I am you," and "You are me." As human beings created in the image of God, we are intricately connected, and in order to imitate the example set by Jesus, we must work together to create the kingdom of God on earth and in heaven. Our awareness must move past the awareness that comes easily by responding to what is closest to us and that which nurtures and supports us in the short run. We must enlarge our sphere of awareness to think globally and to move out of the comfortable places we have created for ourselves and those that make those around us comfortable.[23]

Within such an aspiration lies immense hope — hope for the church and its music.

Toward Imagination

Imagination is the stuff upon which change and transformation are built. What is imagination? It's the ability to see in the mind's eye something that doesn't exist. It's the ability to project into the future something that could make the world better. It's the ability to reshape what is into what it could be. For a church musician, it's the ability to imagine a congregation singing a song they have never sung before and finding a way to teach and inspire them to sing it and eventually make it a part of themselves. It's the ability to hear a musical motif and imagine it as the seed for a new song. It's the ability to hear a passing phrase and imagine it as lines of poetry that could be set to music. It's the ability to see the limits of your own musical world and imagine that world becoming much broader and deeper. It's the ability to see our world segregated into musical cubicles of self-propagating, like-colored individuals and imagine a wall-less, multicolored world. Those who have altered the world have imagined.

Imagination is more than knowledge; many people are able to understand what is but can't imagine what could be. Other people spend

23. Sadler, *Personality and Religion*, p. 132.

their lives gaining more knowledge, believing that their quest for knowledge will change them and their world. But without imagination, knowledge will not be transformative. Craig Nessan reminds us, "While it is possible and important to know many things, knowledge is not what changes us. Instead, what changes us are the dreams that grip us, the idea that things do not have to be like they always have been, the power to imagine another course."[24] Imagination is more than dreams, although dreaming is an important component of imagination. True imagination is the ability to see what could be — to "image" it — to create a picture, a sound, a touch, or a feeling, and to move from where you are into that imagined place. Once you've moved to the imagined place, you have the ability to see where you were, and you have the opportunity to retrace your journey to the imagined place. Once you've done this, you can begin to bring others with you. In time, the imaginary journey can become three-dimensional — moving from the imagination into reality.

Imagination isn't based on facts — indeed, facts are often the toxin that destroys imagination. Nothing ruins imagination more quickly than the person who imposes perceived reality on imagination. The modern world is a fact-filled world in which knowledge reigns as king of the small boxes in which all things are neatly organized. In this modern worldview, facts are the cardboard from which the boxes were constructed; they are the upholstered walls that divide our cubicles; and they are the structures and policies that stifle our imaginations. Facts are the walls that we have constructed to keep our thoughts small, confined, and always local. While in the past some have considered facts immovable and permanent, today we know that facts are always open to interpretation, and they are true only until someone moves beyond them and starts to live life on the other side of the fact-constructed wall.

When I was a young boy not yet in school, my daddy and I drove our pickup to the small Alabama community of Dixie and bought a truckload of hogs from a local farmer. In the group were several sows with young pigs. To allow the hogs to become acclimated to our farm, we put them in a small, enclosed area for a few days to observe them and to be sure that they were calm before turning them into the adjacent cornfield. After several days, they seemed to be adjusting well, so my daddy and I took down the electric fence that enclosed them. Immediately al-

24. Craig L. Nessan, *Beyond Maintenance to Mission: A Theology of the Congregation*, 2nd ed. (Minneapolis: Fortress Press, 2010), p. 42.

most all of the hogs moved into the cornfield and began to enjoy the end-less stalks ripe with golden ears. Only one sow was unwilling to cross the line where the electric fence had been. In spite of our best coaxing, she was unable to cross that barrier. For several days we fed her a limited diet of crushed grain, knowing that she could have made a pig of herself and been in hog heaven in the cornfield. Still, she remained unable and un-willing to cross the imaginary electric fence, which isolated her both from her peers and from the feast that was hers to enjoy. At last, exasper-ated, my daddy resorted to loading her into the truck and driving her across the line where the fence had once been. In her mind, the fence was still there. To her peril, she trusted her knowledge and experience.

Too often, we are like this lone sow. Perhaps her past included be-ing shocked by an electric fence, and the pain that she had endured had scared her. Perhaps she had imagined cornfields in the past, and once she'd taken the risk of moving past the fence, she had been disap-pointed and become cynical. Perhaps she had followed the dreams of others in the past and had been disappointed, and now found it safer to remain alone in a place where at least she felt secure. Perhaps she had once left the safety of her pen and had gotten lost in a cornfield and feared that she might never find her way back again. Whatever her rea-son, she was unable to risk, to imagine, or to dream because she was trapped inside her imaginary cage.

As Christ-followers, we are to engage with the imagination of Christ himself. Nessan puts it this way:

> There is a third dimension of faith that we neglect at our peril, that is, faith as imagination. What Jesus did in his ministry was to tell stories that invited people to imagine what it meant to have a living God who made a real difference in the way things are and the way things turn out. Jesus appealed to the human imagination to envision an alterna-tive world, a world where God makes all things new. Imagination is the lost dimension of faith itself.[25]

As Christ-followers, we often claim to act on faith when in reality we're acting on faith in ourselves or our institutions. In my many years of ministry, I have rarely seen a congregation (or its leaders) actually move toward a project, a goal, or a ministry that moved beyond the group's

---

25. Nessan, *Beyond Maintenance to Mission*, p. 42.

perceived understanding of the facts. Most of the time, these churches and their leaders were acting completely and wholly within their own power rather than in the imaginative faith that Christ lived and taught. These churches and their leaders failed to envision an alternative world and to trust God himself to take them to places that were beyond the limits of their perception of the facts. Until the church begins to imagine in God-sized images, it is destined for the continued bland grayness that is indicative of our fallen human condition.

Worship is the act in which God changes us. We come to worship to engage with God and submit our brokenness to God, who can heal us and make us whole. As we move further from weekly worship, we lose perspective, and little by little we lose sight of the reality that God is God and that we are not. We are in our most broken condition when we begin to believe that we are sufficient in and of ourselves. Worship is submitting ourselves to God to be realigned according to God's standards, allowing God to recalibrate our lives to God's priorities, and allowing God to tune our lives to sing God's grace. Everyday examples suggest the kind of work that God needs to do. Often when I visit the chiropractor, he tells me that one of my legs has become shorter than the other and that one shoulder is out of line with the other. He's able to pull and tug a muscle in another part of my body to lengthen my leg and lift my shoulder. And recently we purchased a piano that needed some "finetuning." Because we moved it from a place about four hours away, the piano was weary from transport when it reached its new home. After we let it sit for several days to allow it to "get adjusted," we had to bring it back in tune. Similarly, when we worship, God moves us around so that we are realigned to God's ways and God's being.

When we worship, we move into an alternative world, one in which the perceived reality of the rest of our world often has little bearing on what God might want to do with us and where God might want to take us. Nessan says, "While we ourselves engage in imagining the kingdom of God, God is in the very act of enacting that kingdom in our midst."[26] God desires for us to be changed into God's image, and worship is the act of submitting ourselves to the change that only God can enact within us. Nessan continues, "When we gather for worship, we enter into and engage with a time of bold imagination. We dare to appropriate the very vision of existence that Jesus inaugurated, the vision of the

26. Nessan, *Beyond Maintenance to Mission*, p. 42.

kingdom of God, in which all our conventional wisdom yields to the wisdom of God's mercy and grace."[27] The world that we enter when we worship is a world in which we allow the imagination that God has placed within us to engage with the transformative power of Christ himself. However, we must not believe that worship is all up to us. In worship, we imagine and submit, and God takes our best efforts and our most broken offerings and transforms them toward God's likeness. Even as we suspend time and engage in imagining the kingdom of God as it ought to be, God is at work transforming the stuff of our everyday lives into a form that more closely approximates the kingdom itself.

While our imagination will not change the reality of our world, it can move us to places where we are able to imagine personal and corporate change. Imagination allows us to bring the past to the present and the present into the future. Imagination allows us to bring past, present, and future together in order to bring about a new condition: "Insight is gained into the way things could and ought to be."[28]

However, the church has been slow to challenge and engage the imagination. Perhaps because the church has been deeply moored in the "reality" of modernity, we have resisted imagining a different world. Within this failure is one of the biggest ironies of our time. While God is the most imaginative being with which humankind could ever engage, the church is one of the least imaginative places in our culture! The hope of the church lies in its ability to move from the *perceived* reality of humankind to the *assured* reality of God's self.

As we begin to find our way forward, what remains of the "old house" that we discussed at the beginning of this book? By now it has been stripped of its years of clutter, decades of cosmetic updates, and continually shifting facades. The cordoned-off spaces have been opened up, and the carpet covering the foundational cracks has been ripped out. How shall we re-imagine this structure? What shall we retain, and what shall we discard? What relics of the old structure will we keep to ground us and underpin our memory? How will we position bedrocks to keep the story alive without miring us and stifling imagination? How much of the old structure will be stripped away in order to serve the future?

I have my own story about an old house. Shortly after my wife and I adopted our second child, Isaac, we innocently stopped at an open

---

27. Nessan, *Beyond Maintenance to Mission*, p. 45.
28. Nessan, *Beyond Maintenance to Mission*, p. 44.

house for an older home in our town. We quickly became attached to the 1930s vintage home with its large, rounded doors, its solid wood craftsmanship, its native hardwood floors lurking under layers of carpet, and its sprawling front porch. Within a few days we decided to make an offer on this old house and speculatively put our home on the market. To our surprise, our home sold quickly, and we found ourselves owning a decades-old home that had to be renovated in order to function for our young family.

Decisions were myriad. Where should we start? How much could we afford? Which infrastructures were solid, and which were too worn to sustain a renovation? With the advice of our friends and some experts, we began by assessing the home's structural soundness, the ability of its electrical and plumbing systems to support increased voltage and water pressure, and the ability of the roof to keep us safe and dry. From there, we made decisions about the house's historical value to us and our community in tandem with our family's functional needs. While we imagined our children crawling up expansive stairs and rolling their toys down them, we also imagined them and their friends posing for prom photos. We were committed to a renovation that would both sustain us for the present and launch us into our imagined future.

In this book we've made a similar assessment of the church's "old house." As we've looked at the church's music and its re-imaging process, we've observed cracks in the foundation — provincialism, misappropriation of power, lack of inclusivity, failure to be ecumenical — and we've attempted to shore up these fissures with new paradigms embedded in a Godward focus, a biblical intent, and an expansive view of God's world and its people. The load-bearing walls of grace, flexibility, community, hospitality, missional practice, and multiple musical languages have been supported. The living and working areas of this house have large, expansive spaces that allow for different views representing all people of the world. There are no more floor-to-ceiling walls inside, which can encourage us to retreat to safe, quiet places in order to protect what we've created in our isolation. New spaces encourage a free flow of people and ideas, and we have an ongoing awareness that all conversations will and should be overheard by others working around us. Our work is shared; at all times, others have access to our ideas.

Because natural light keeps us externally focused and shields us from the darkness that comes from thinking too small and imagining too little, the structure has expansive windows that allow light from every angle of the world to infuse our work and imagination. Light promotes growth, encourages honesty, and assures clarity, and it protects us from being cordoned off into shadowed spaces where our perspective is clouded and suspicions thrive. Well-lighted spaces allow us to circulate among each other so that our work is open, informed, and influenced by others who also cannot risk the costs of isolation.

Since the music of the church will no longer be limited to one space or one dominant structure, new spaces must be imagined and created around the world in which creativity will flourish, and these new spaces will be in constant dialogue with other communities with similar goals throughout the world. As we inhabit this yet-to-be-claimed space, we will begin to imagine new forms, genres, and material, and we will begin to refurbish older, thread-bare ones.

We must nurture communal spaces in which conversation can thrive, stories can be shared, and new ideas can be vetted. The church and its music leaders must have space to gather without agenda or predetermined outcomes. With space and time, stories will come forth, hearts will connect, and new directions will emerge. Hospitable spaces will allow gifts to be reciprocally shared and received, the spiritual and physical act of bread-breaking to be embodied, the wounded to receive care, and the chronically ill to receive the nurture and treatment they need.

Lastly, any imagination of the new church's music structure must include ample play space — a large, rambling playground where our imaginations can be re-ignited, where we can rediscover the child-like world of risk-taking and acting out adult roles until we are mature enough to step into them again. A well-used playground is a training place, a place to rekindle imagination, to relearn laughter and smiling and the joy of play. By participating in play, we learn to see beyond color, gender, economic status, social standing, cultural capital, and education. A playground can be a leveling place — a place where joy is the goal, and laughter and play are shared among all.

This is our hope for the music of the church, and it is also our hope for the church itself. Based on imaginative thought, the music of the church can serve as a catalyst to transform the unimaginative church into an organism alive with the imagination of God. If the best we can do is pretend that God can do better, then that's enough. God can supply the rest. God can take our best efforts and transform them into imaginative places where God is ultimately able to create even more imaginative paths.